IMAGES of America

DETROIT'S HISTORIC EASTERN MARKET

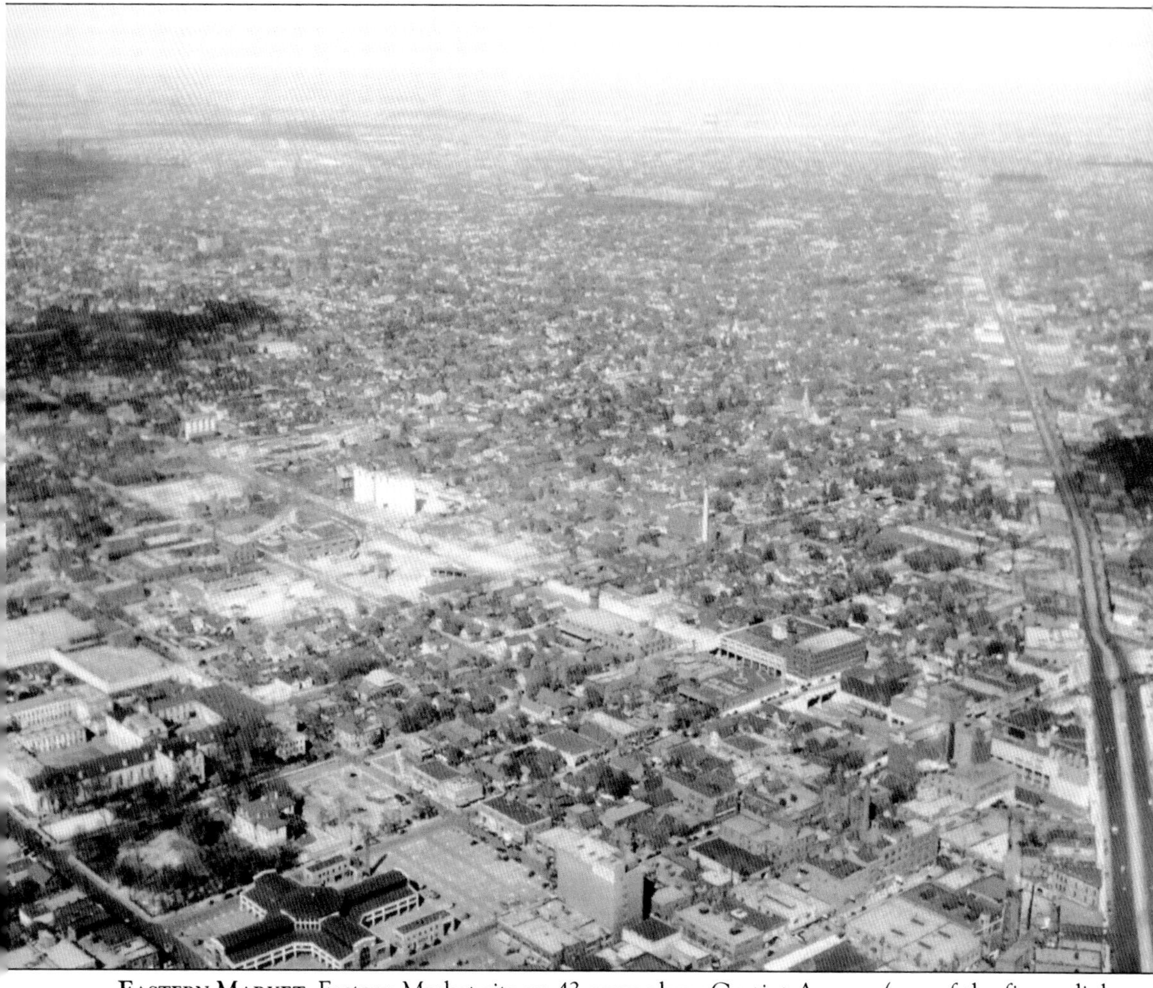

EASTERN MARKET. Eastern Market sits on 43 acres along Gratiot Avenue (one of the five radial streets that originate from Campus Martius Park downtown), just northeast of downtown Detroit. (Courtesy of Walter P. Reuther Library, Wayne State University.)

ON THE COVER: The first public market in Detroit was established in 1802 by the third ordinance of the first Detroit City Charter. (Courtesy of Walter P. Reuther Library, Wayne State University.)

IMAGES
of America

Detroit's Historic Eastern Market

Randall Fogelman and Lisa E. Rush

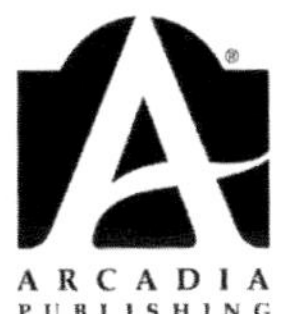

ARCADIA
PUBLISHING

ISBN 978-0-7385-8440-9

Published by Arcadia Publishing
Charleston, South Carolina

Printed in the United States of America

Library of Congress Control Number: 2009943817

For all general information, please contact Arcadia Publishing:
Telephone 843-853-2070
Fax 843-853-0044
E-mail sales@arcadiapublishing.com
For customer service and orders:
Toll-Free 1-888-313-2665

Visit us on the Internet at www.arcadiapublishing.com

This book is dedicated to the diverse group of farmers, vendors, merchants, shoppers, visitors, buskers, tourists, and friends that comes together to make Eastern Market a uniquely authentic place.

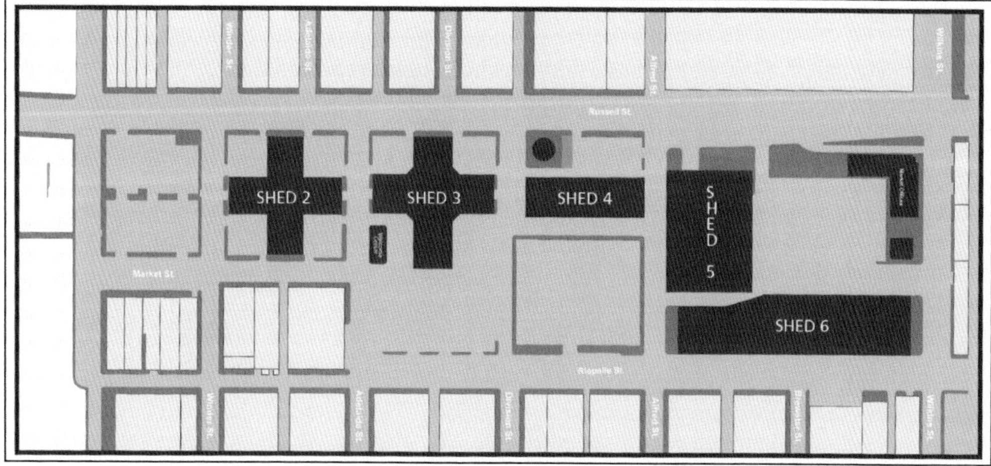

Market Campus. The core of Eastern Market, occupying almost 14 acres, is made up of five principal sheds, various outbuildings, and parking lots. (Courtesy of Eastern Market Corporation.)

Contents

ACKNOWLEDGMENTS

This book would not have been possible without the help, assistance, generosity, guidance, patience, stories, family histories, photographs, and expertise of the following people: Larry Arnone, Doshia Barton, Ronnie and Rosemary Bedway, Tommy and Mary Bedway, Kate Beebe, Abe Berry, Mike Bieke, Curtis B. Blessing, Peter Blum, Frank Boscarino, Carol Brennan, Sally Brownfield, Maggie Bullwinkel, Tom Burkhart, the staff of the Burton Collection, Terry Campbell, Dan Carmody, Heidi Christein, Tony Ciaramitaro, Elizabeth Clemens, Virginia Clohset, Gerald Cook, Pete Cornils, Richard Crabb, Nancy Day, Bert Dearing, Ed Deeb, Patrick Degens, David DeVries, Pamela M. DeWeese, PhD, Jacel Egan, Jela Ellefson, Terry Farnum, Tom Featherstone, Jerome Ferretti, Carol Fink, Marilyn Florek, Deborah Goldstein, Liz Gurley, Ben Hall, Bob Heide, Barry Holtzman, Barbara Hughes, Phoenicia Jackson, John Jones, Jim Kaiser, Martin Korchak, Steve Levine, Dianne and John Little, Jack LoPiccolo, Adam Lovell, Dave Mancini, Jerricka Martin, Charles Martinez, Dominic Moceri, Dominic J. Moceri, Mary Moceri Hoehner, Joe Moore, Mark Mowatt, Joe Muer III, Jason Murphy, Sandy and Mike Novak, Tizzie Onderko, David O'Neil, Dominic and Fran Palazzolo, John Pearson, Jim Pellerito, Amy Perryman, Alex Pollock, the volunteer tour guides of Preservation Detroit, Christine Quane, Don Rafal, Marian Rafal, Tracy Rivard, Fiona Ruddy, Christine Sauve, Merle Scheibner, Don Schneider, Derek Seay, Sandy Shalton, Eric Smith, Janet Sossi Belcoure, Jim Sutherland, Ruth Synowiec, William Tallenger, Margaret Thomas, Mallory Tomaro, Katie Toussaint, Kendall Vaughn, Anna Wilson, Tom Wing, Rose Wright, Jason Yelencich, Michelle Zastawny, and George Zumbro. Thank you!

Unless otherwise noted, the images in this volume appear courtesy of Alex Pollock (AP); the Archdiocese of Detroit (AoD); the Bedway family (BF); the Burton Historical Collection, Detroit Public Library (BHC); Busy Bee Hardware (BBH); David O'Neil (DO); the Detroit Historical Society (DHS); Eastern Market Corporation (EMC); Eric Smith (ES); Gerald Cook (GC); Historic Trinity (HT); Joe Moore (JM); Joe Muer III (JMIII); Lisa Rush (LR); Mike Bieke (MB); Old St. John's (OSJ); Curt Clayson at Clayson Studios (CCS); Mike and Sandy Novak (MSN); and the Walter P. Reuther Library, Wayne State University (WRL).

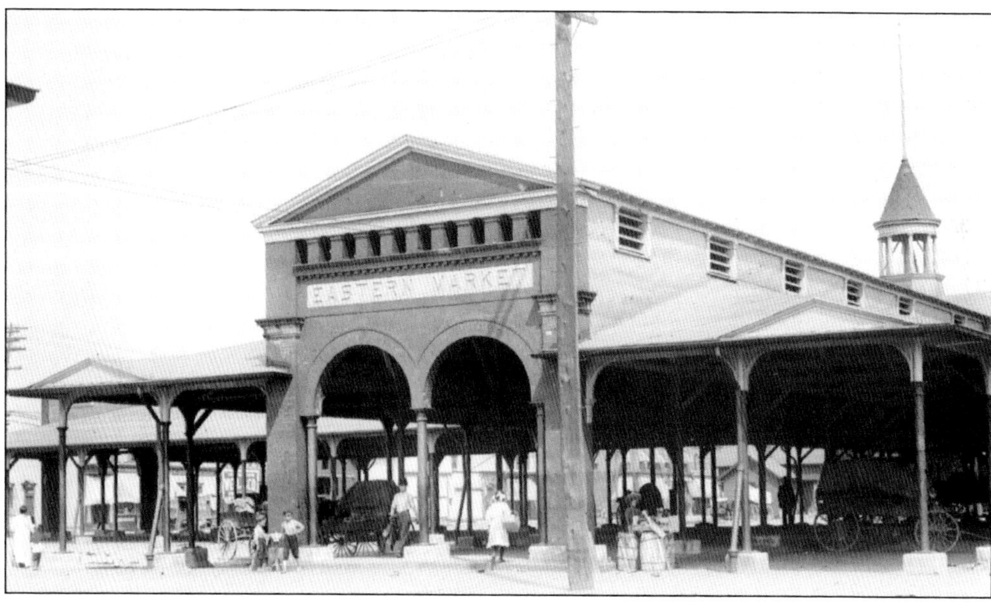

INTRODUCTION

The first public market in Detroit was established in 1802 by the third ordinance of the first Detroit City Charter. At the time, most of the 500 settlers in Detroit lived at Fort Pontchartrain, on the Detroit River, in an area now bounded by Larned and Griswold Streets and Cobo Center. The market was to be established outside of the fort "next to the river, between the old bake house and the upper lines of the pickets [of the fort]." Those market stalls, like most of the original buildings of early Detroit, were destroyed in the great fire of 1805. Subsequently, the market was rebuilt at the foot of Woodward Avenue and was known as Woodward Avenue Market. By 1843, a new two-building market called City Hall Market, or Central Market, was constructed adjacent to the city hall at Cadillac Square. This remained the main city market until 1891.

Meanwhile, the land outside of Fort Pontchartrain was used for farming by the early settlers of Detroit, many having received land grants directly from Detroit's founder, Antoine de la Mothe Cadillac. The long, narrow farms, called "ribbon farms," on the east side of the fort were mainly settled by the French and stretched from the Detroit River to where Harper Avenue is today. In 1742, the Gouin family purchased the farmland where Eastern Market now stands. The family farmed it until 1832, when Charles Francis Gouin died and his estate was put up for sale. Coincidentally, the city cemetery downtown was nearly filled, and city officials were interested in acquiring inexpensive land for a new cemetery. The Gouin family farm was available at a low price, and the city purchased 55 acres at auction in 1834 for $2,100. That land became the Russell Street Cemetery. The cemetery was where the market sheds are today, from High Street (now the eastbound service drive of the Fisher Freeway) at the southern edge to roughly Eliot Street on the north, and then from Russell Street on the western edge to about 50 feet east of what would later become Riopelle Street.

Not all of the land allocated for the cemetery was used for those purposes. In 1870, the Hay and Wood Market was moved from nearby Hastings Street to where Shed 3 is today. In 1861, the original Detroit House of Corrections (DeHoCo) was built on land located approximately where Shed 5 is today. DeHoCo remained in the Eastern Market area until 1931, when it was moved to land in Northville and Plymouth Township.

By the 1870s, the city ordered that there could be no more burials in the Russell Street Cemetery, although the land was not vacated for another 10 years. Most of the bodies were removed, but a few were missed and discovered later when the original Shed 1 was built, and a few more were discovered during the excavation of the Fisher Freeway almost 100 years later.

Besides having the cemetery, the Wood and Hay Market, and the prison, the Eastern Market area was becoming the center of the German community in Detroit. Germans first settled in the area now known as Greektown, and as the population grew, the community moved north along Gratiot Avenue and brought their traditions with them, especially their breweries and churches. These traditions are still evident in the Eastern Market district, with four of the churches in the district having German roots and several buildings still standing that were formerly home to German-owned breweries.

By 1891, the city was beginning a period of tremendous growth, and the City Hall Market land at Cadillac Square was becoming too valuable to use as a market. The market was then split into two, with the western farmers relocating to Western Market, at Michigan Avenue and Eighteenth Street, and the eastern farmers relocating to Eastern Market, on recently cleared land at the south end of the Russell Street Cemetery. The third and last city market, at Chene and Ferry Streets, was added as a municipal market in the early 1920s, and although it still stands, it has not functioned as a market since the 1980s. Western Market, always smaller than Eastern Market with only two sheds, was completely demolished when Interstate 96 was built.

Retail and wholesale businesses developed in Eastern Market, mainly around Sheds 1 and 2, with various other food purveyors and market-related businesses along the western edge. Most early wholesalers, or dealers, were on the eastern edge of the market area, with Detroit's growing meatpacking industry along Orleans Street aided by the proximity of the railroad tracks. The southern edge of the market was anchored by the retail meat market known as Gratiot Central Market.

Eastern Market flourished in its early years and was known for being well run. By the 1950s, however, many changes were occurring in Detroit and in the food industry, making farmers' markets largely irrelevant for consumers.

Because of urban renewal in the 1960s, much of the residential land along the south and west edges of the market was targeted for demolition. This area, anchored by Hastings Street, had been the center of the growing African American community in Detroit. The newly cleared parcels, along what is now the service drive of the Fisher Freeway, were mostly purchased by existing wholesalers, including Wolverine Packing and several produce distributors, who remained in Eastern Market by building larger facilities with ready access to the freeways instead of moving to another part of the city.

While much of this effort focused on the growth of wholesale businesses, it was apparent that Eastern Market needed some attention to continue to attract retail customers in the early 1970s. The first of these was a series of colorful murals adorning the historic sheds and buildings. Flower Day was started, and it is now the largest one-day plant sales event in the United States. Various other publicity events were staged to create awareness, and Eastern Market again enjoyed new interest from a new generation of consumers.

By the early 2000s, Eastern Market needed an update again. A task force consisting of the two Eastern Market associations, the Eastern Market Advancement Coalition (EMAC) and the Eastern Market Merchants Association, was joined by the public-private Greater Detroit Partnership (GDP) to plot the course for the future of the market. The Urban Land Institute (ULI) was brought in to help develop a comprehensive, shared plan that included all Eastern Market stakeholders and would revitalize Eastern Market.

In August 2006, the management and promotion of Eastern Market was transferred from the City of Detroit to the newly formed Eastern Market Corporation (EMC), a nonprofit organization responsible for the operations of the market. Backed by a 21-member board of directors, EMC has been quite successful in changing the destiny of the market. Since EMC assumed management, over $10 million in capital improvements have been made to the market core, bolstered by enormous private-capital investments in improvements to businesses throughout the market district. New farmers and vendors have been recruited, the campus and the district are cleaner and safer, new events and market days have been added, and customer counts have increased dramatically. With all of these positive changes, Eastern Market will continue to feed the body and soul of Detroit for many years to come.

One

The Sheds

Eastern Market began as a single shed in 1891 and multiplied over the next century to its current five buildings that make up the 14-acre market core. In these buildings, farmers from southeastern Michigan and nearby environs sell their products to the public on Saturdays and Tuesdays. The sheds are also home to a thriving nighttime wholesale market in which grocery stores and produce houses buy their wares from farmers and vendors.

Each of the five buildings is different and represents a very different period of the market's history. Shed 2, built in 1898, exemplifies Victorian architecture, with its stall sizes scaled for horses and wagons, not trucks. Shed 3, built in 1922, is an incredible example of municipal architecture, with a design scaled for small trucks to accommodate a Detroit on the move. Shed 4, built in 1938, is a simple steel-framed canopy; the lack of ornamentation or architectural detail of any kind evokes a city coming out of the Great Depression and headed to war. Shed 5, built in 1981, embodies the hopes and dreams of the early 1980s, an era with big architecture that has yet to stand the test of time. Finally, Shed 6, built in 1966, while functionally obsolete from the very beginning, as the roof is too high to offer any real protection from the elements, stylistically offers a wonderful example of mid-century reinforced-concrete architecture.

Great efforts have been taken since 2006 to preserve the significant architectural elements of the five structures while modernizing them to accommodate the Eastern Market of today. Between 2006 and the spring of 2013, over $10 million has been spent renovating and restoring the sheds.

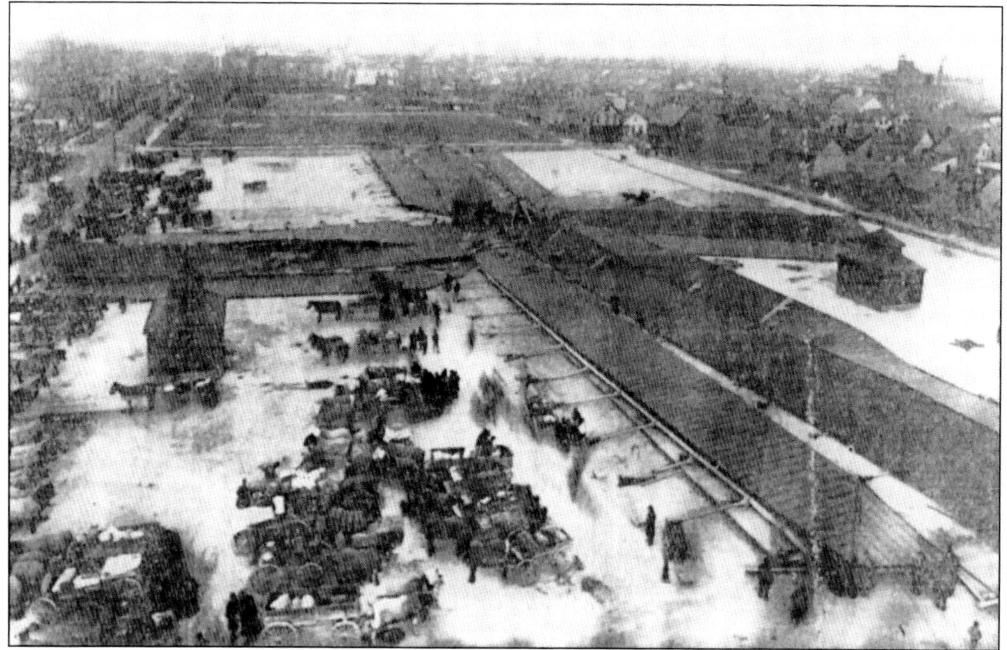

The Original Shed. By 1882, the Russell Street Cemetery had been relocated, and within a couple of years, an informal market began on Russell Street at High Street (now part of the Fisher Freeway service drive). The first structure, consisting of iron support poles with a raised roof and market offices in the center, was constructed in 1886. This building, later described as "a flimsy affair, which had not been sufficiently anchored," blew down during a fierce winter storm on December 23, 1890. (EMC.)

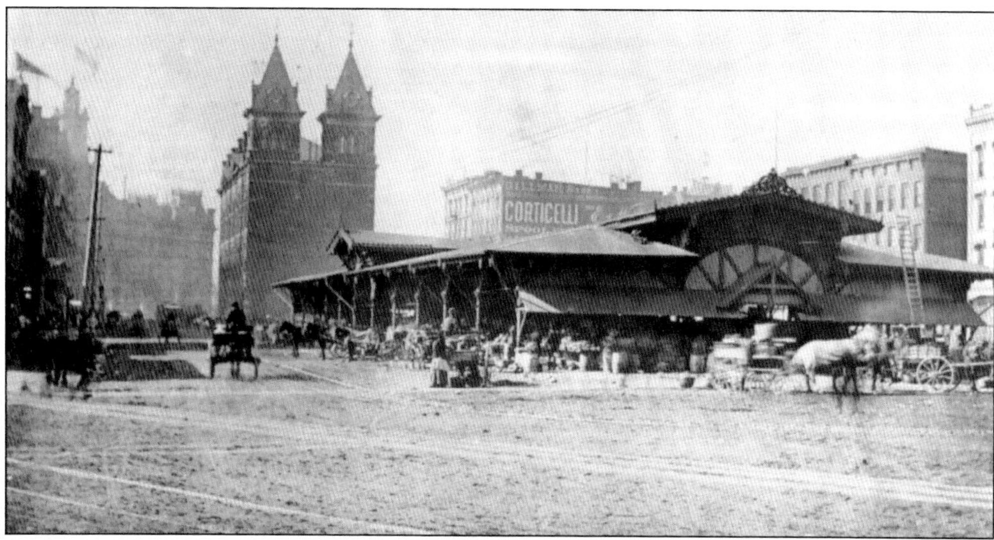

Central Market. As the city grew, it became apparent that Central Market, or City Hall Market, was not large enough to accommodate the growing population, and expansion was not an option. A plan was hatched to create two separate markets in the city: Eastern Market and Western Market. The site of the informal market on the corner of Russell and High Streets was an obvious choice for the establishment of a new market, and in 1891 the area was officially designated as Eastern Market. (BHC.)

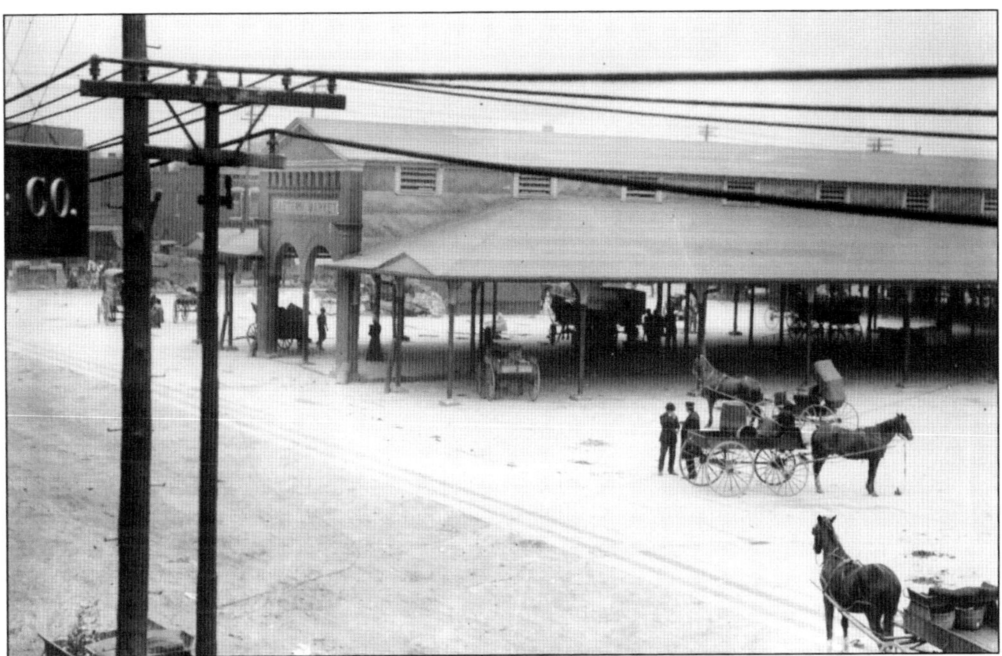

SHED 1. The new market required a building, which would come to be known as Shed 1. Designed by architect Richard E. Raseman, it was to be built on the exact same block where the previous market building had blown down. (WRL.)

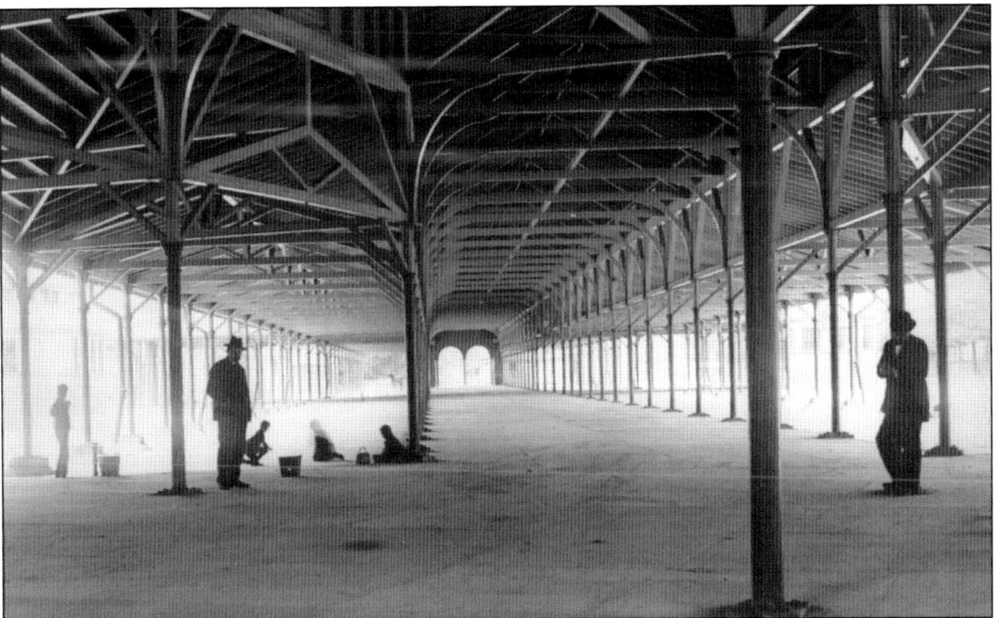

SHED 1 INTERIOR. The new Shed 1 was an open-air sheltered pavilion in a cruciform shape. The exposed-wood framed roof was supported by cast-iron columns, and the deep stalls allowed farmers to back their wagons right into the shed. The building, approximately 450 feet from north to south and 330 feet from east to west, occupied the entire block, bounded by Russell, Vernor, Market, and High Streets. When it was completed on April 26, 1892, the building had more than 150 covered stalls, as well as many more uncovered stalls around it. (BHC.)

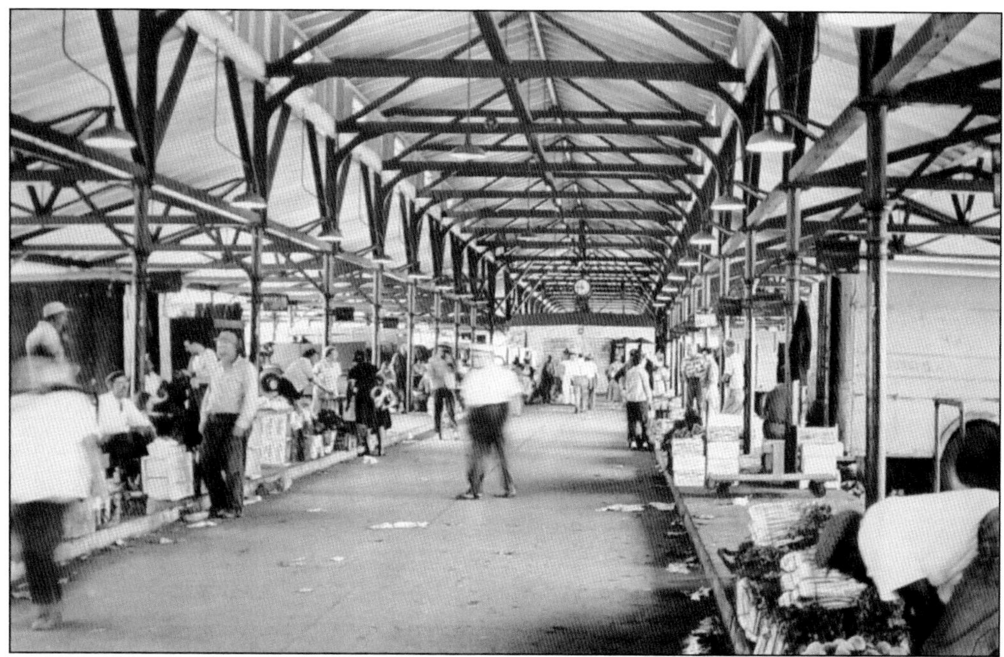

Street Widening. In the 1930s and 1940s, both Russell and Market Streets were widened. In order to accommodate the enlargement plan, approximately 30 feet was removed from both the east and west wings of Shed 1. (EMC.)

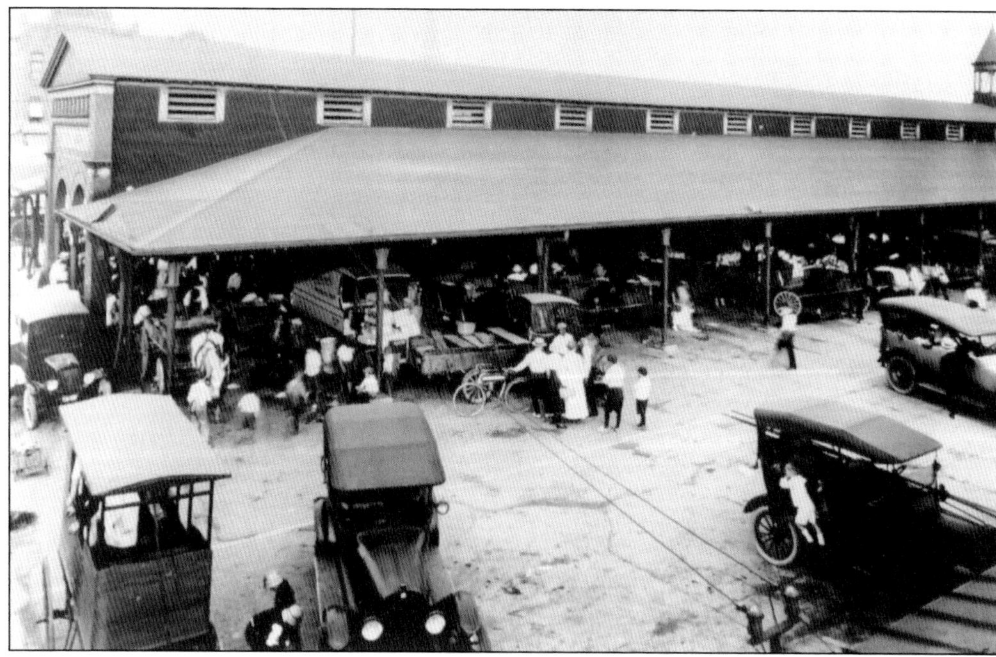

Shed 1 Is Demolished. Unfortunately, Shed 1 was demolished in 1967 to make way for the construction of the Interstate 75 connector. Vendors occupying Shed 1 stalls were relocated to other parts of the market. The freeway construction required only part of the land, and the remainder of the parcel was used as an informal parking lot. In the mid-1990s, the gravel lot was paved, sidewalks and lighting were added, and a very tall flagpole was erected. (EMC.)

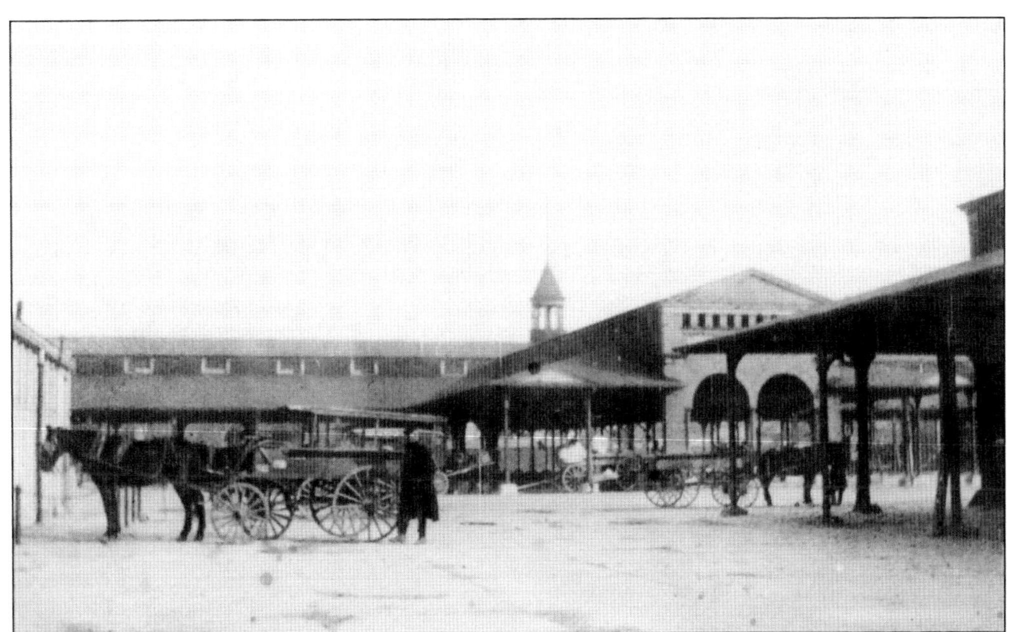

Shed 2. As the market grew, more covered space was needed. A building permit was granted on December 5, 1898, for a new, one-story wooden market shed. Architect Richard E. Raseman was once again commissioned to design the building. The new structure was built on the block directly north of Shed 1, a site bounded by Russell, Winder, Market, and Adelaide Streets. (BHC.)

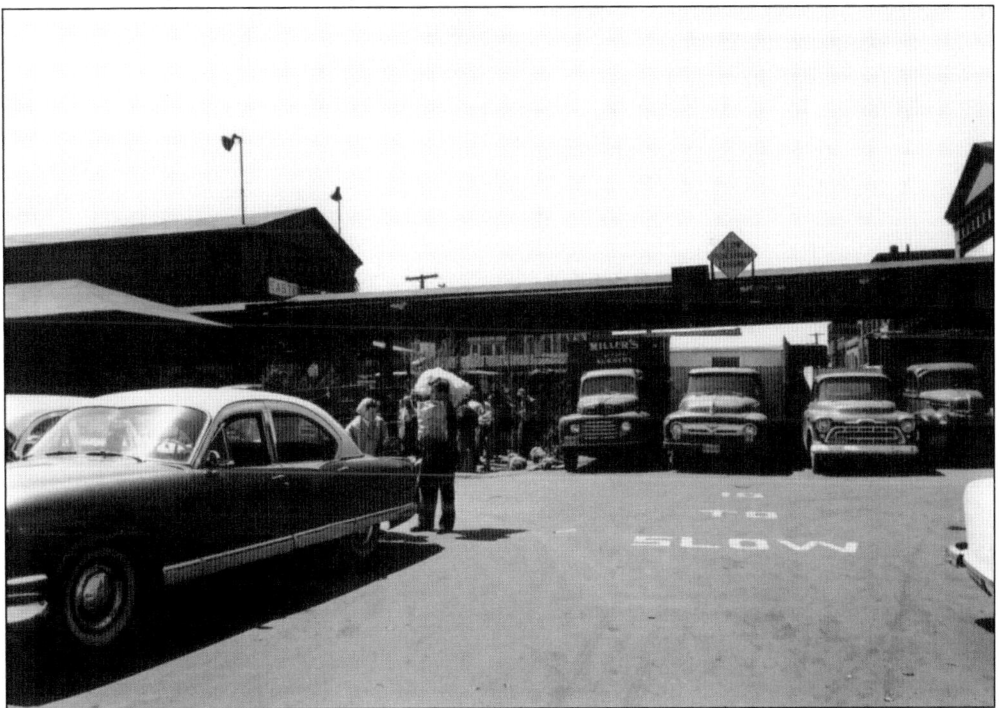

Shed 2's Design. Raseman opted for consistency with his earlier design for Shed 1, and the two buildings were almost identical, with Shed 2 being just a bit smaller. Eventually, a canopy was added, connecting the two sheds and providing additional covered space for vendors. (BHC.)

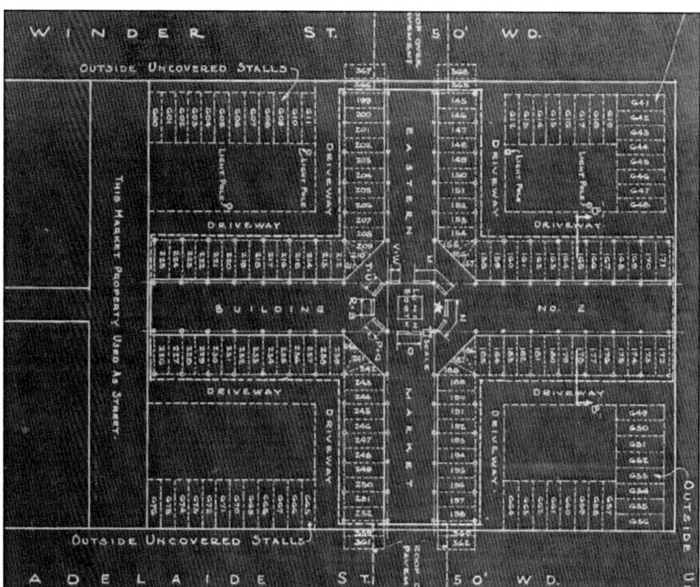

SHED 2'S BLUEPRINT. Measuring approximately 250 feet from north to south and 315 feet from east to west, the shed was built by contractor Henry P. O'Connor for $10,000. The building featured a lunch booth in the center and included more than 140 stalls. (EMC.)

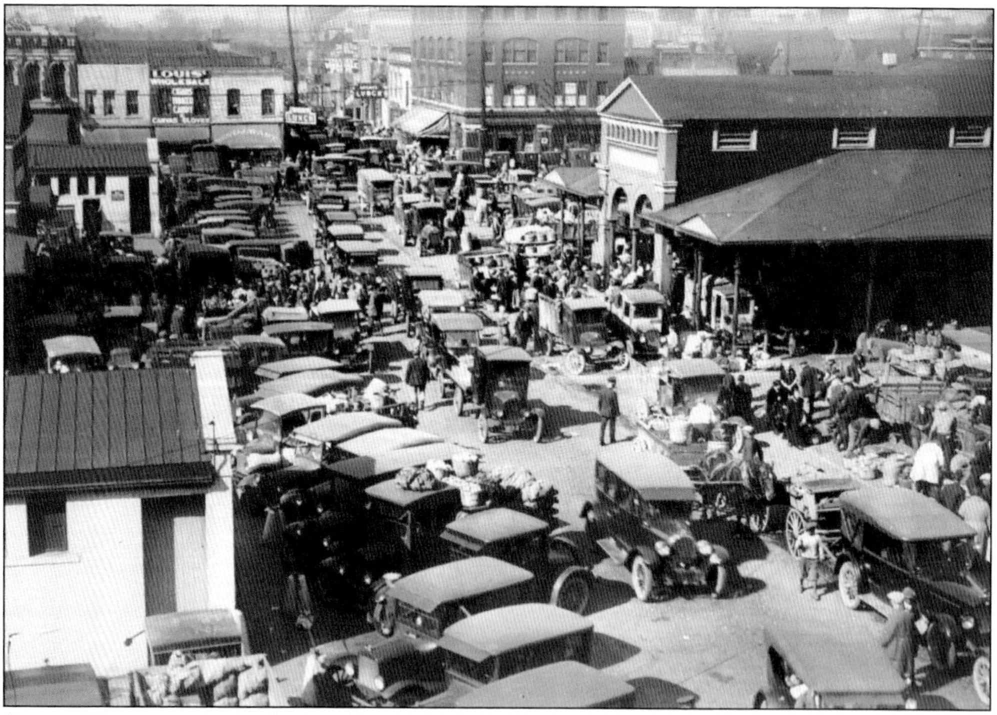

STREET WIDENING. To make way for a widened Russell Street, 35 feet was removed from the west wing of the building. The east wing also had 35 feet removed in order to enlarge Market Street. The historic brick facades were rebuilt to match the originals. (WRL.)

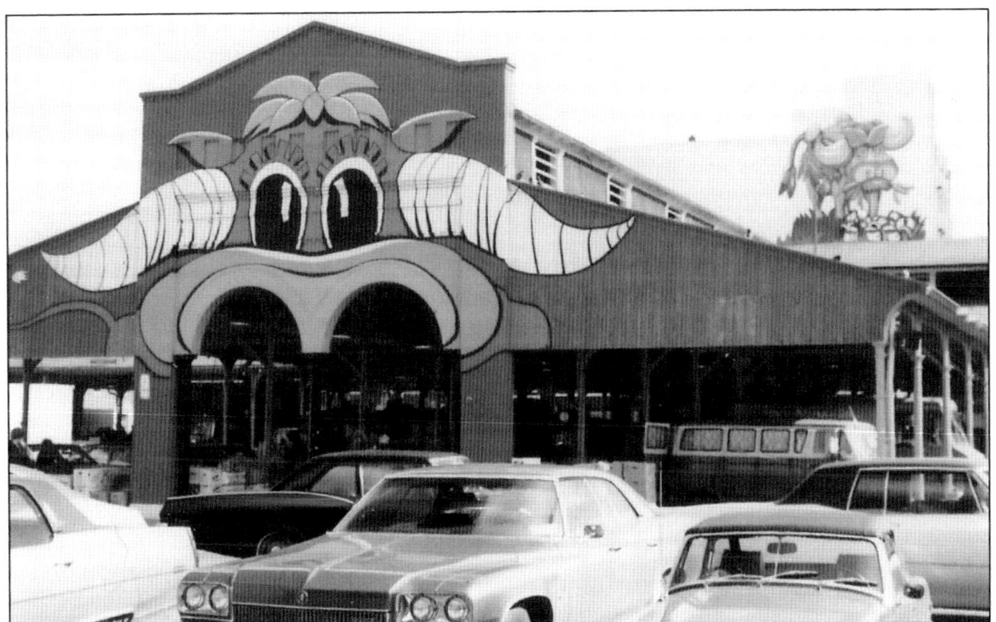

SHED 2'S BULL. In 1971, in an effort to spruce up the market and bring in more customers, Detroit architect Alex Pollock designed three murals that transformed the shed into a figurative chicken, pig, and bull. (MSN.)

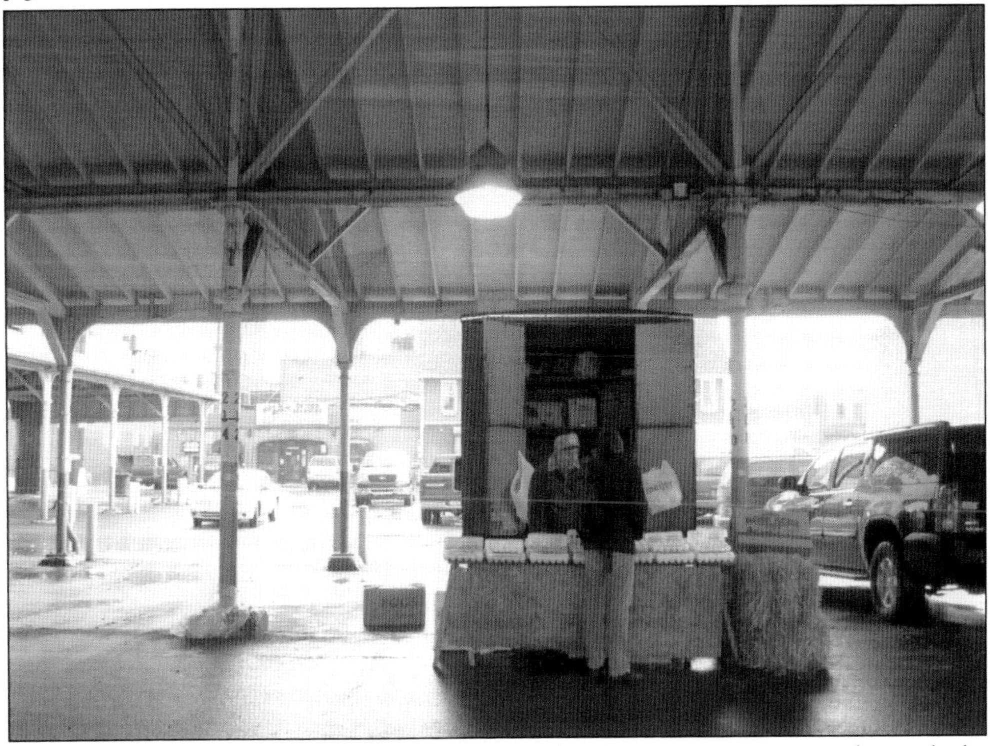

SHED 2 RENOVATION. In October 2007, Eastern Market Corporation, in partnership with the Detroit Recreation Department, began renovations on historic Shed 2—the first in its 110-year history. (EMC.)

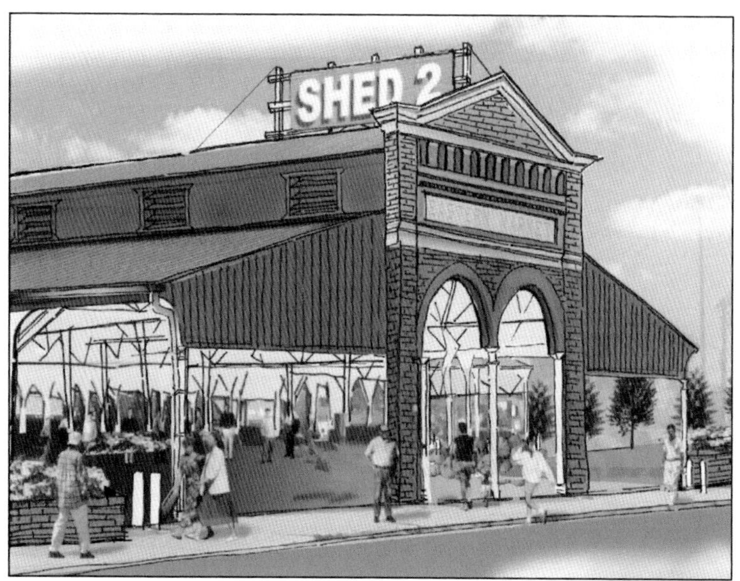

SHED 2'S RENDERING. The Detroit architectural firm Gensler was chosen for the renovations of Shed 2, along with local contractor WCI Construction. Existing vendors were temporarily moved to a large tent on the north side of the market, while many layers of paint were carefully removed and existing concrete and asphalt eliminated. (EMC.)

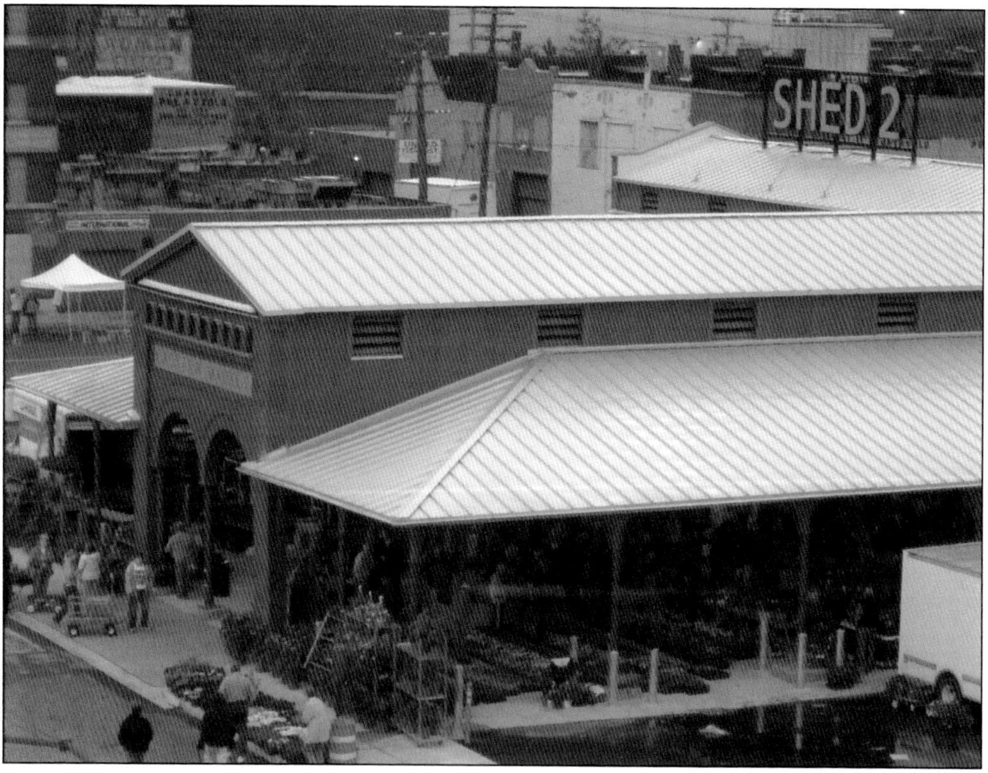

SHED 2 REIMAGINED. The work done on Shed 2 was not a strict historical restoration, but rather a renovation that honored the history and architecture of the building while modernizing it for the comfort of both the vendors and their customers. The shed received a new galvanized-metal standing-seam roof (the type often seen on agriculture buildings), new wiring and lighting, fresh concrete throughout, water spigots, stall lines, banner holders, and a "Shed 2" roof sign. (EMC.)

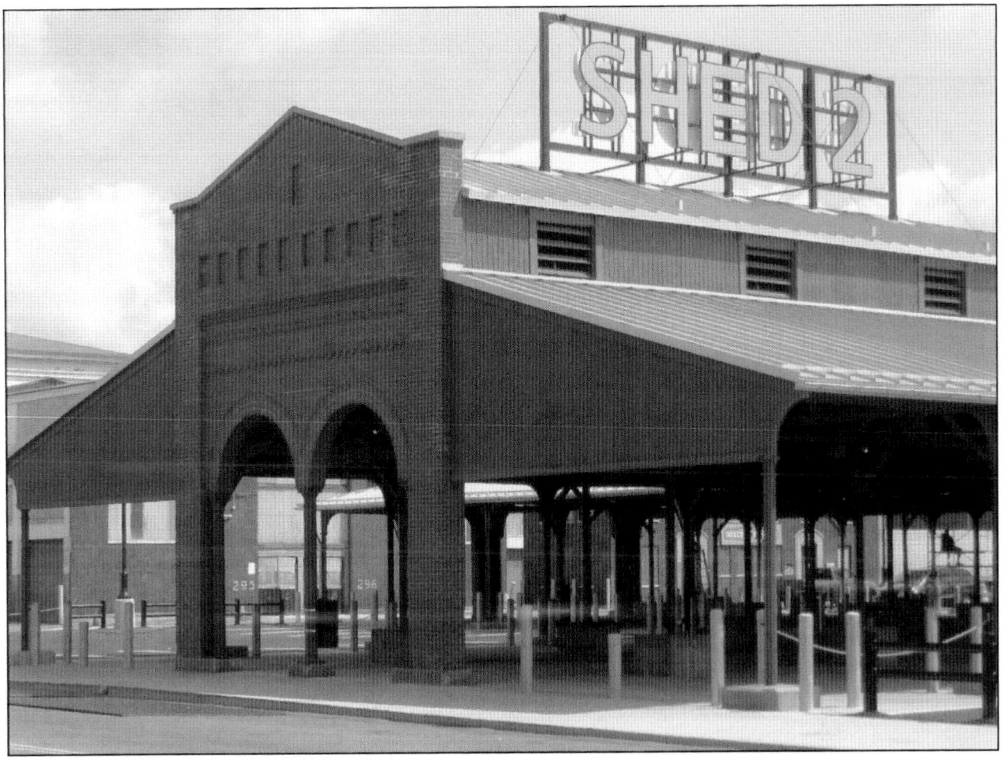

Shed 2's New Sign. While the building has always been known as Building 2 or Shed 2 by longtime Eastern Market vendors, it was not common knowledge to most visitors to the market. The signage helped customers identify the shed and created an improved sense of place and community among visitors and vendors alike. (EMC.)

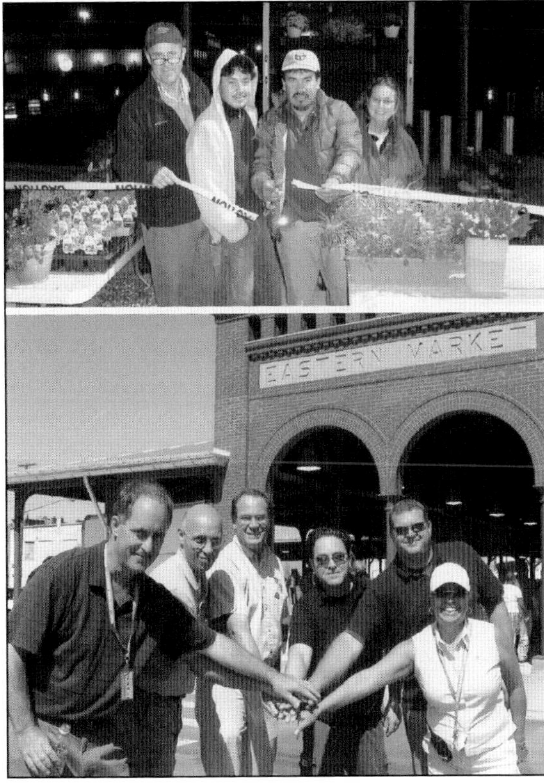

Shed 2 Reopens. Early in the morning on May 17, 2008, vendors returned to the shed just in time for Flower Day weekend. In the end, the renovation took over 10 months and cost nearly $2 million. The funds came from the City of Detroit and private foundations that were anxious to see the market improved. Shed 2 was formally rededicated on August 16, 2008. Dignitaries, Eastern Market Corporation staff and board members, district business owners, and longtime supporters of the market were on hand to cut the ceremonial ribbon. A rededication plaque was permanently affixed to the southern facade of the building. (EMC.)

THE DEPARTMENT OF PUBLIC WELFARE.
Detroit, Mich., Nov. 19, 1920.

NOTICE TO CONTRACTORS

PROPOSALS WANTED FOR ADDITION TO EASTERN MARKET

ADELAIDE, RUSSELL, DIVISION AND MARKET STREETS DETROIT, MICHIGAN.

Sealed proposals will be received at the office of the Public Welfare Commission, City Service Building, Detroit, Michigan, until Monday, December 13, 1920, 12 o'clock noon, for construction of additions to Eastern Market, Adelaide, Russell, Division and Market Streets, Detroit, Michigan, in accordance with plans and specifications on file in the office of the Architects, John Scott & Co., 2326-30 Dime Bank Building, Detroit, Michigan.

Proposals to be made in duplicate and the envelope endorsed with the item bid on and the name of the bidder.

Proposals to be made for the complete work or separate divisions as follows:

(1) Mason Work, Cut Stone and Plastering.
(2) Steel and Iron Work.
(3) Carpenter Work.
(4) Painting and Glazing.
(5) Steel Sash.
(6) Rolling Steel Doors.
(7) Reinforced Cement Roofing Tile.
(8) Roofing and Sheet Metal Work.
(9) Marble Work and Marbleoid Floors.
(10) Plumbing and Heating.
(11) Electrical Work and Lighting Fixtures.
(12) Garbage Incinerating Plant.

SHED 3'S ORIGINS. In 1920, the site of what was known as the Hay and Wood Market was chosen for the construction of Shed 3. The lot was bounded by Russell, Adelaide, Division, and Market Streets and was located immediately north of Shed 2. (EMC.)

SHED 3'S BLUEPRINT. On June 23, 1921, a building permit was issued to general contractor W.E. Wood Co. for the construction of Shed 3. In contrast to the outdoor canopy style of Sheds 1 and 2, this was a fully enclosed brick, steel, and reinforced-concrete structure designed by the architectural firm John Scott & Co. Scott was best known for the Beaux Arts–style Wayne County Building downtown, which was constructed in 1902. (EMC.)

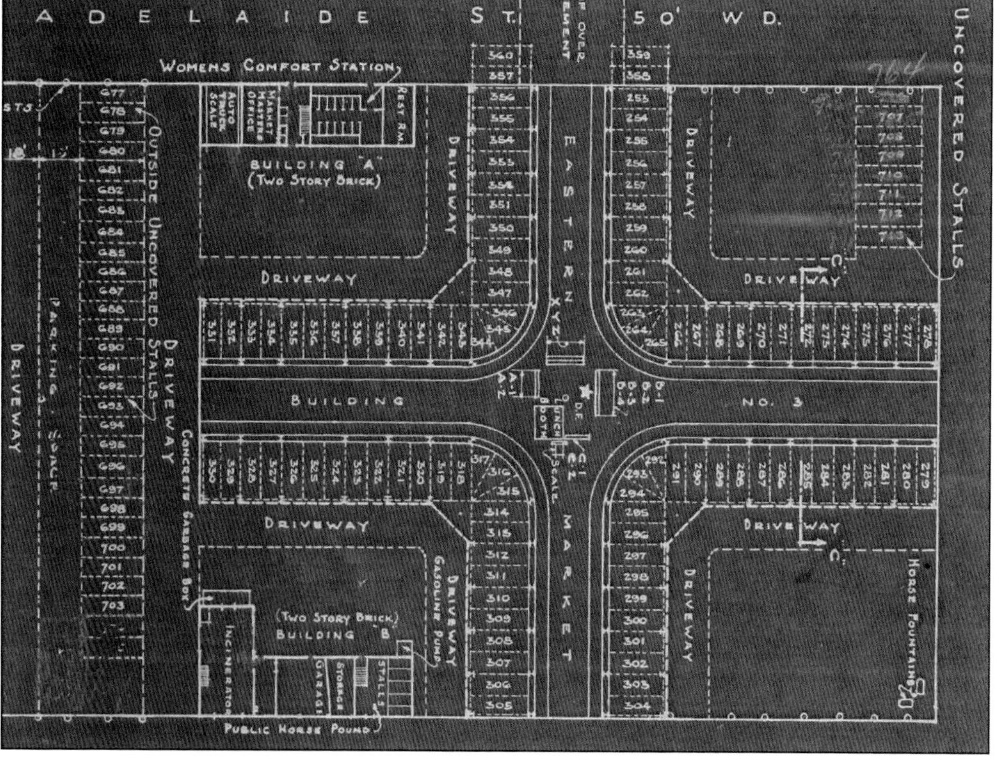

An All-Weather Shed. The 1921 annual market report read, "The contract already let for a fine market building which will function especially as a winter market, having rolling steel doors all around, to protect buyers and sellers from the cold winds which will sweep the market, and other bad weather . . . this will be the first market building of its kind and the best." (EMC.)

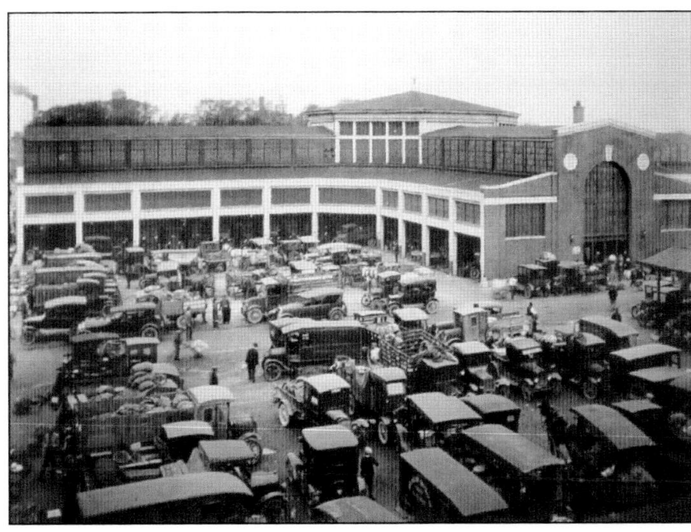

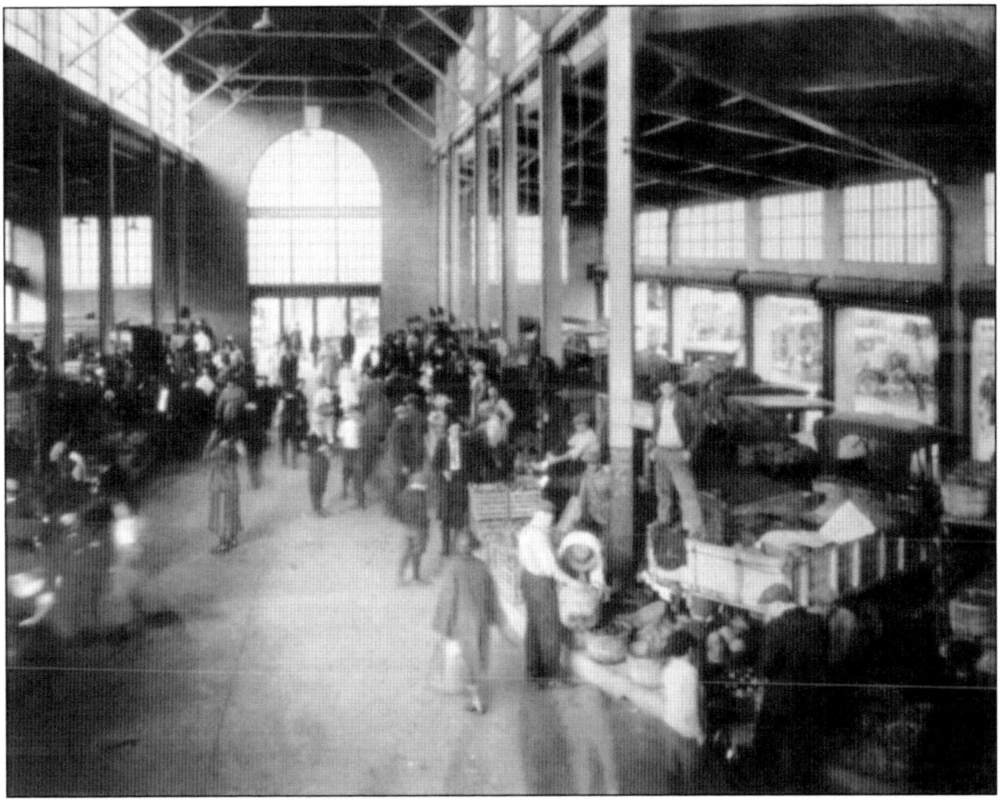

Shed 3 Opens. When completed and open for use in August 1922, the building had over 100 stalls for farmers and vendors. In addition to the shed, two outbuildings were constructed. Building A, on the south side of the shed, housed the market master's office, a truck scale, and a women's "comfort station," or restroom. Building B, on the north side of the shed, housed an incinerator, a garage, and a public horse pound. The total cost of the project, including the outbuildings, was $165,000. Looking towards the future, the building was designed to allow for possible expansion of a Shed 3 east wing toward Riopelle Street. (AP.)

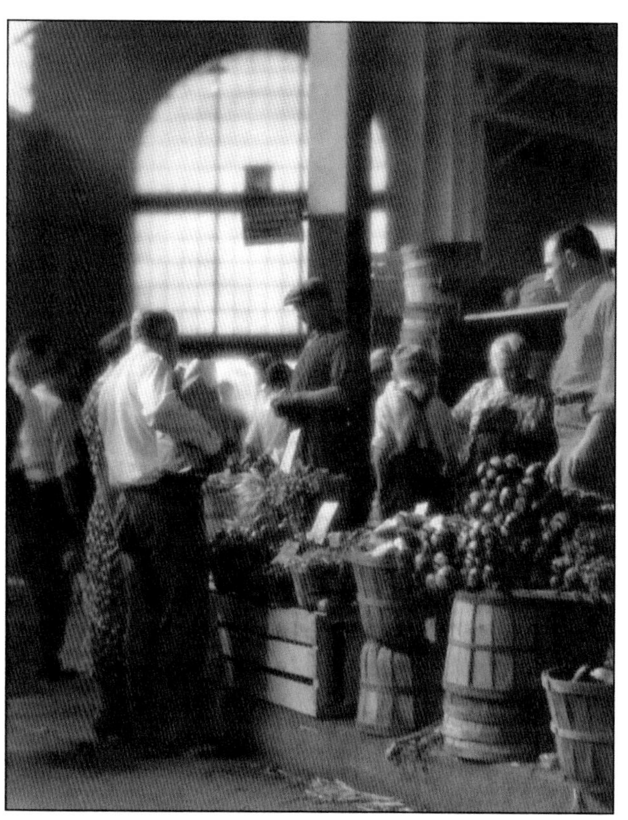

Widening of Russell Street. The expansion on the east wing of the building never happened. In fact, a decision was made to truncate the west wing of the building approximately 30 feet for the widening of Russell Street. This historic west facade, complete with cement medallions and a keystone depicting the city of Detroit, the state of Michigan, and symbols of agriculture, was rebuilt 30 feet to the east. (BHC.)

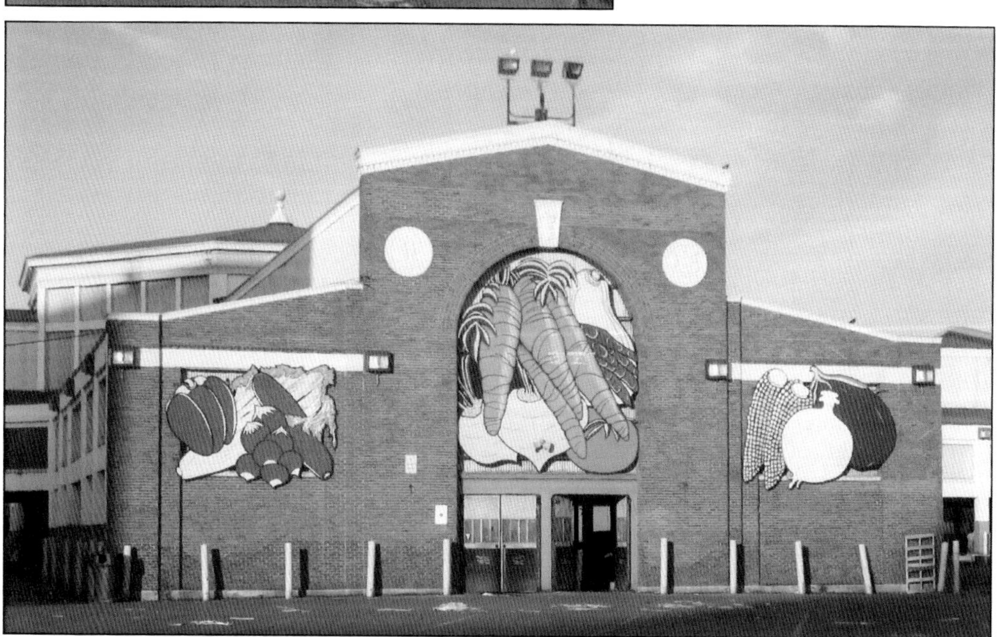

Shed 3's Quick Fix. In 1971, Eastern Market's management asked Detroit architect Alex Pollock to come up with a solution for the rising cost of replacing broken windows. The glass windows were taken out and replaced with heavy-duty plastic. Pollock designed large vegetable cutouts on marine-grade plywood, which were placed over the plastic. (Courtesy of Christine Sauve.)

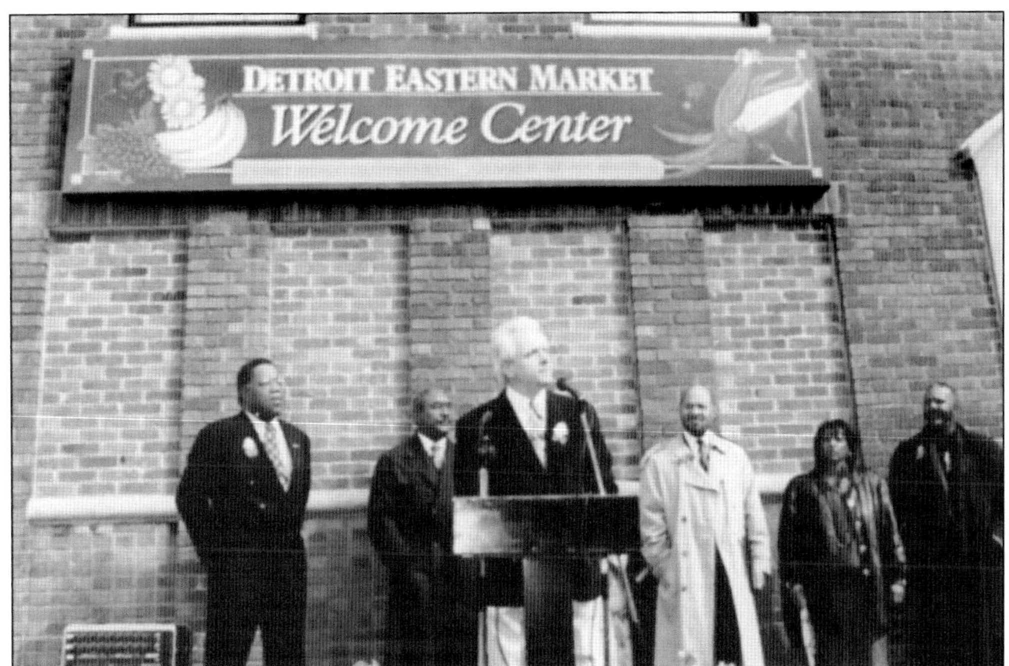

WELCOME CENTER. In the late 1990s, under then-mayor Dennis Archer, Building A was renovated into a welcome center. Unfortunately, due to limited resources and a lack of volunteers, it closed. The welcome center reopened in July 2007 as an information office and the headquarters for the Eastern Market Bridge Card Program. Five years later, its upper floors were renovated by EMC to house Michigan State University Extension staffers who focus on nutrition and new food and product development. (EMC.)

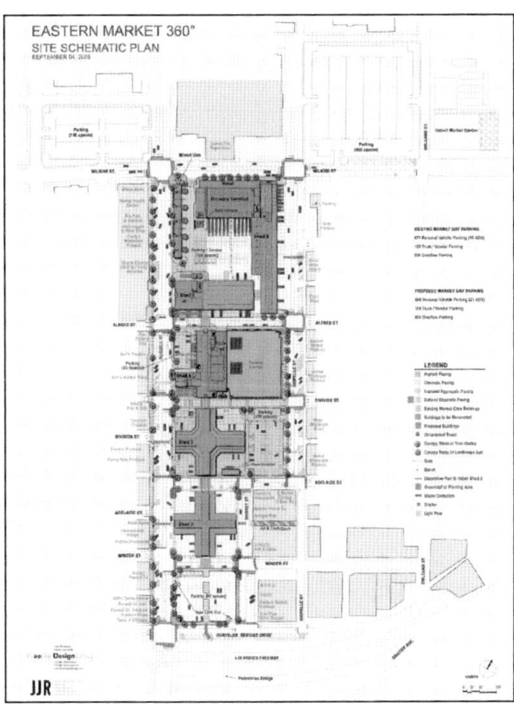

EASTERN MARKET 360°. In 2008, Eastern Market Corporation chose the Detroit-based Kraemer Design Group to design the next phase of market improvements. The new plan for the entire campus was called Eastern Market 360°. Later that year, a joint venture between Detroit-based minority firm KEO Construction and the Detroit office of the international construction firm Turner Construction was chosen to oversee construction-management services. (EMC.)

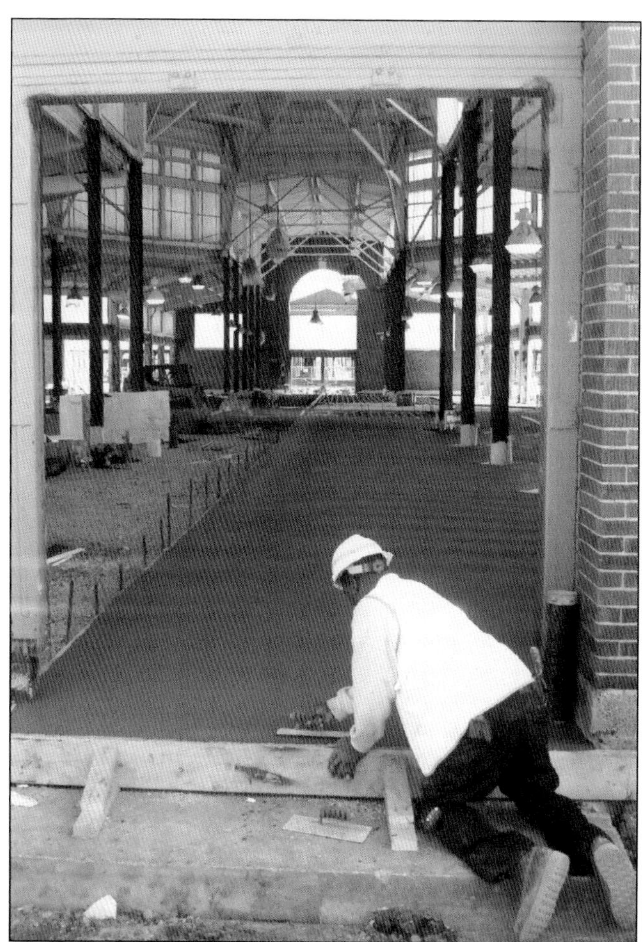

Shed 3 Renovation Begins. Construction began in January 2009. All vendors were relocated to the heated Shed 5 for the winter while the initial construction phase began. By April, the new concrete floor was poured, and the shed was used for the public market on Saturdays while work continued during the slower weekday periods throughout the summer and fall. (EMC.)

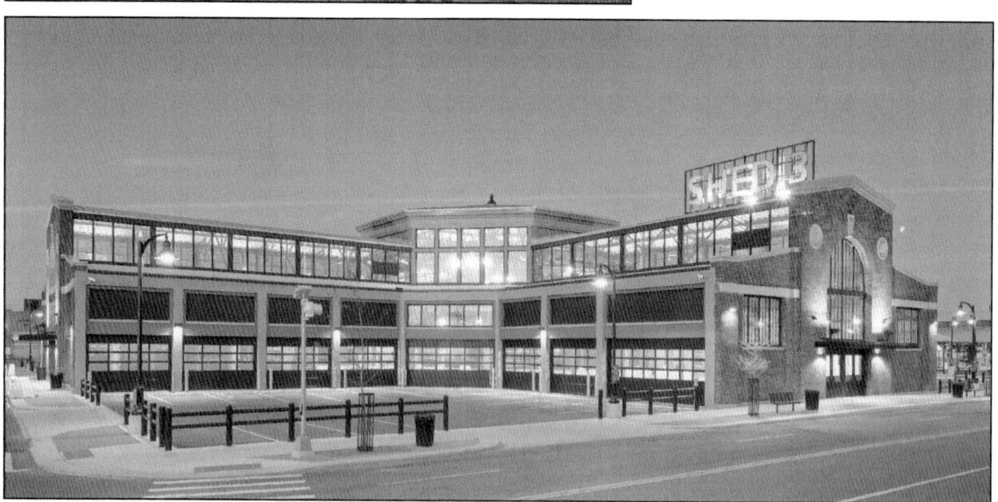

Shed 3's Rendering. The shed received a new galvanized-metal standing-seam roof, new electrical wiring and architectural lighting, new concrete throughout with energy-efficient windows and garage doors, asphalt parking lots, new sidewalks, signature site fencing, multiple water sources, and a "Shed 3" roof sign. (CCS.)

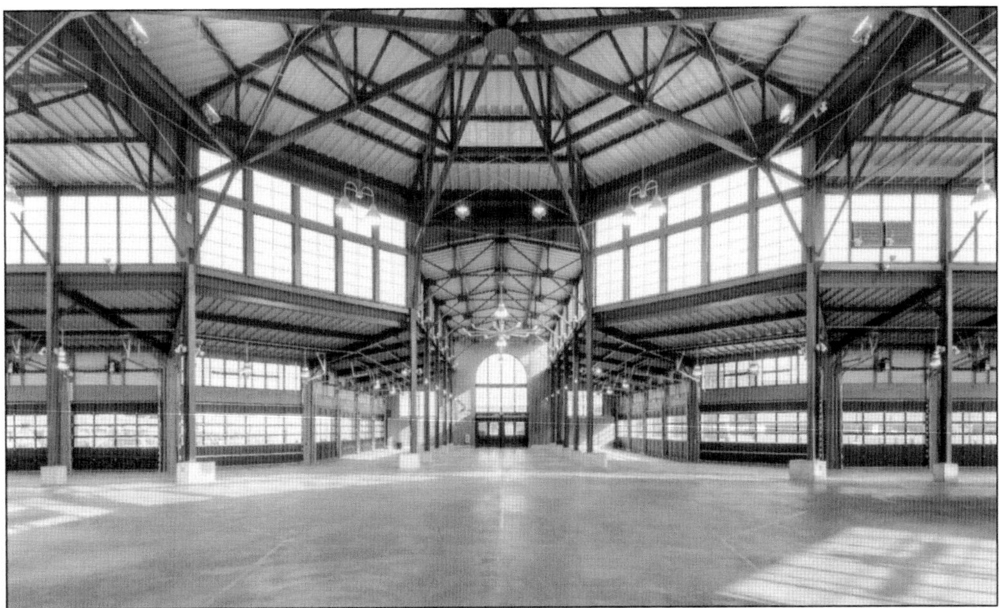

Shed 3's Features. Many features were added to make the shed more comfortable for both vendors and market visitors year-round, including ceiling fans and air curtains for the pedestrian entrances. Plastic piping was laid into the cement for a future hookup to a geothermal field that will provide radiant floor heating. (CCS.)

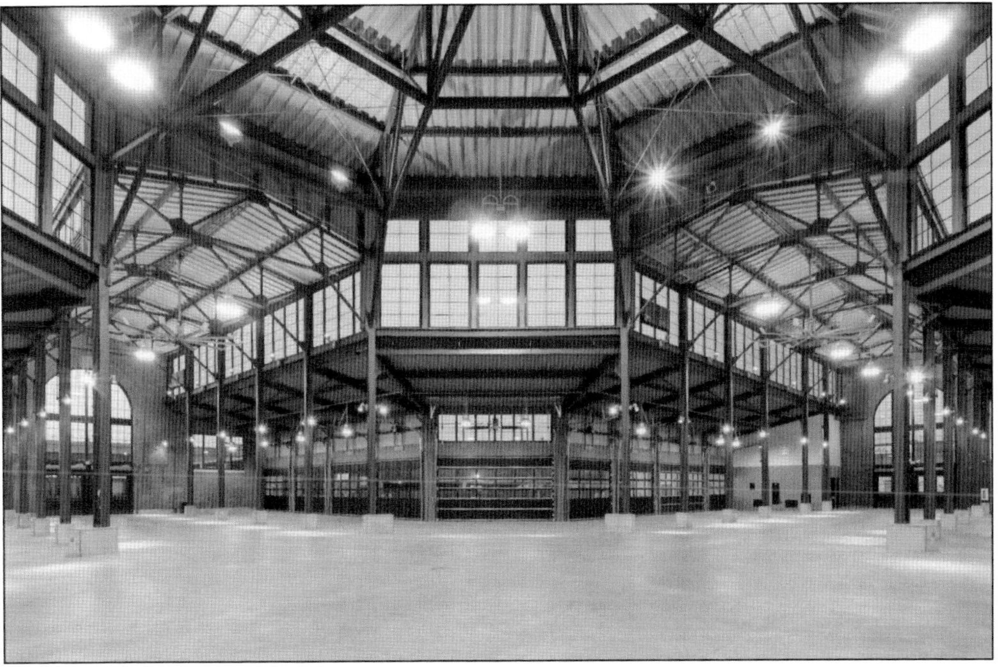

Shed 3 Renovation. Construction work on Shed 3 was completed by November 2009 after 11 months and a cost of $6.2 million. In 2010, the renovation work was recognized by the Michigan Chapter of the Society of Civil Engineers (Quality of Life Project of the Year), the Construction Association of Michigan Magazine (2010 Special Issue Recognition Award), and the Construction Real Estate for Women Association (Impact Award). (CCS.)

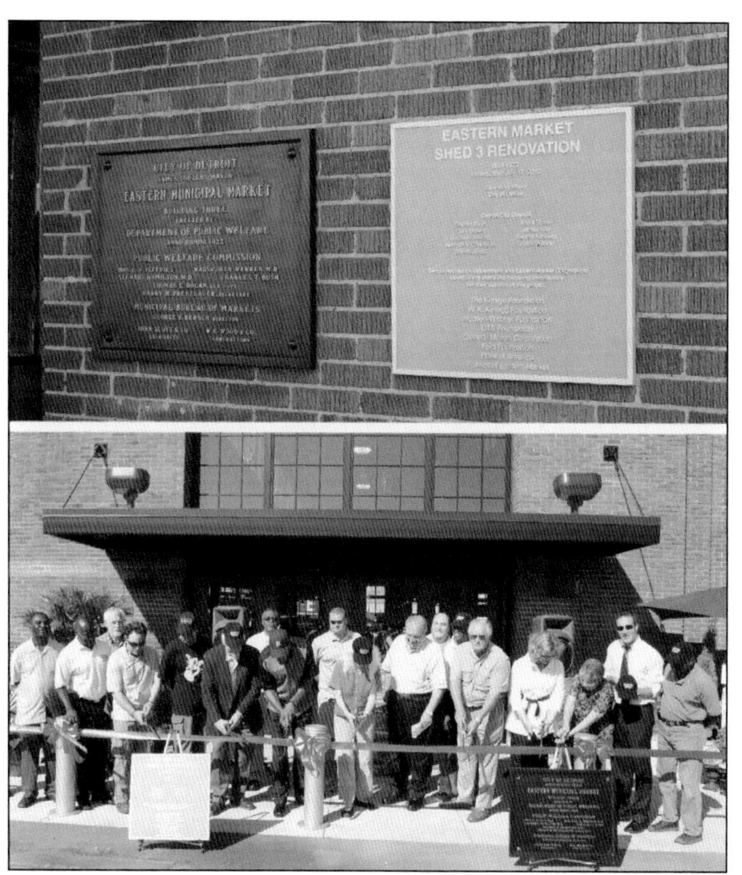

Shed 3 Rededication. EMC officially rededicated Shed 3 on July 17, 2010. Mayor Dave Bing was joined by farmers, vendors, construction team members, EMC staff and its board of directors, and members of the philanthropic community who had been involved on various levels to help fund the project. A new dedication plaque was hung on the west facade of the building next to the original 1922 dedication plaque, which had been found and rehung after years of being in storage. (EMC.)

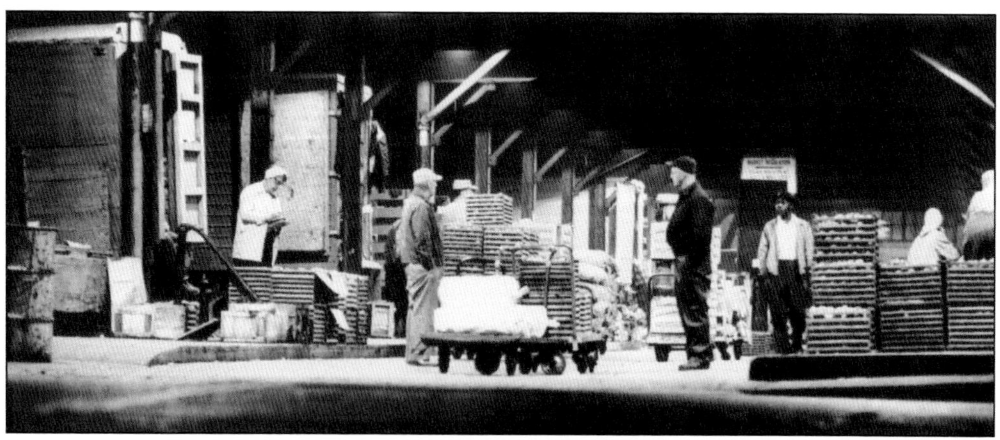

Shed 4 and Shed 5, behind the Scenes. Deeming the "physical facilities inadequate" in 1935, the Detroit Bureau of Markets approved expansion projects for all three city markets. In 1937, the area was paved, and when the remaining project funding was finally secured, Sheds 4 and 5 were built in 1938 and 1939. (BHC.)

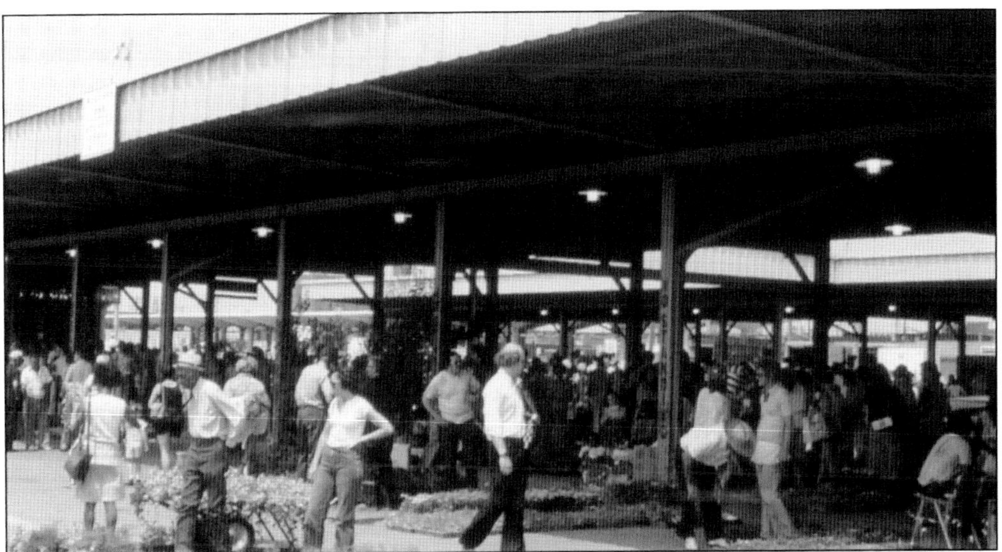

SHED 4 AND SHED 5 STRUCTURE. The two buildings were unadorned canopy structures with walkways down the middle. The simple, efficient design featured vertical steel beams with steel roof supports and a wooden roof deck. Together, Sheds 4 and 5 formed a 60-foot-by-465-foot *H*-shaped structure and covered 224 market stalls. (EMC.)

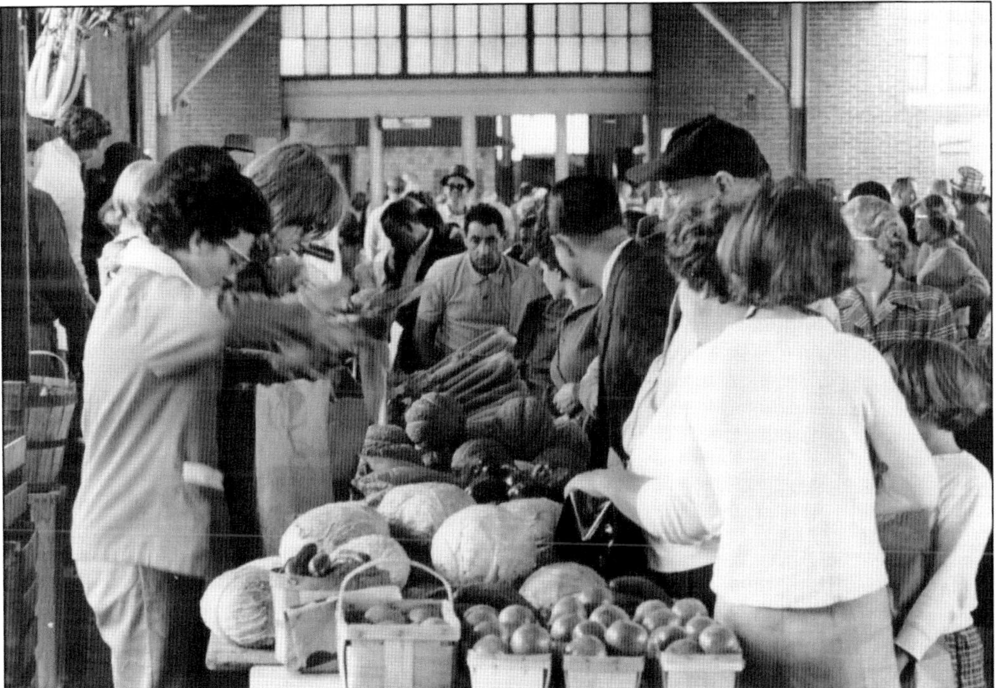

A NEW SHED 5. The original, open-air Shed 5 was torn down in 1980 to make way for a new, enclosed Shed 5 and the construction of a new 330-car municipal parking deck. The parking deck was located on the site of the old Shed 5, and the new Shed 5 was to be placed on Alfred Street between Russell and Riopelle Streets on land that had served as a parking lot for many years but had been the location of the Detroit House of Corrections until it was torn down in 1931. (EMC.)

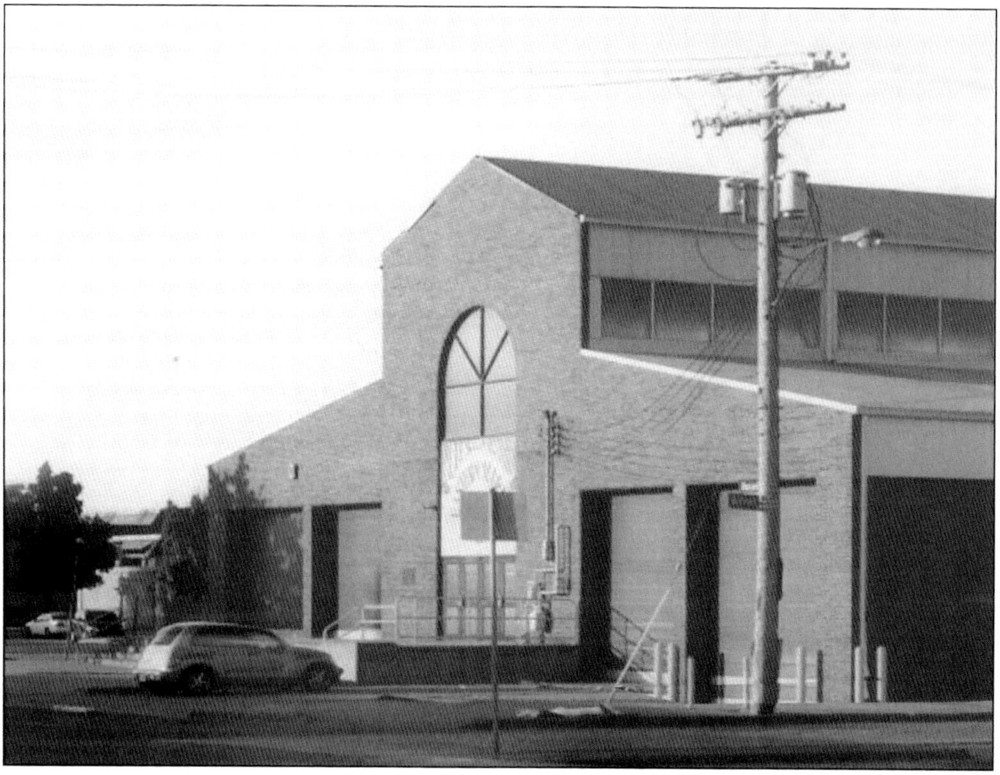

SHED 5 COMPLETED. The new Shed 5 was completed in 1981. The 22,000-square-foot building, designed by Nathan Johnson and Associates and built by Turner Construction, featured large garage doors to accommodate large trucks, overhead radiant heat, and a raised platform in the front that was home to a concession stand. (EMC.)

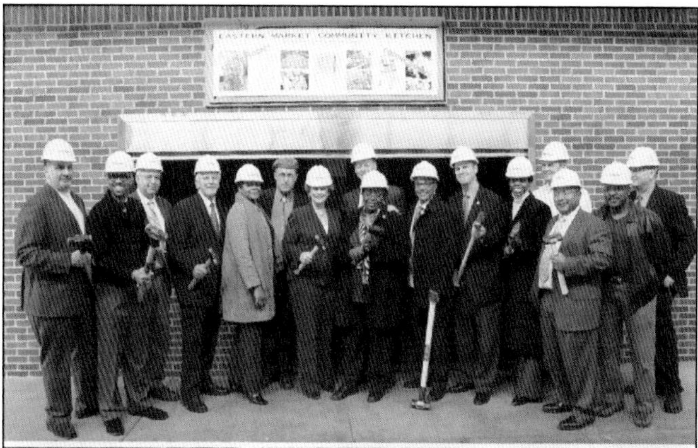

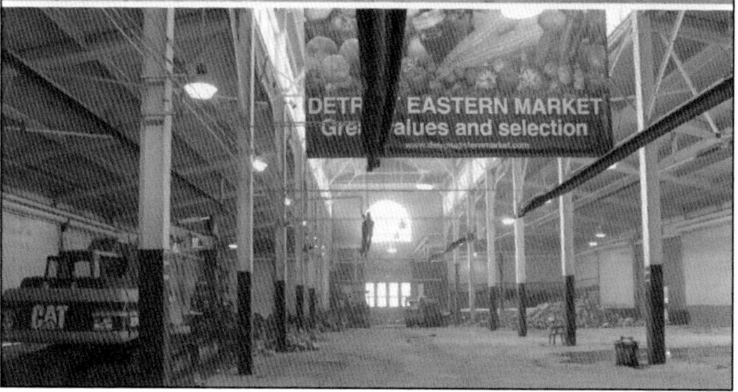

SHED 5 RENOVATION. Work began on Shed 5 in January 2012. Though it was the newest of the sheds, it had been out of date almost from the time of construction in 1981 and needed major renovation work to bring it up to the caliber of the recently renovated Shed 3. (EMC.)

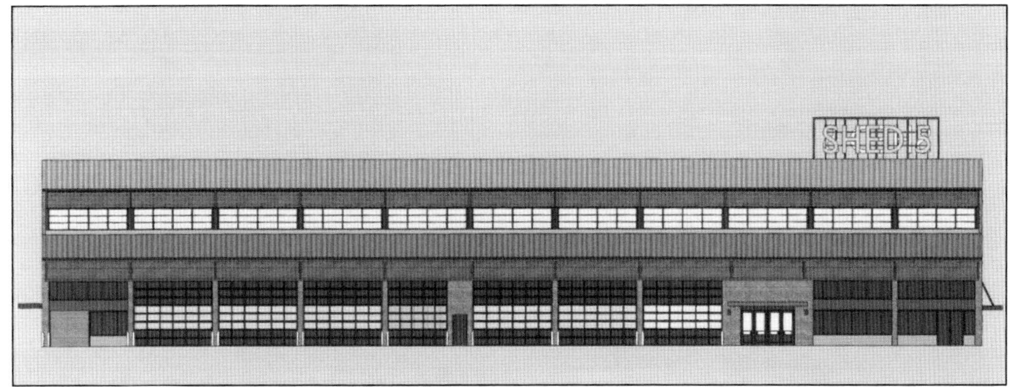

Shed 5's Rendering. When completed, Shed 5 will feature many of the amenities found in Shed 3, including restrooms, energy-efficient lighting, new windows and automatic garage doors, and radiant heat in the floors. (EMC.)

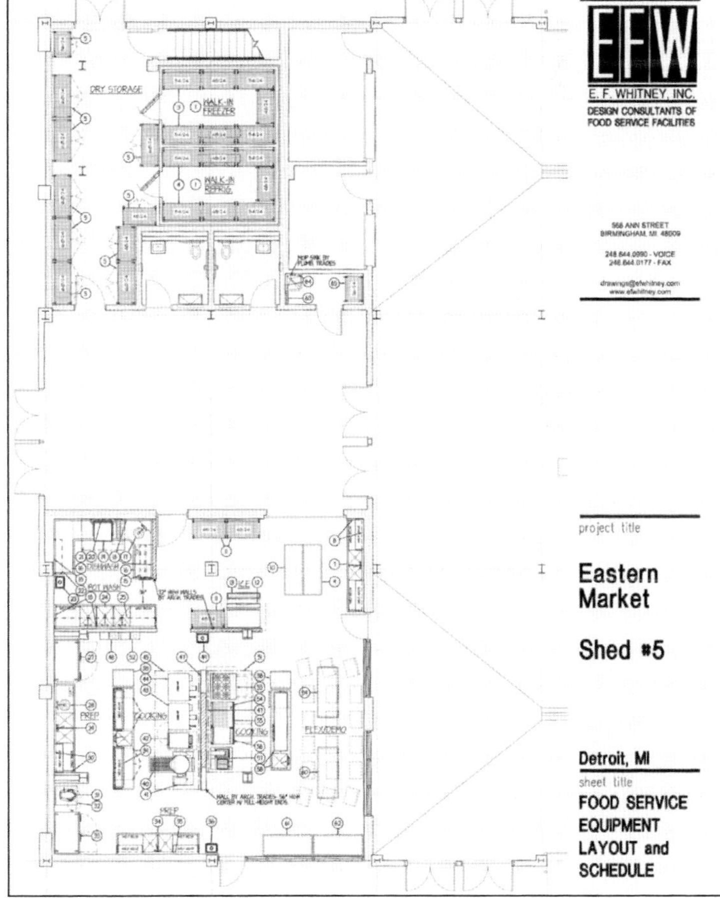

Shed 5 Community Kitchen. To foster new food entrepreneurship, provide urban farmers a place to wash and process their harvest, teach food safety and cooking classes, and host catered events at the market, EMC is building a community kitchen in Shed 5. The full-service, 1,200-square-foot kitchen will be outfitted with equipment that is being donated by Whole Foods Market. (EMC.)

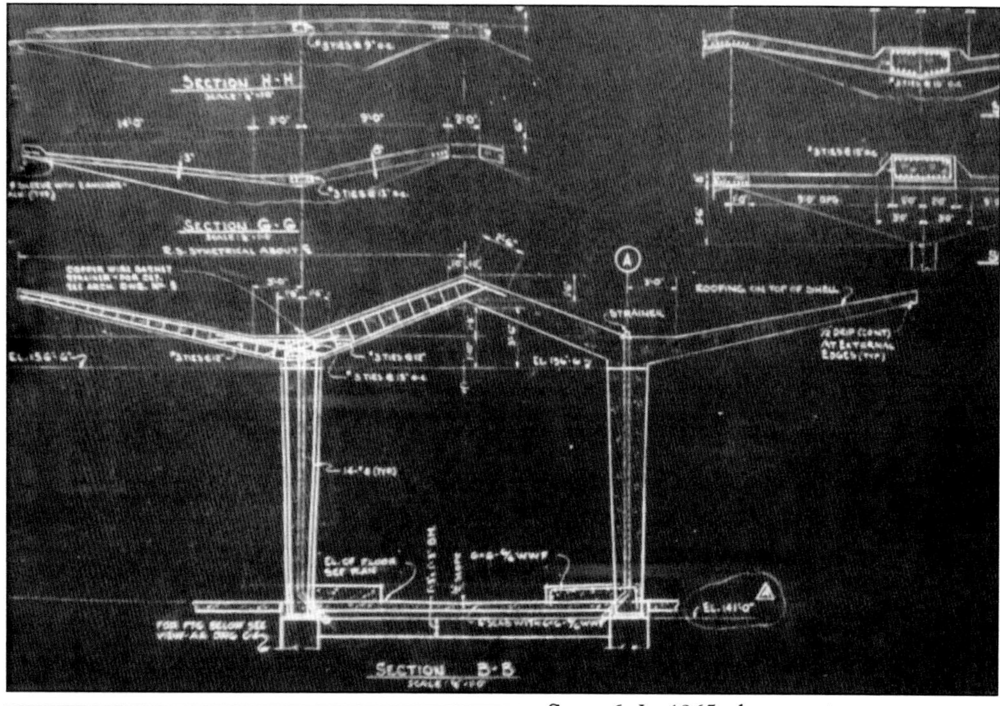

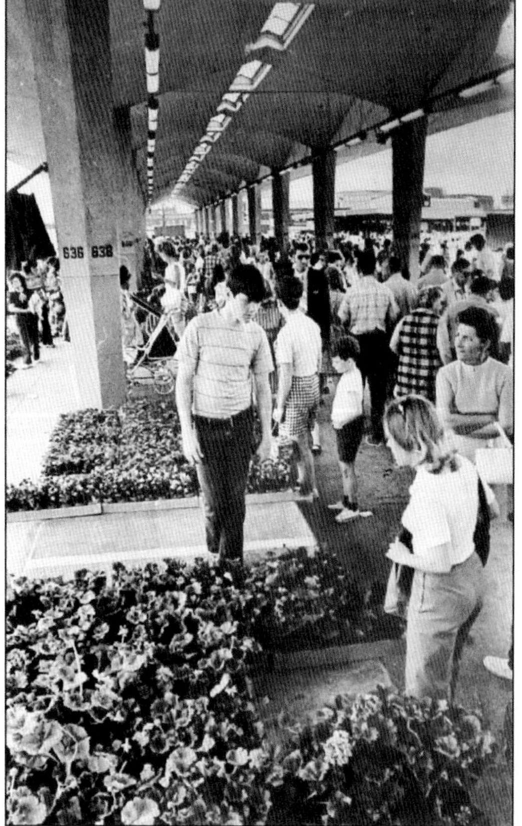

SHED 6. In 1965, three projects were undertaken at the Eastern Market: a new administration building at the corner of Russell and Wilkins Streets (currently the home of Eastern Market Corporation), a new truck scale in front of the administration building, and a new shed structure, Shed 6. Situated along Riopelle Street between Wilkins and Alfred Streets, Shed 6 is a modern canopy of steel-reinforced concrete with a tall, concave roof. (EMC.)

SHED 6'S DESIGN. Designed by the architectural firm of Giffels and Rossetti, the shed was constructed specifically to accommodate vendors from the pending closure and demolition of Western Market (1966) and the pending demolition of Shed 1 to make way for the freeway expansion (1967). The 26,000-square-foot shed features a roof with skylights to allow natural light to reach the pedestrian walkway down the middle, raised concrete platforms for vendor sales, and extra-large stalls to accommodate larger trucks. (EMC.)

Two

Farmers and Vendors

Eastern Market is not strictly a farmers' market; it is known instead as a public market. Almost since the very beginning, both farmers and produce dealers have sold at the market. For farmers, the market offered a place to sell their products directly to consumers and yield the highest return. The produce dealers were often recent immigrants who found that sector a low-barrier entry into American enterprise. Many of the market's brick-and-mortar businesses can trace their start back to an ancestor who worked as a produce dealer at Eastern Market.

There has always been a sense of community among farmers and vendors. The weekly outing is the revenue source, but it also is a chance to connect with fellow merchants and share their produce and lives with shoppers. Unlike a grocery store, the connection between producer and consumer is personal and direct. Oftentimes, the bonds between Easter Market's farmers and customers reach back two or three generations.

With the growing awareness of the importance of supporting local businesses and eating locally grown food, farmers' markets have proliferated across the United States and in metropolitan Detroit. Despite the competition, Eastern Market has continued to thrive, and vendors and customers alike feel a special connection to this historical, authentic place.

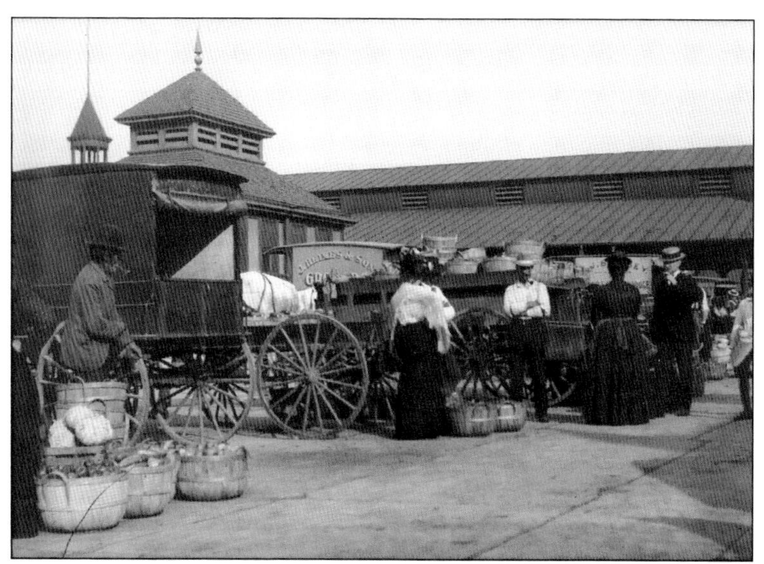

THE FIRST FARMERS. Eastern Market's first vendors came via horse and wagon, mainly from what were still rural farming communities within a 15-to-20-mile radius east of Gratiot Avenue. Selling at the market required a two-day trip, and the farmers often slept on bales of hay on their wagons at night. (BHC.)

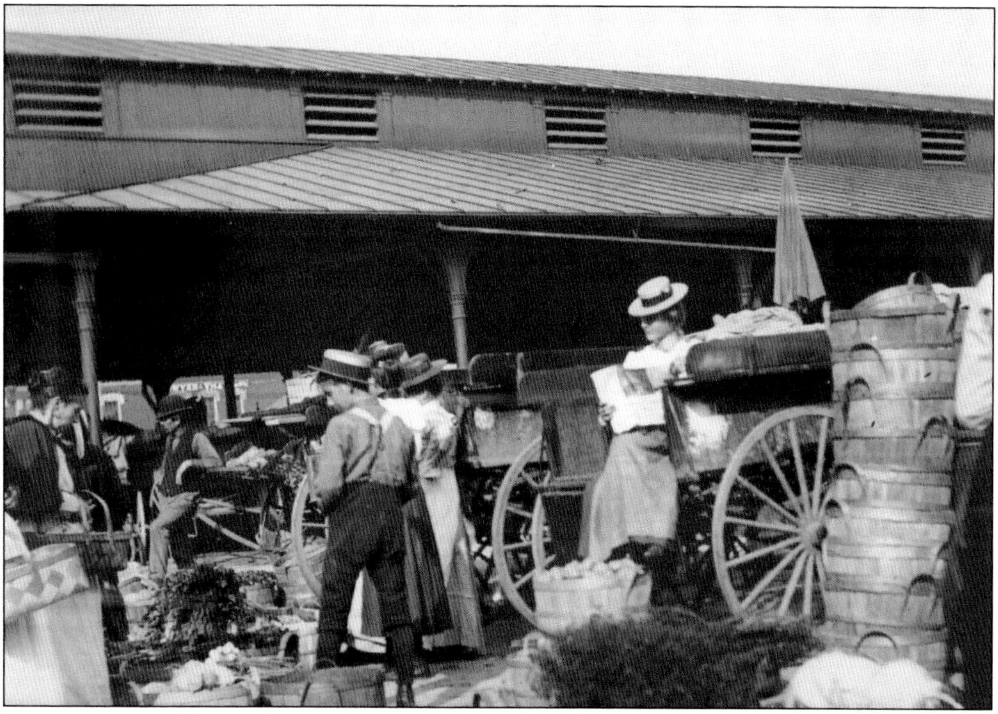

EARLY GROWTH. The market soon became a hub of retail and social activity, as both the German American community and a newer Italian immigrant neighborhood expanded along Gratiot Avenue. The Gratiot thoroughfare also became a vital link after the introduction of downtown-bound streetcars. Selling and buying at the market was a family and social event. For a time, shoppers and farmers set up a routine where each ethnic group would shop on a different day, with the farmers and vendors catering to each group's tastes on those specific days. (BHC.)

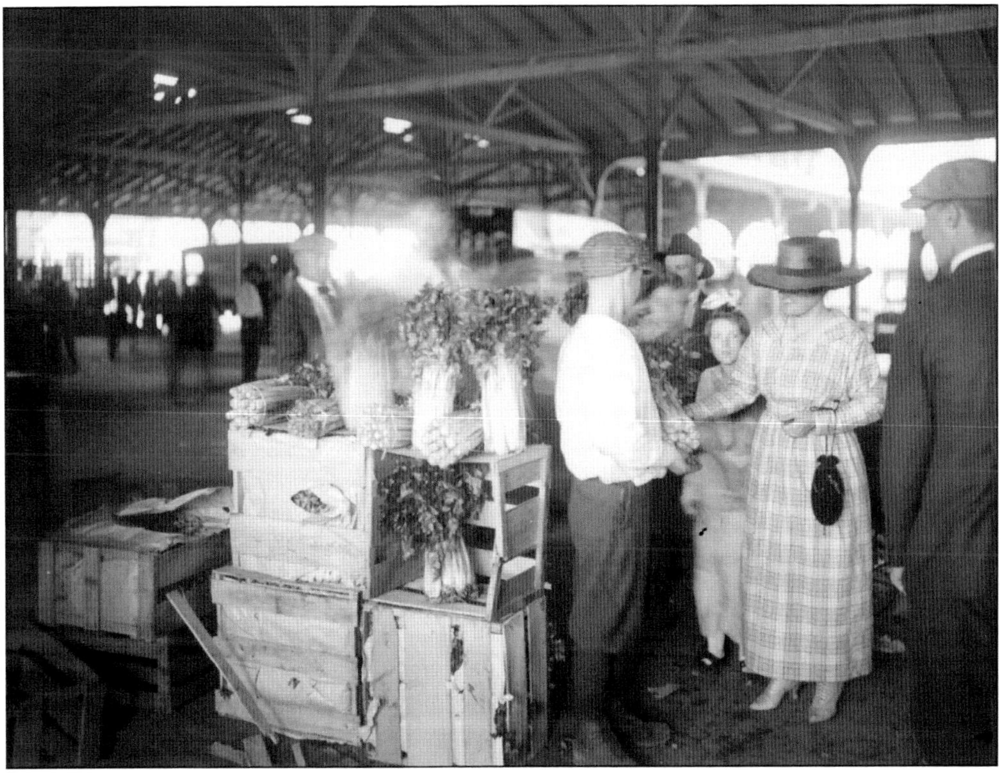

Ethnic Diversity. By 1920, about 20 percent of Michigan's farm operators were foreign born. Germans were employed as farmers more than any other migrant group, and this was especially so in the Midwest. Germans and Belgians were the predominant sellers at Eastern Market. Many settled on farms along Gratiot Avenue, which evolved into predominantly German American neighborhoods not far from the rapidly growing African American community centered around Hastings Street. (WRL.)

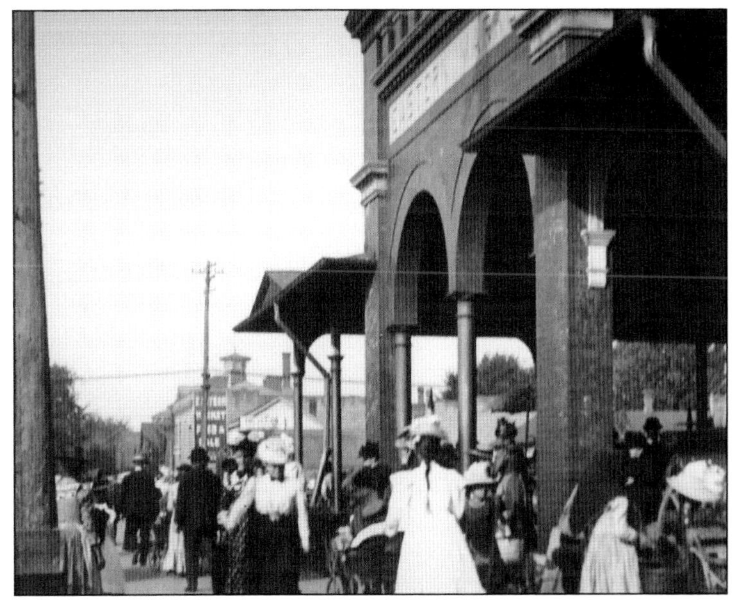

Saturdays at Eastern Market. Saturday was the busiest day at the market, with many farmers saving their best produce for that day. In 1899, between 13,000 and 15,000 shoppers came to the market on Saturdays, compared to an estimated 5,000 to 6,000 visitors on weekdays. The market opened to wholesalers between 6 a.m. and 9 a.m. and retail buyers from 8:00 a.m. until the end of the day. (BHC.)

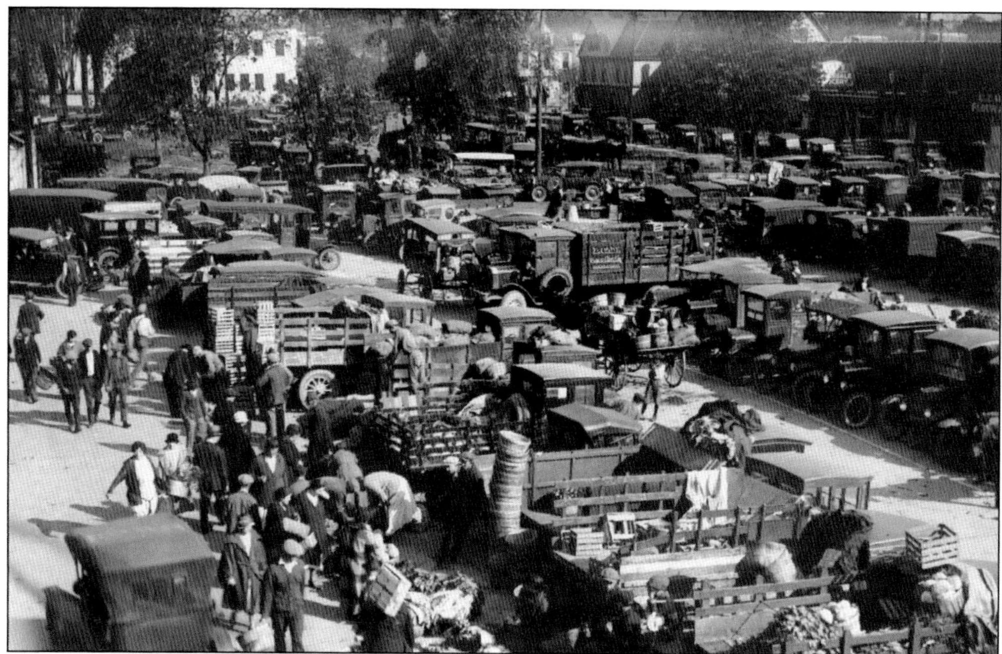

Better Methods of Transportation. With the introduction of the motor truck in the 1920s, farmers could come to Eastern Market from much greater distances than they had by horse and wagon. Using a motorized truck to haul their wares meant that farmers could now travel from within a 300-mile radius of Detroit. (WRL.)

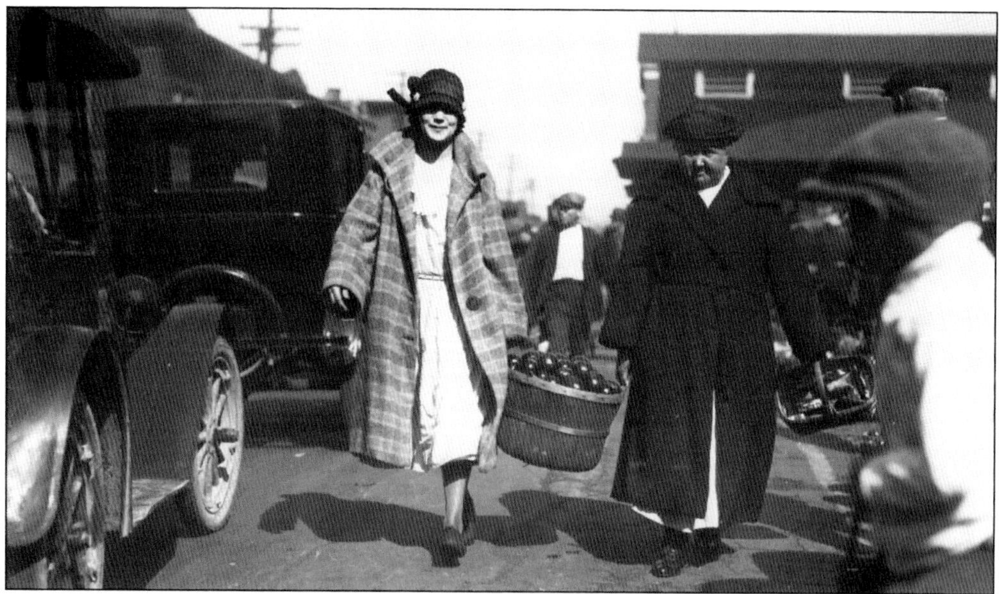

High Cost of Living. During the Depression, Detroit was ranked as among one of the most expensive cities for a US worker to live in. It was estimated that the average family of modest means spent 45 percent of their income on food. Newspapers and reformers spoke about the high cost of living and searched for ways to alleviate the situation. Farmers' markets were one obvious source of relief, allowing direct exchanges between buyers and sellers and eliminating the middleman. (WRL.)

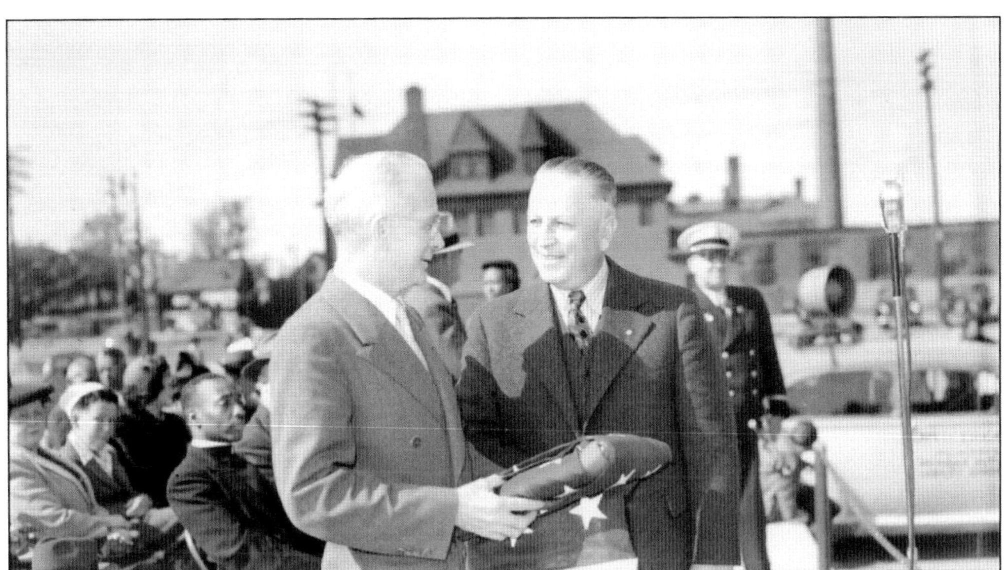

MARKET DIRECTOR GEORGE V. BRANCH. Under the reformist new Detroit City Charter of 1918, the two public markets, Eastern Market and Western Market, were shifted from the board of public works to the department of public welfare. The first mayor under the new charter, James Couzens, was in favor of expanding the market structure and hired George V. Branch as the new market director. Branch carried out these changes and developed the markets into a tightly regulated and consumer-oriented institution. He remained market director until his retirement in 1951 and is credited with many of the changes still in practice today. (WRL.)

DETROIT FARMERS' MARKET REPORT

DEPARTMENT OF PUBLIC WELFARE
MUNICIPAL BUREAU OF MARKETS
2093 18TH STREET
DETROIT, MICH.

VOL. 12 THURSDAY OCTOBER 1, 1931 NO. 160

SPECIAL NOTICE

On and after Thursday Oct. 1st., no producer or dealer selling on the Eastern Municipal Market shall hire any helper unless such helper has been approved and registered by the Bureau of Markets. Helpers may apply for registration at the Market Master's Office.

PRODUCT	SUPPLY	FARMERS' MARKET PRICES UP TO 9 A.M.						
		FANCY GRADE		NO. 1 GRADE			NO. 2 GRADE	
		LOW	HIGH	LOW	HIGH	MOST	LOW	HIGH
Apples, bu.	mod	1.25	1 50	.60	1 00	.75	.40	50
Beans, wax bu.	mod			1.50	2.00	1.75 (green 1.50-2.00 bu.)		
Beets, dz bchs	mod (.40-.50 bu.)			25	.40	.30		
Cabbage bu	mod (curly .60-.75 bu.)			.50	.75	.60 (red cabbage .65-1.00 bu.)		
Cantaloup	hvy		1 50	.75	1.25	1.00	.40	.60
Carrots, dz bchs	hvy (.60-.85 bu.)			.25	.35	.30		
Cauliflower bu.	mod			1.00	1.50	1.25	.75	1.00
Celery doz bchs.	mod	.60	.65	.40	.50	.45	.15	.25
Cucumbers bu	hvy (pickles 1.00-2.00 bu.)			.60	1.00	.75 (dills 1.00-1.50)		
Eggs, doz.	mod (whsl 7.50-8.10 30 doz. case)						(retail .28-.35)	
Endive, bu.	mod	1.50	2.00	.50	1.00	.75		
Grapes	mod (.25-.35 12 qt basket)(.75-1.25 bu.)							
Lettuce bu leaf	mod ((H H .60 7# basket)			.75	1.25	1.00	.50	.60
Onions, Green doz. bchs.	lgt (picklers 1.25-1.75 bu.)			.30	.60	.40 (dry .90-1.35 bu.)		
Parsley, bu.	mod (curly .25-.40 dz bchs.)			.40	.60	.50		
Parsnips bu.	lgt			.75	1.25	1.00		
Peaches bu	lgt			1.50	2.00	1.75 (hales 3.00-4.00)		
Pears bu.	mod	2.00	2.50	1.50	2.00	1.75	1.00	1.25
Peas, bu.	lgt			2.00	2.50	2.25	1.00	1.50
Peppers, sweet bu.	mod (hot .50-.75)			.50	.75	.60 (red .75-1.25)		
Plums	mod	2.25	2.50	1.50	2.00	1.75	1.00	1.25
Potatoes bu.	mod			.60	.75	.70	.35	.50
Poultry, live, lb								
Hens	mod (leghorn .18-.20)			.21	.24	.23	(retail .25-.28)	
Broilers	lgt (leghorn .18-.20)(rocks .22-.24 lb.)							
Ducks	lgt			.16	.18	.17		
Geese	none							
Poultry, Dressed, lb	lgt retail (hens & springers .30-.35)(ducks .30-.35)							
Radishes, bu.	mod (long .30-.40 dz bchs.)			.75	1.25	1.00 (black .60-.75 bu.)		
Spinach	mod			.75	1.25	1.00		
Squash, hubbard, bu	mod (Italian 1.00-2.00) (Table Queen & Sweet Potato .75-1.25)			.60	.90	.75 (summer .35-.50)		
Sweet Corn, 5 doz sack	lgt			.50	.75	.60		
Tomatoes, bu.	hvy	1.00	1.50	.40	.75	.50	.30	.40
Turnips dz. bchs	mod (.75-1.00 bu.)			.25	.50	.35 (greens .40-.60 bu.)		

Rhubarb .35-.60 dz bchs. Quince 2.00-2.50 bu.
Celery Cabbage .50-1.00 bu. Collards bu .35-.50 Crab Apples 1.00-1.50 bu. Veal .14-.16 lb.
Pimentos .50-1.00 bu. Watermelons .60-1.00 bu.
Butter .30-.40 lb. Bagas .75-1.00 bu. Mustard .40-.60 bu. Escarole .40-.60 bu.
Leeks .40-.60 doz. bchs. Vegetable Oysters .60-.75 dz bchs. Egg plant .40-.50 bu.
Sorrel .35-.50 bu. Dill .35-.50 dz. bchs. Chard .30-.50 bu. Pumpkins .60-.75 bu.
Romaine .50-.75 bu. Kohlrabi .30-.40 dz bchs. Kale .30-.40 bu. Broccoli .75-1.00 bu.
Okra 3.00-4.00 bu. Lima Beans 1.50-2.00 bu. -.25-.35 qt. Horse-radish 3.50-5.00 bu.

*The above represents wholesale prices and conditions and does not cover sales in small quantities to consumers except when marked "retail." —Market reported by H. B. Chamberlain

CHANGES UNDER BRANCH. Under Branch's leadership, price-speculation practices were eliminated by publishing a daily market report that publicly displayed pricing as well as product supply and demand. Ordinances were implemented to protect the farmers and their customers. Branch also instituted a special Saturday afternoon wholesale market, where dealers could sell surplus produce "that could not be held over" at a lower cost, providing less affluent shoppers more options. (EMC.)

PRODUCER

STALL NO.

SALES TAX NO.

DETROIT MUNICIPAL MARKETS

Changes in Market Regulations. Farmers (producers) and wholesalers (dealers) were required to be licensed and were assigned a specific stall location. These signs were required until the 1970s, and although they are no longer required, many longtime farmers and dealers continue to display their signs when selling at the market. (EMC.)

MARKET HELPER

NAME DiFILLIPPO, Dominic BADGE NO. 1 4 2

ADDRESS 3477 Jos Campau

AGE 39 WEIGHT 195 EYES Hazel HAIR Black

HEIGHT 5'-10" RACE W. SCHOOL PERMIT NO.

SOCIAL SECURITY NO ---- DRIVER'S LICENSE NO. ---

DATE BADGE ISSUED 8/4/49 ISSUED BY Rogers

(SIGNED)

CONDUCT RECORD

RIGHT THUMB PRINT

REGISTERED HELPER 1420 DETROIT MUNICIPAL MARKETS

Market Helpers. The growers at the weekday wholesale market often hired market helpers to assist in delivering merchandise to their buyers. The helpers were relatively unskilled laborers who transferred produce from the growers' trucks on carts, or "larrys," to the waiting purchaser. Parking spots were laid out in squares, with a square manager supervising the loading and unloading of trucks. This allowed the grower to remain at his spot and provided a small wage for helpers, who generally used this to supplement full-time employment elsewhere. All market helpers were required to be registered with the market office and were fingerprinted and photographed. Market helpers were then free to negotiate their wages, hours, and working conditions with the specific grower. (EMC and DO.)

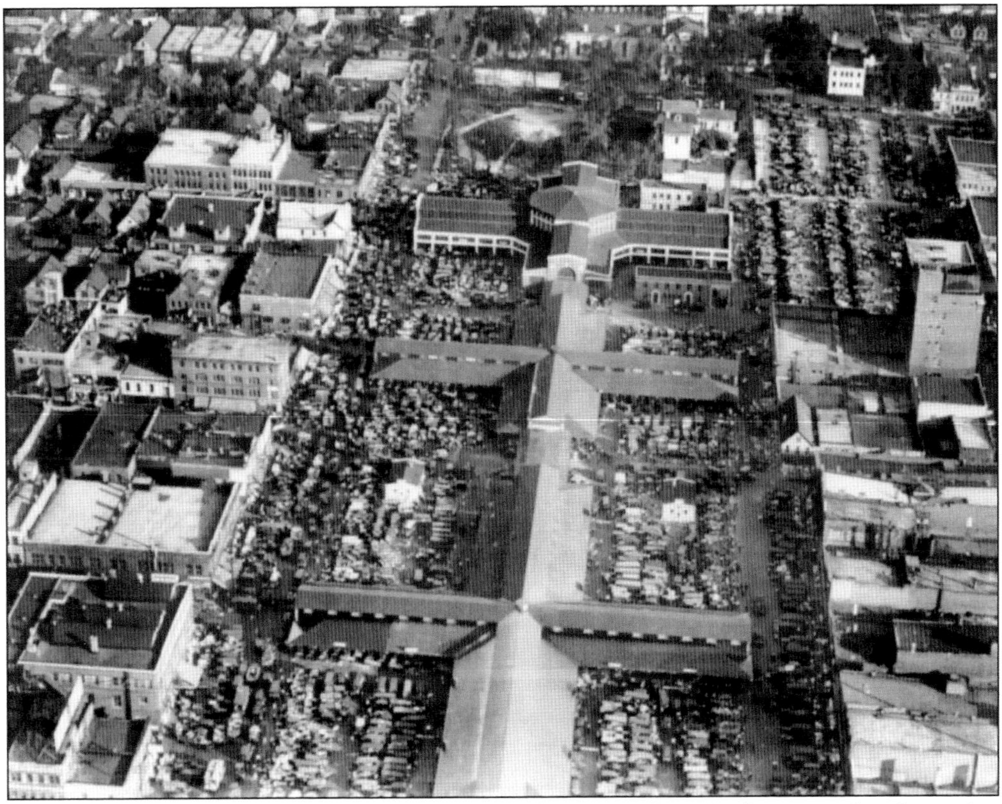

"One of the Best Run Farmer's Markets in the Country." By 1924, five years after the market reorganization under Branch, a series of articles for a farm periodical surveyed farmers' markets and concluded that Detroit had one of the best. It was "clean, well-run, and non-partisan . . . a place where the interests of farmers and consumers prevailed rather than those of politicians." Newspaper articles at the time reported that Eastern Market was said to be the largest in the world. In those five years, the number of registered producers had more than doubled, from 400 to 832, and there were 111 Saturday afternoon dealers. It was estimated that a third of the city's produce passed through the market sheds. (DO.)

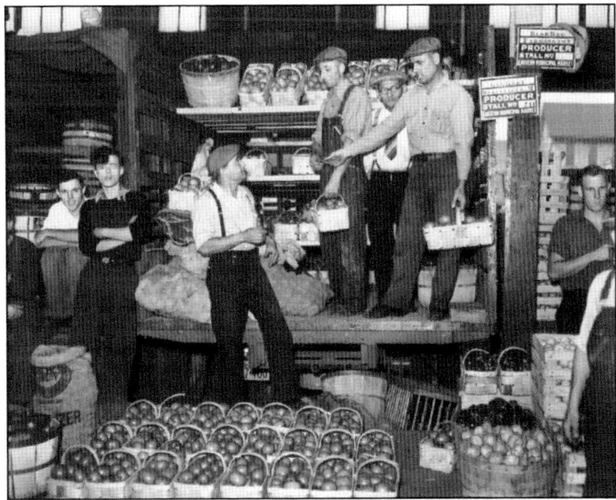

During the Great Depression. Detroit's public markets, which by the 1930s also included the Chene-Ferry Market in addition to the Eastern and Western Markets, flourished during the Great Depression. According to city reports, 1933 was its peak year, with more than 161,000 truckloads brought in by growers to sell. With unemployment at its peak, jobless laborers returned to farming to produce truck gardens for their livelihood. The city's public market facilities offered a dependable place to sell produce as well as steady customers. (WRL.)

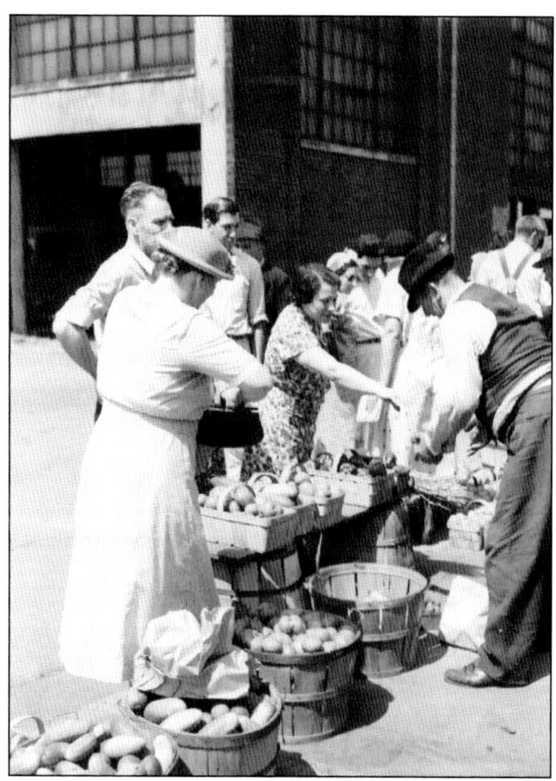

Wartime Food Rationing. During World War II, Detroit's markets flourished once again as a welcome solution to food shortages. Until 1944, shoppers at public markets did not need to use the ration coupons that were required at retail establishments. Black-market prices were a standard practice, which were even published in the market news bulletins. (WRL.)

Poultry Sales. In addition to produce, live turkeys, chickens, and rabbits (which were considered poultry) were sold at the market for many years. (EMC and WRL.)

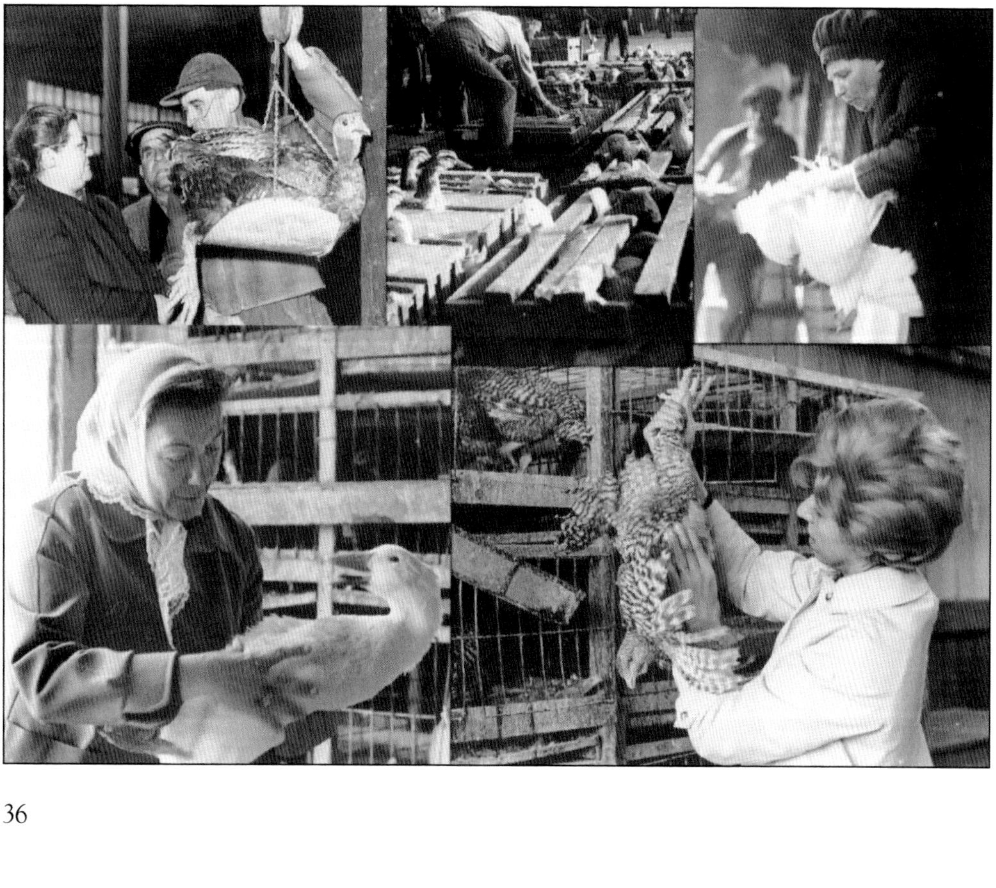

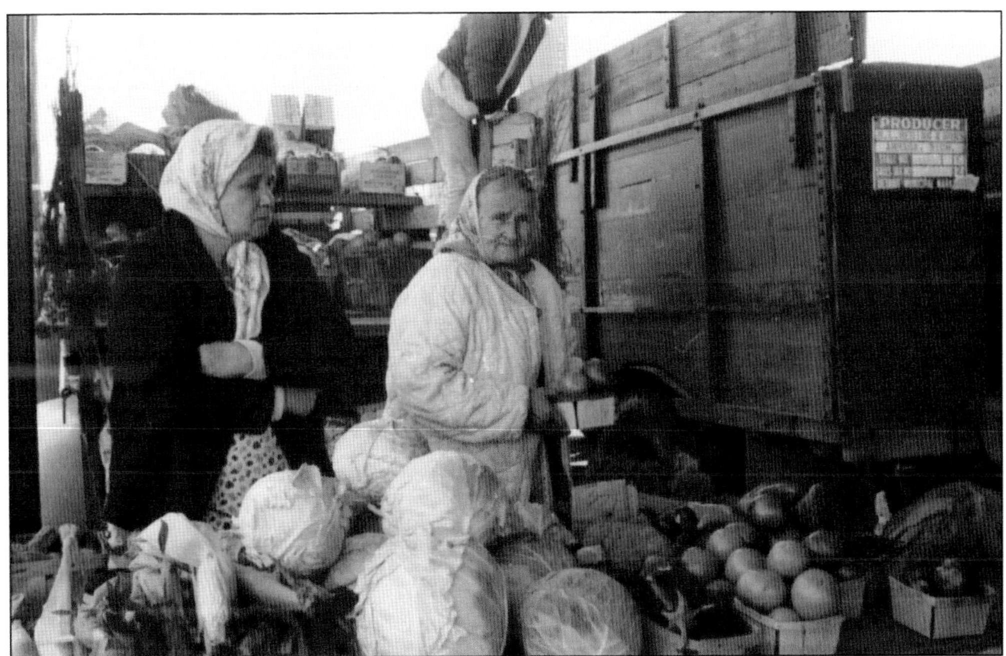

DECLINE OF THE MARKETS. After World War II, market visitor and sales data began a steep decline. Supermarket chains expanded in Detroit and its suburbs, while agricultural innovations allowed wholesalers and retailers to contract directly with farmers. Many longtime merchants simply retired. In 1966, a total of 49,097 truckloads were sold at the market, but just one year later that number had dropped to 21,700 truckloads. By 1968, the market was operating at a deficit, and the city considered closing it altogether. (WRL.)

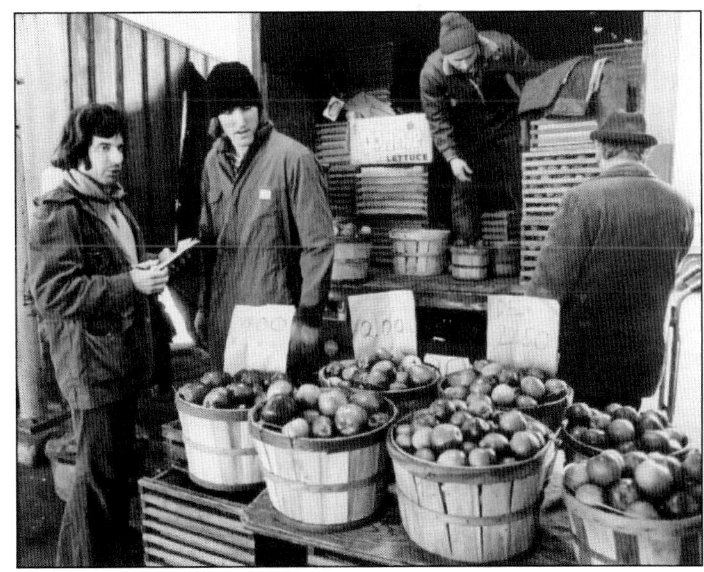

MARKET REVITALIZATION. In the early 1970s, Eastern Market underwent a face-lift, most notably the collection of murals decorating many of the buildings. The publicity resulting from the murals and the "back to nature" movement of the time fueled a renewed interest in Eastern Market, and by 1973 the market was operating in the black again. (EMC.)

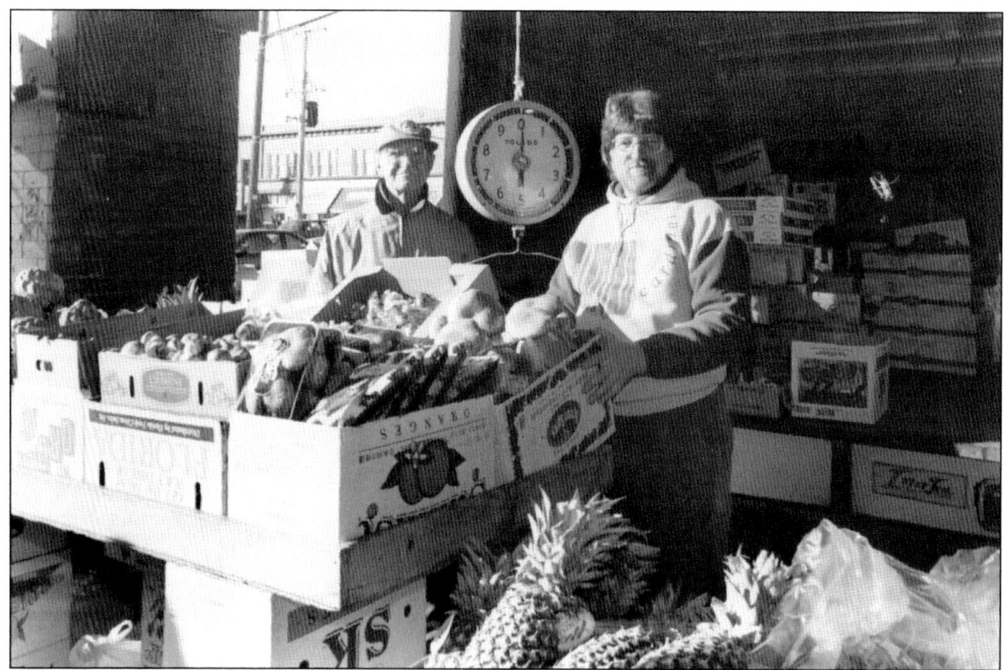

Stall Assignments. A complicated system based on seniority, proximity to other sellers with the same merchandise, yearly or seasonal rental prices, and other factors determined which stall was rented to which producer or dealer. The most senior sellers were located in stalls facing Russell Street and in Sheds 1 or 2. If a seller chose to give up his spot, the next-most-senior seller was given the option of taking over that stall. (Courtesy of Don Schneider.)

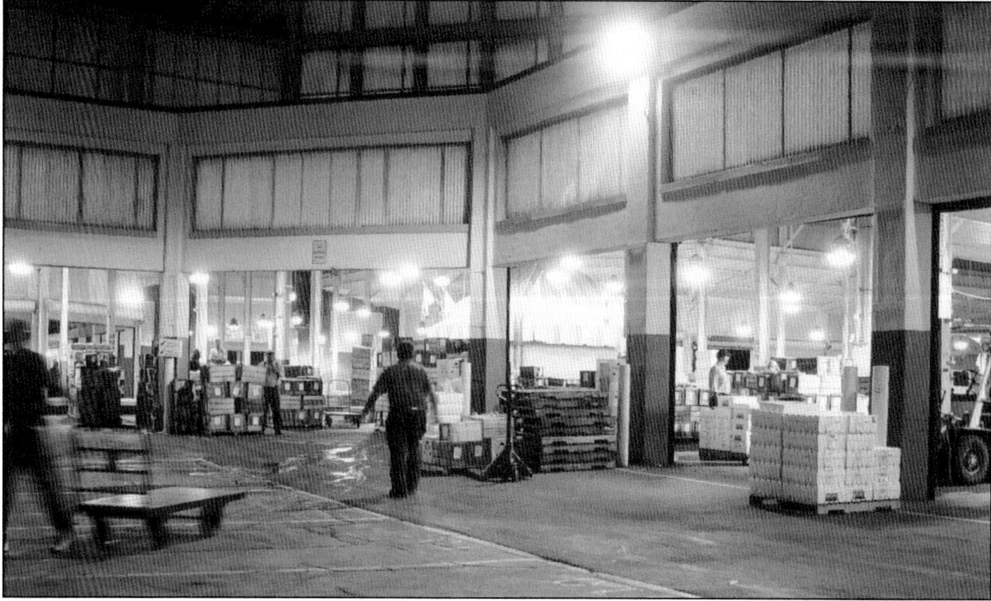

Wholesale Market. While most Detroiters are sleeping, Eastern Market is buzzing with wholesale activity. Monday through Friday, from 12:00 a.m. to 6:00 a.m., farmers from all over the region sell their produce to buyers from local independent grocery store chains and produce distributors. (EMC.)

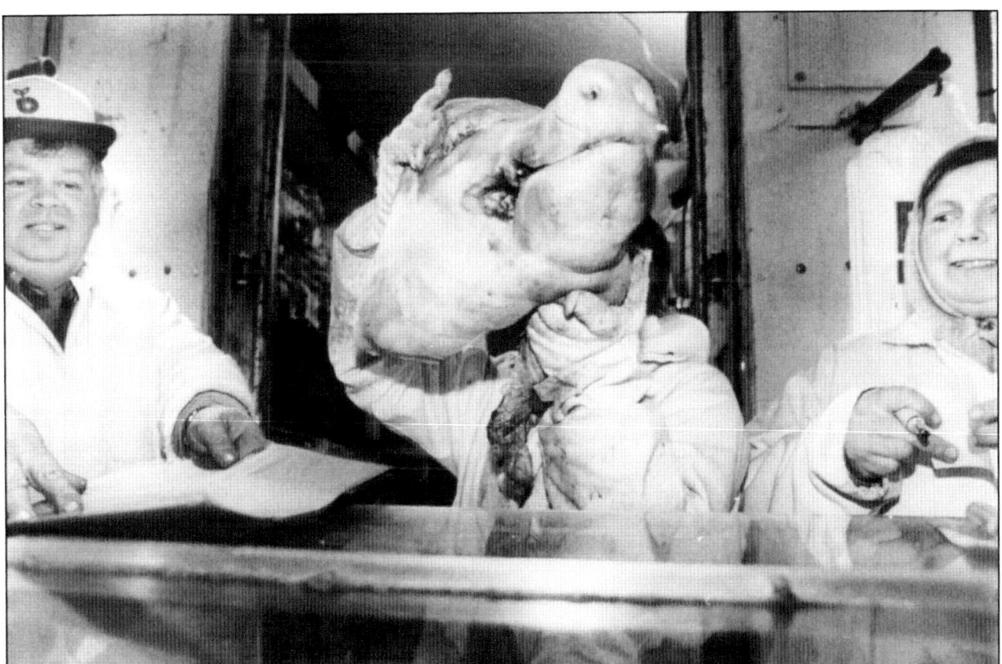

Pork Sales. Since the 1970s, during the cold-weather months, temperatures have been cold enough to allow farmers to sell freshly slaughtered pork from the unheated sheds. This tradition continues today with portable refrigerated meat cases and refrigerated trucks. (EMC.)

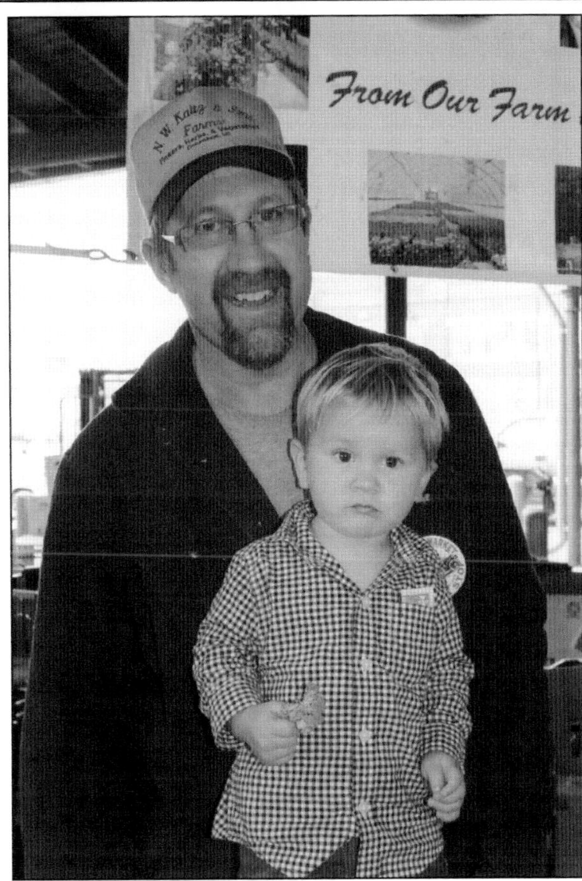

Today's Farmers. Today, farmers come from all over Michigan, northern Ohio, and even Ontario, Canada, to bring their farm-fresh produce to shoppers at Eastern Market. While some farmers travel great distances, the majority of Michigan farmers who come to the market are either from just north of Detroit (centered around Macomb County) or just south of Detroit (centered around Monroe County). Farms range in size from a couple of acres to over 1,000 acres, and many of the families selling at the market are second-, third-, and even fourth-generation local farmers. (EMC.)

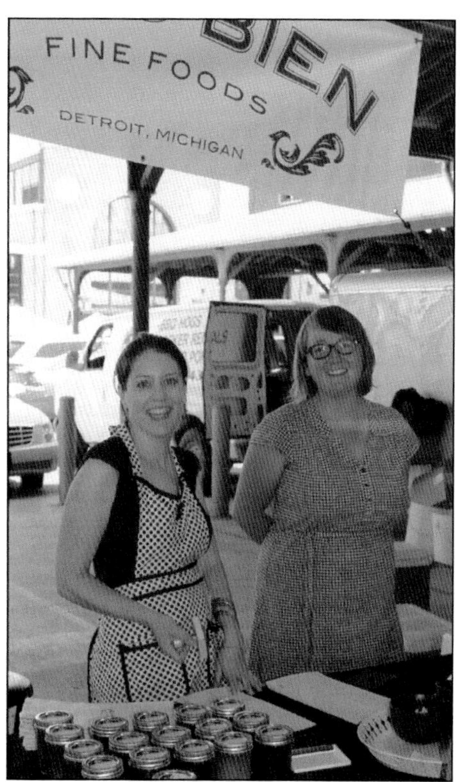

Specialty Goods. Since Shed 2 was renovated in 2008, its east and west wings have been home to a growing number of manufacturers of Michigan-made specialty products, such as jam, salsa, baked goods, pickles, cheese, sausage, granola, spices, and more. For many of these local businesses, Eastern Market is the first place they sell a product to the public, as it offers a great place to interact with a large customer base without the investment in a traditional brick-and-mortar location. In addition, a limited amount of prepared foods and food trucks can also be found for those looking for a quick snack. (EMC.)

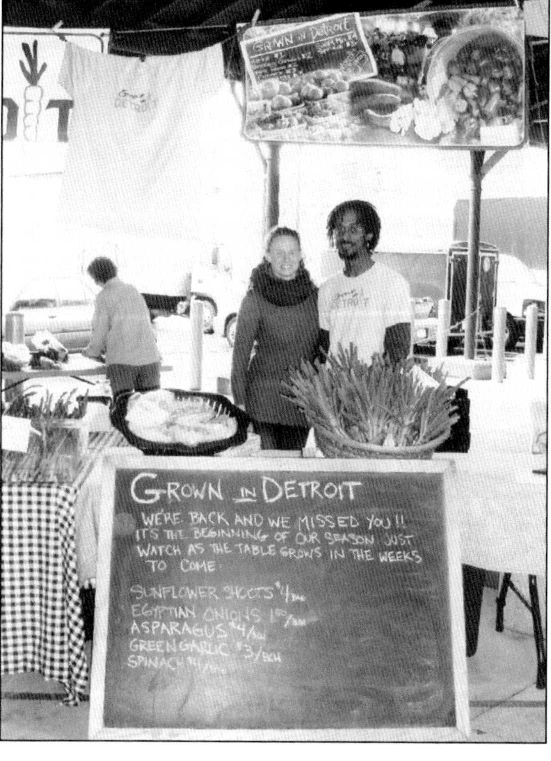

New Farmers. Detroit has received national media attention for its newfound role as a leader in the urban agriculture movement. Produce that is grown in the city, aggregated each week from some of the nearly 1,400 urban gardens in the city, can be found in Shed 2 under the proudly displayed "Grown in Detroit" sign. (EMC.)

Three

Churches

In 1701, two days after the French arrived in Detroit and established Fort Pontchartrain, construction began on a church. As evidenced by the emphasis early settlers placed on establishing a congregation, organized religion played a very important role in the history and development of Detroit. Eastern Market is no exception to this rule.

For many, a church is the center of the community. A common ancestry and practice of religion brings people together. This was especially true for the many different ethnic groups that settled around the market district. In addition, the actual houses of worship often reflected both the social status and cultural heritage of the congregations. The churches near Gratiot Avenue—Historic Trinity, St. Joseph's Roman Catholic Church, and St. John's-St. Luke's—were originally built as smaller neighborhood churches closer to downtown Detroit.

As the congregations grew and the communities migrated eastward along Gratiot Avenue, the churches were rebuilt larger and more ornately than their predecessors, often reflecting traditions and architecture from the immigrants' land of origin. Each church usually consisted of several buildings and often included a school.

This continual migration also had the symbiotic effect of freeing up existing church buildings to allow smaller congregations to "move up." An example of this is the Sacred Heart Church. After the original German community continued its northeast migration, the existing church became the center of the African American Catholic church in Detroit.

Each of these four churches remains active today. The congregations have grown, garnering new members from the city. Also, many descendants of original members still return to their family churches even though they no longer live in the area.

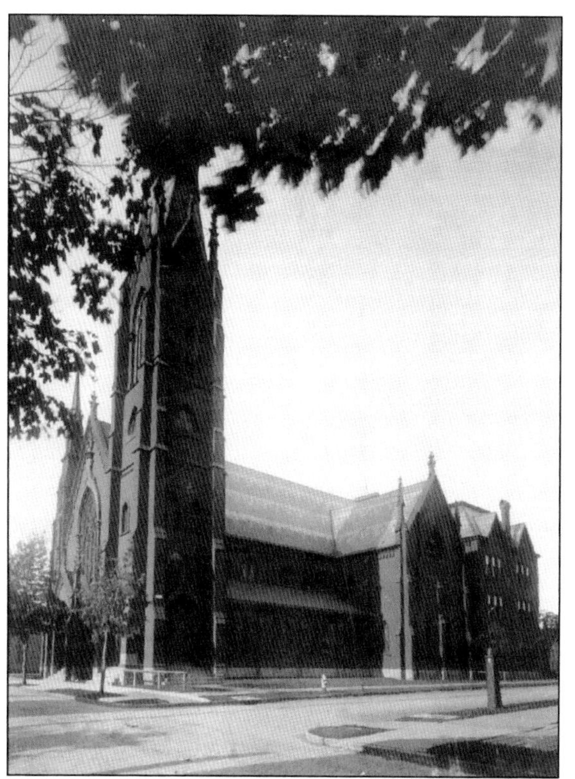

St. John's-St. Luke's Exterior. St. John's, the oldest German Protestant church in Detroit, held its first religious services on August 18, 1833. The congregation's first building was on the corner of Farrar and Monroe Streets near downtown. A new building at 2120 Russell Street was dedicated on September 20, 1874. This 500-seat Gothic Revival structure was designed by architect Julius Hess and is still the congregation's home today. (OSJ.)

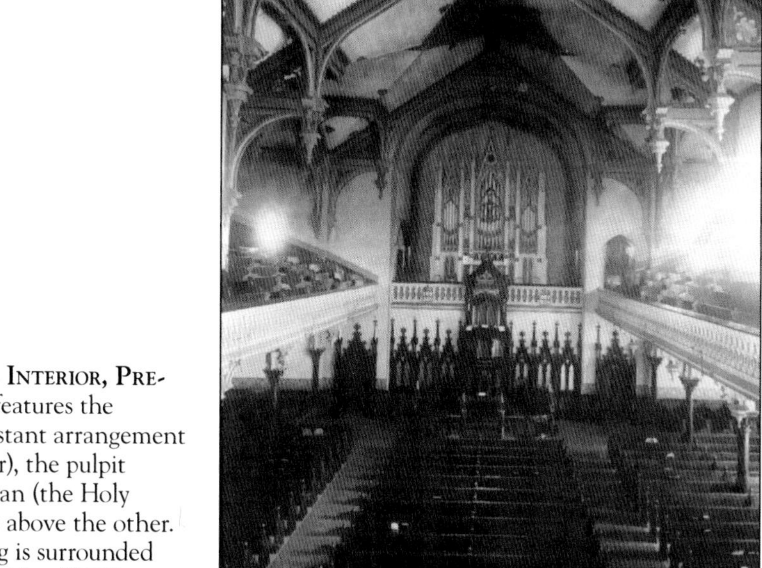

St. John's-St. Luke's Interior, Pre-1915. The sanctuary features the typical German Protestant arrangement of the altar (the Father), the pulpit (the Son), and the organ (the Holy Ghost), with each one above the other. The main floor seating is surrounded by balconies on three sides. (OSJ.)

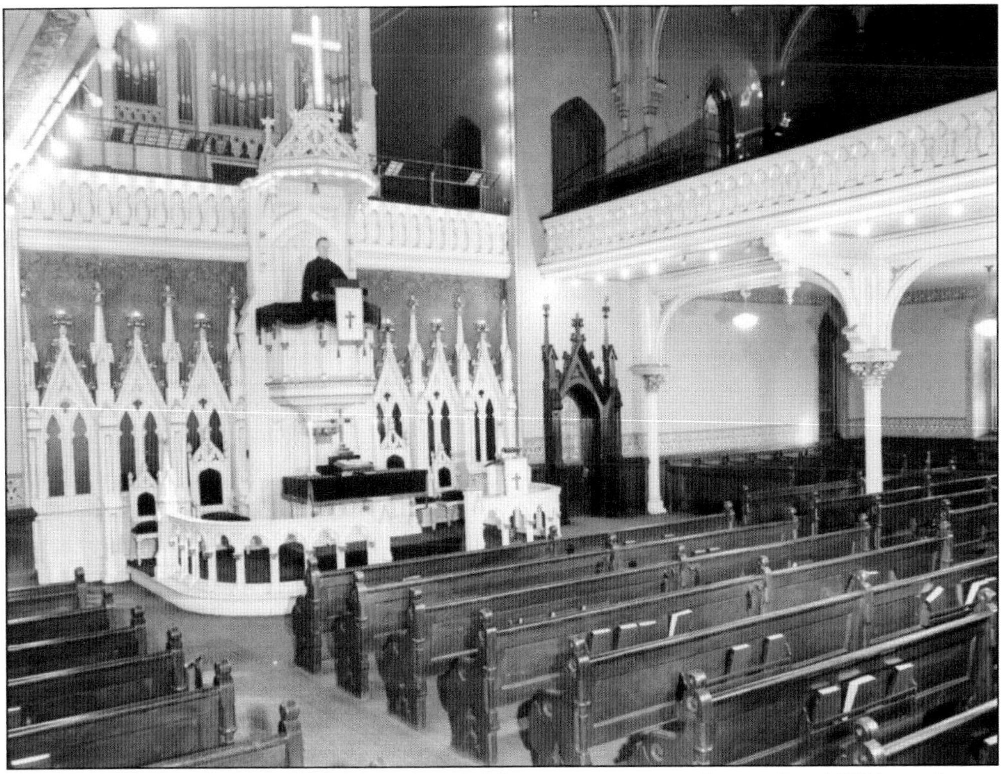

St. John's-St. Luke's Interior, Post-1915. The interior was modernized in 1915 by architect Hans Gehrke. The renovation included extensive state-of-the-art lighting and covering of original dark wood with white paint. (WRL.)

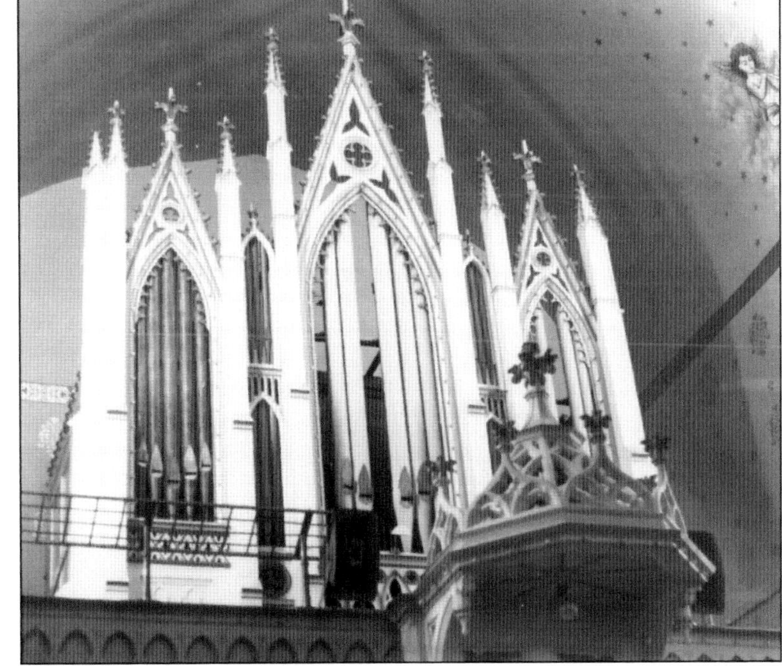

St. John's-St. Luke's Organ. The building is home to the original pipe organ, constructed by Gottlieb F. Votteler of Cleveland. It has a traditional tracker operation and was completely restored in 1983. (OSJ.)

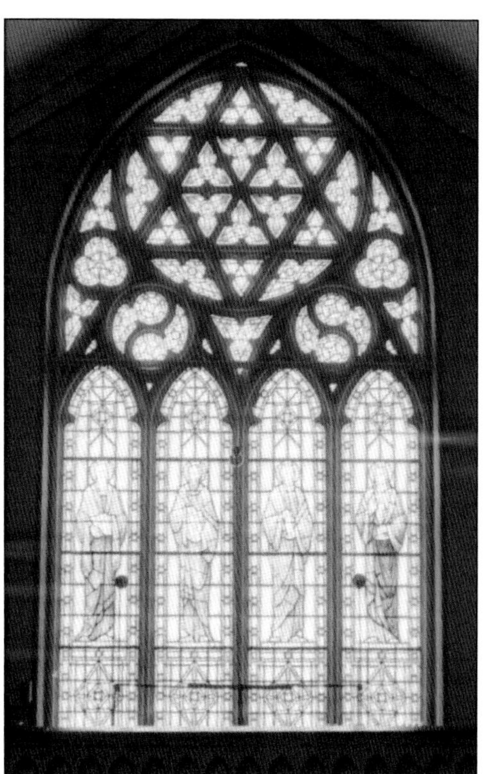

St. John's-St. Luke's Stained Glass. The Judeo-Christian Memorial Window, featuring the Star of David and the figures of Matthew, Mark, Luke, and John, was installed in 1947. It was created especially for the church by Detroit Stained Glass Works, which operated in Detroit from 1861 to 1970. (WRL.)

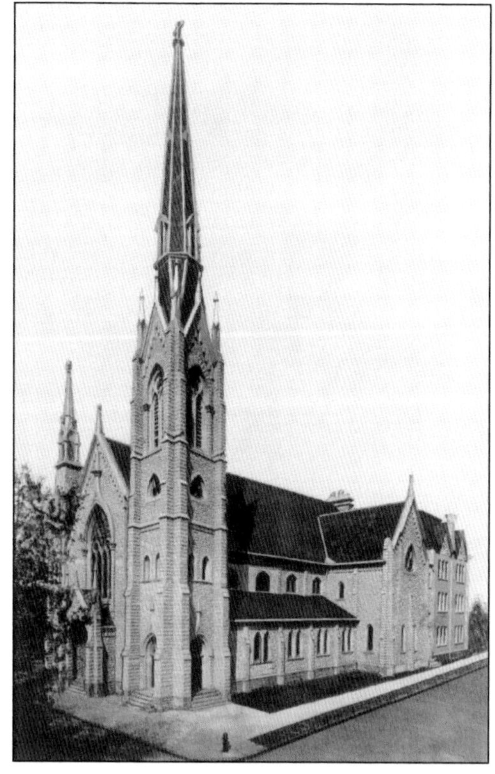

St. John's-St. Luke's Merger. The congregation of St. Luke's, with their own building on East Warren and Rohns Streets, was founded in 1888. The two congregations merged in 1969 when St. Luke's moved into the existing St. John's Gothic Revival building. The combined congregation has been known since that time as St. John's-St. Luke's. (OSJ.)

ORIGINAL HISTORIC TRINITY CHURCH. Trinity Lutheran Church, organized on November 10, 1850, was the first Lutheran church of the Missouri Synod in Detroit. Worship services were first held in buildings near Rivard and Larned Streets. In 1866, a larger, redbrick church was built at 1345 Gratiot Avenue, at the intersection of Rivard Street, to accommodate the growing number of German Lutherans in the area. The new building was constructed at a cost of $22,000 and seated 800 congregants. The church held services in German until 1913, when an English-language Mass was introduced. (HT.)

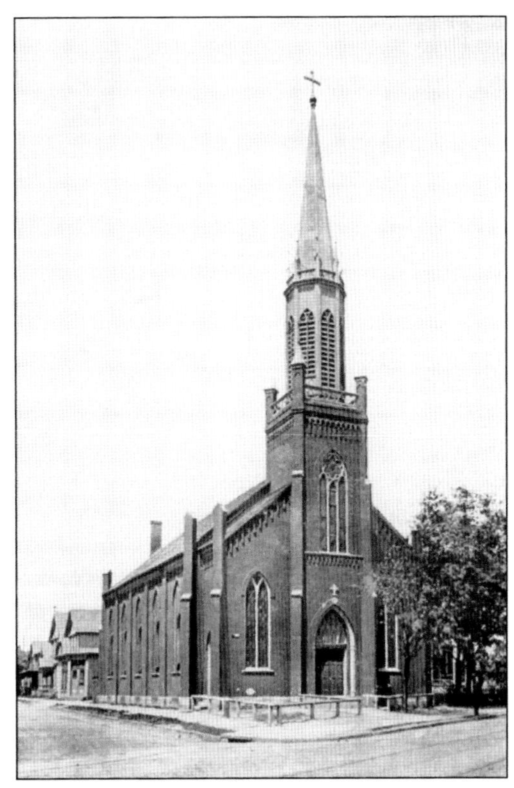

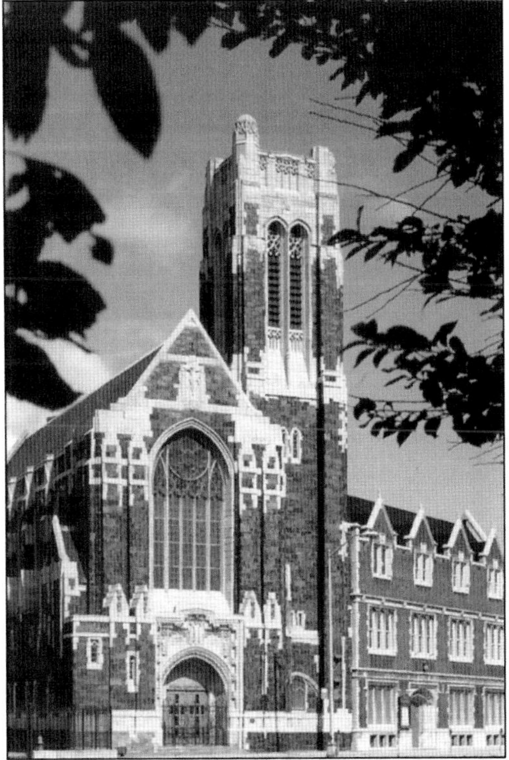

HISTORIC TRINITY GROWS. In the late 1920s, Charles Gauss, a businessman and a member of the church, offered to pay for a new church building at the same location in gratitude for his daughter's recovery from polio surgery. The brick church was demolished and a new pier-and-clerestory edifice, reminiscent of 16th-century Gothic churches in Europe, was built of varied-color granite and Indiana limestone. The building was dedicated on Ascension Sunday in 1931. (HT.)

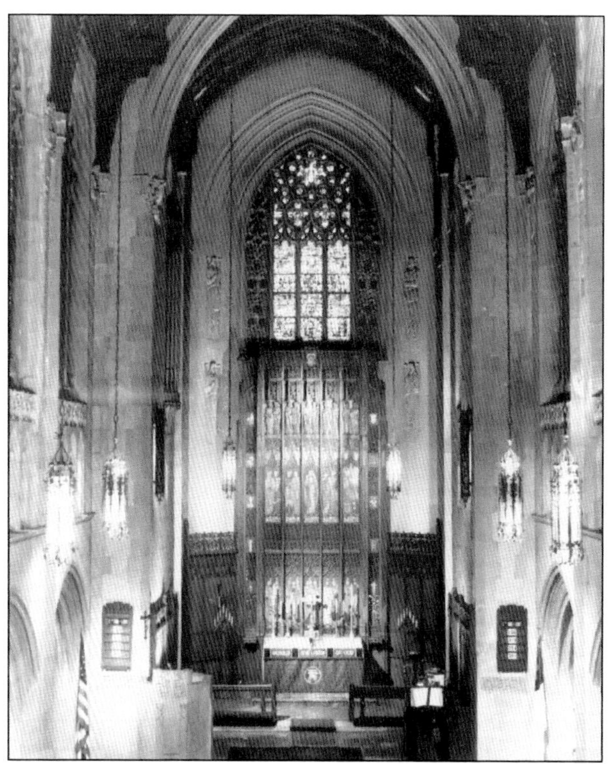

Historic Trinity Shines. The church is a beautiful example of Gothic art and architecture. Designed by W.E.N. Hunter and created with the help of some of the city's finest artisans, the church features a slate roof and floor, stained glass, stone and wood carvings, tile work, and paintings, all depicting symbols of the Lutheran faith. (HT.)

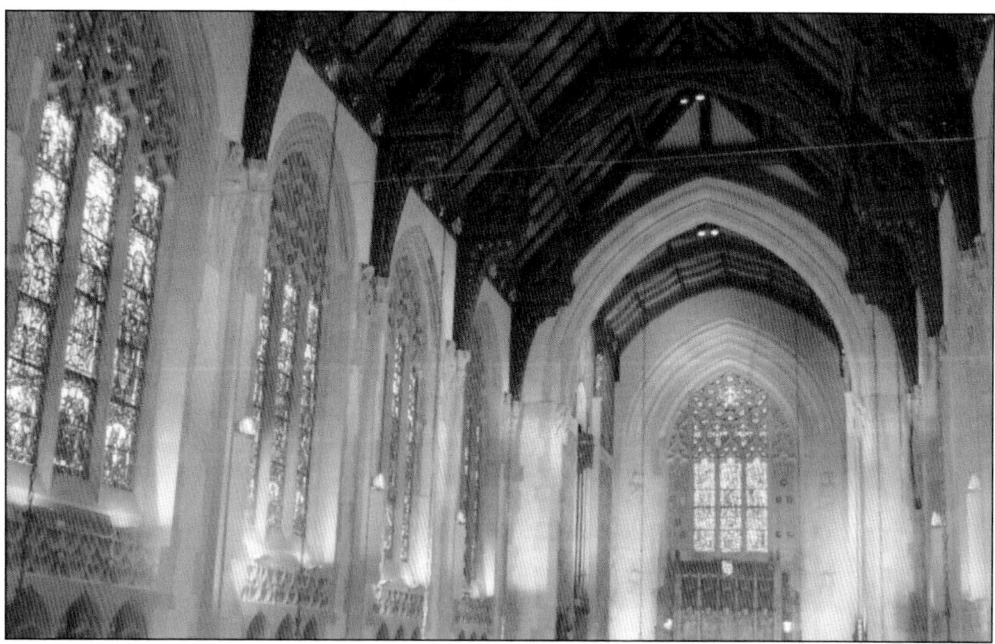

Historic Trinity's Stained Glass. The large stained-glass windows were designed, manufactured, and installed by Henry Lee Willet of the Willet Stained Glass Company of Philadelphia. The altar window depicts the Resurrection and the Ascension, the balcony window includes a verse from John 1:15 ("I am the vine and ye are the branches"), and the nine windows in the nave feature notable figures from the Old and New Testaments. (HT.)

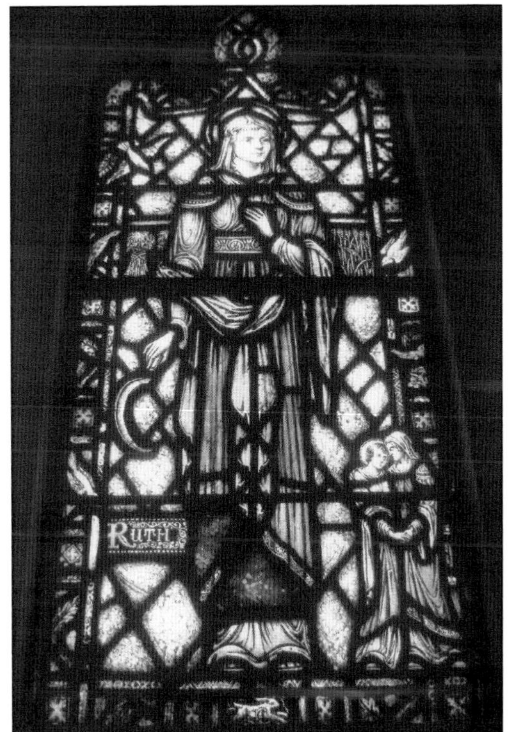

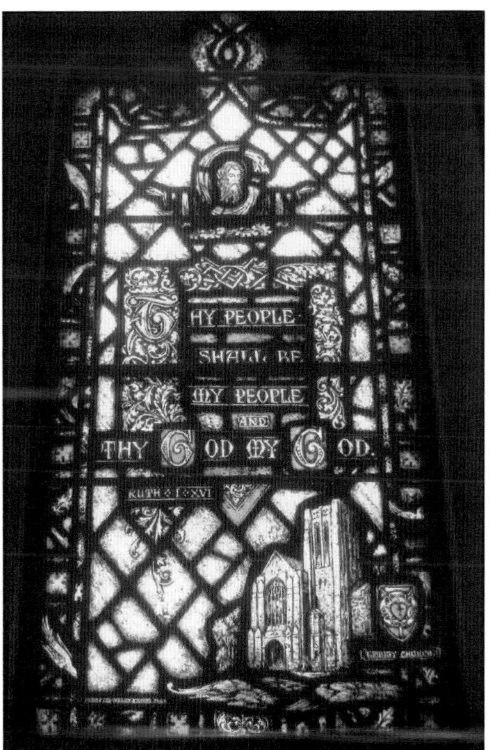

Historic Trinity's Ruth Window. The left side of the chapel window, signed by artist Henry Lee Willet, depicts the biblical story of Ruth. Polio survivor Marion Gauss, the daughter of church benefactor Charles Gauss, was the model for Ruth. The right side of the window depicts Trinity Lutheran Church, along with a rendition of Martin Luther's Coat of Arms. (HT.)

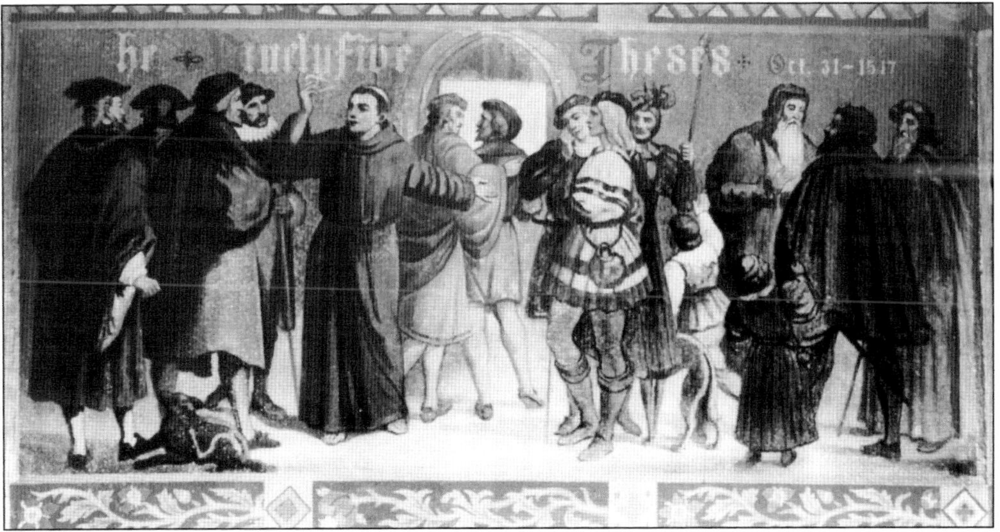

Historic Trinity's Murals of the Reformation and Renaissance. In the Pastor's Study, eight murals depict key events of the Reformation, including Martin Luther's posting of his *Ninety-Five Theses* on the door of the Castle Church in Wittenberg, Germany. (HT.)

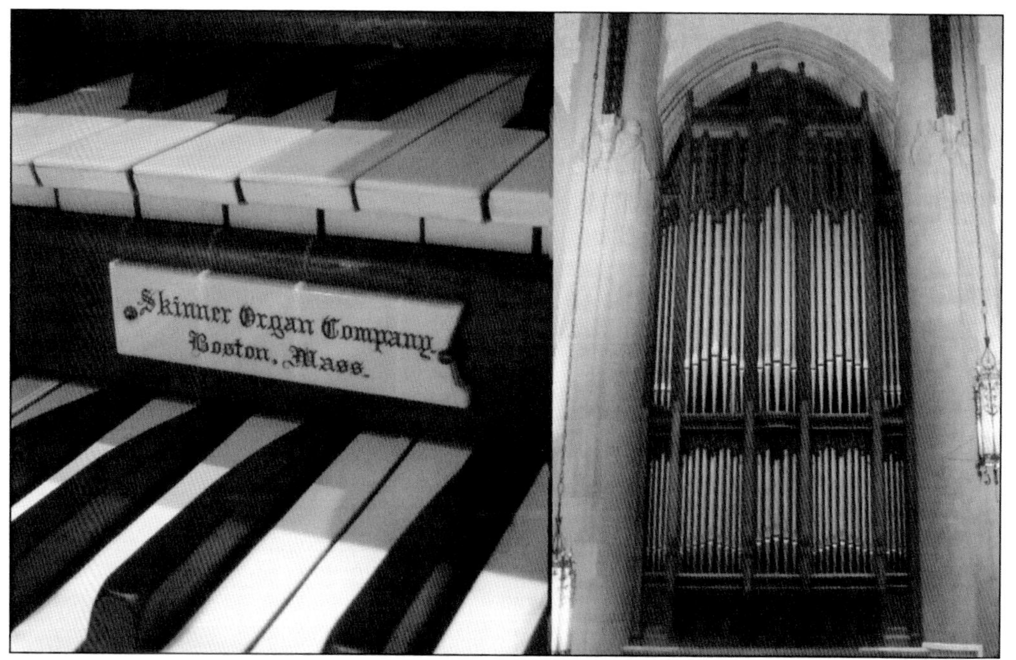

HISTORIC TRINITY'S ORGAN. The church's organ, an Opus 808, was built by premier organ builder Ernest M. Skinner in the 1920s and designed as a miniature English Cathedral organ. (EMC.)

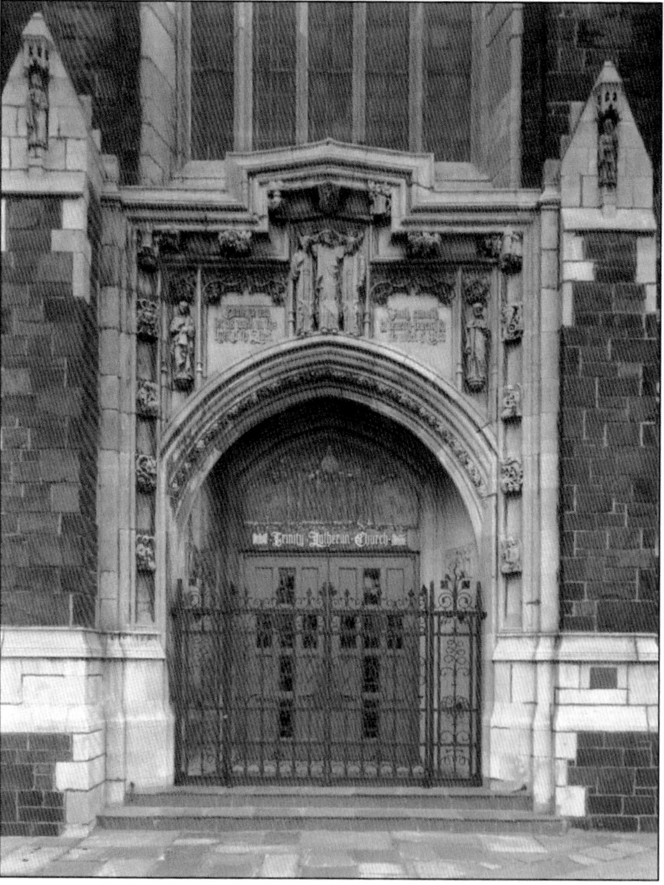

HISTORIC TRINITY. Trinity is considered the mother church of Lutherans in southeast Michigan. Some 132 churches across the metropolitan area trace their roots to Trinity Lutheran Church, which was renamed Historic Trinity Lutheran Church in 1986. (HT.)

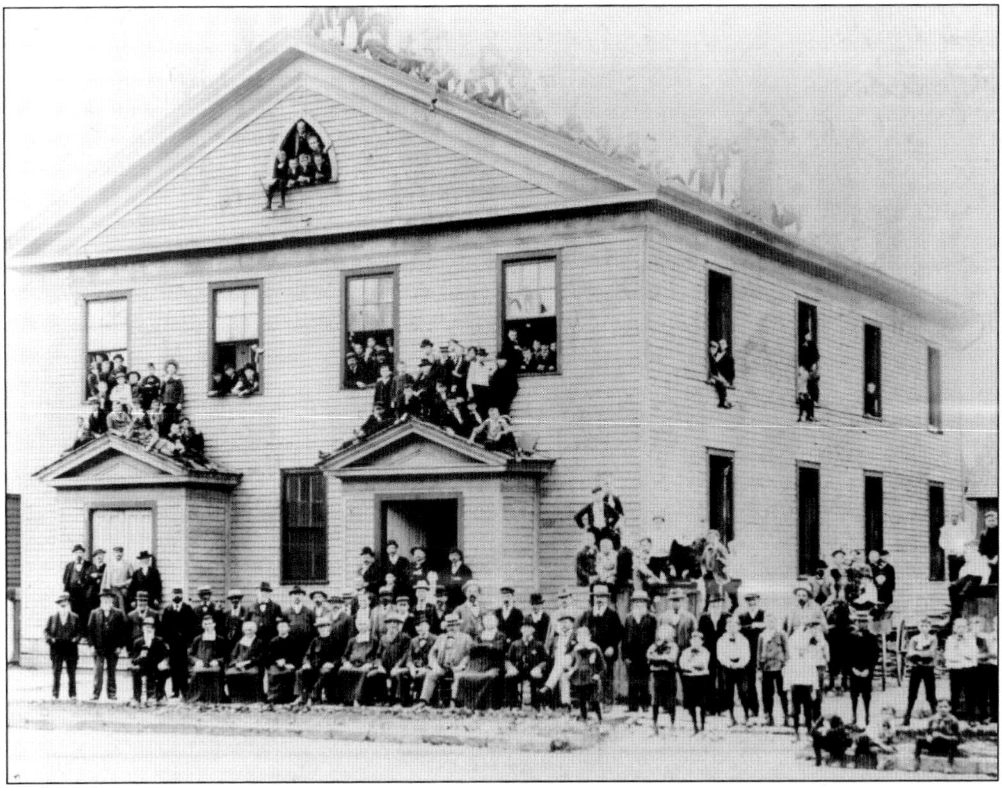

St. Joseph's Original Building. St. Joseph's Church was founded in 1855 as a German congregation of the Roman Catholic faith. A daughter church to St. Mary's Catholic Church in Greektown, St. Joseph served the newly settled farmers moving east along Gratiot Avenue. Their first church was built in 1856 at Gratiot Avenue and Orleans Street. It was later used as a school after a new church was built. (BHC.)

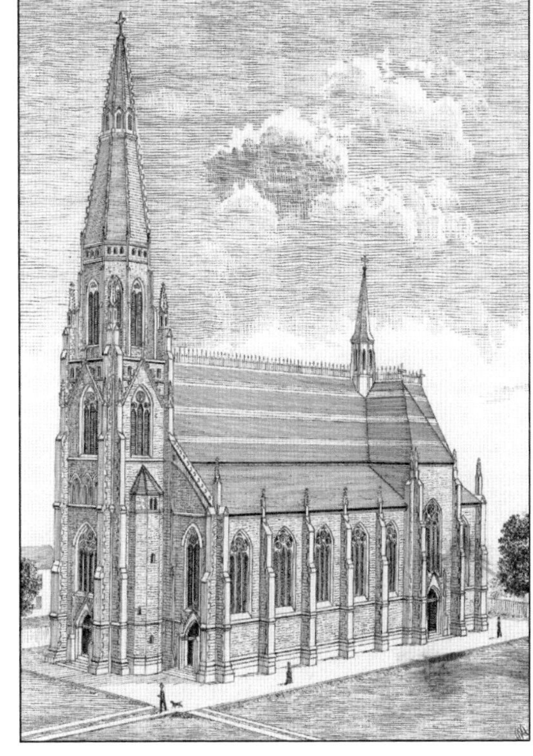

St. Joseph's Exterior. Construction began on a new Victorian Gothic Revival building in 1870. Designed by German-born architect Franz Georg Himpler of New York City, the building was completed and formally dedicated on November 16, 1873. (EMC.)

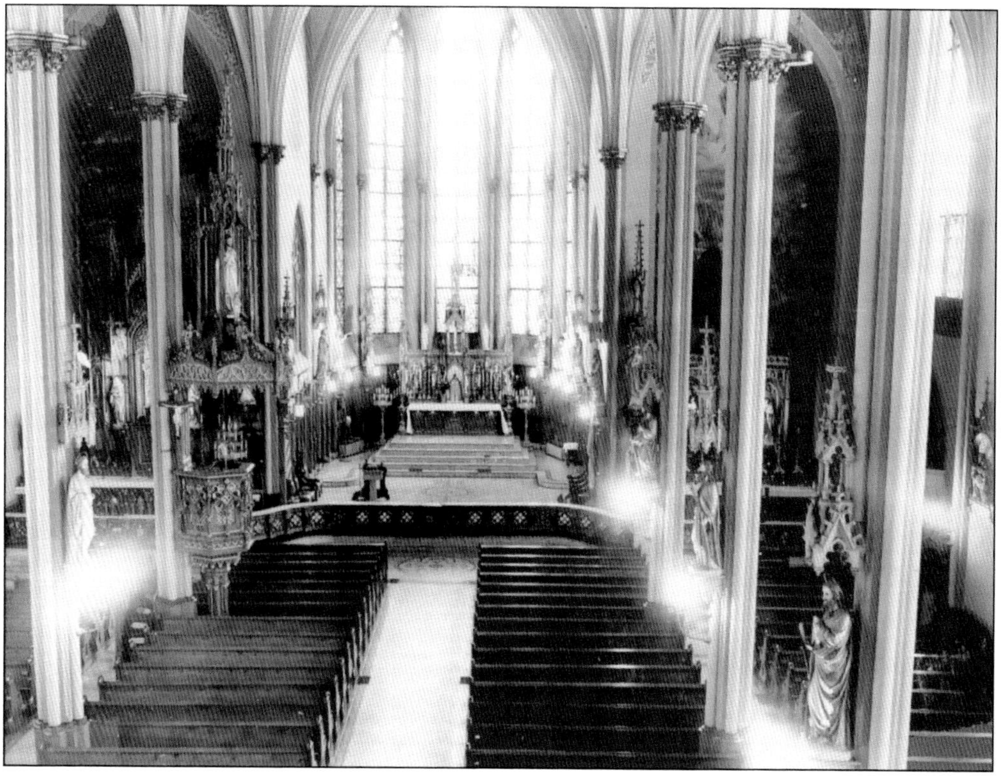

St. Joseph's Interior. In the 1870s, it was typical for a church's interior architectural details to be molded out of plaster; however, at St. Joseph's, many of the features, including the altar and statues, were hand-carved from wood in Germany. The building features extensive stained-glass windows created by both the Franz Mayer and Company in Munich, Germany, and Friedrichs & Staffin, the forerunner of the Detroit Stained Glass Works Company. (AoD.)

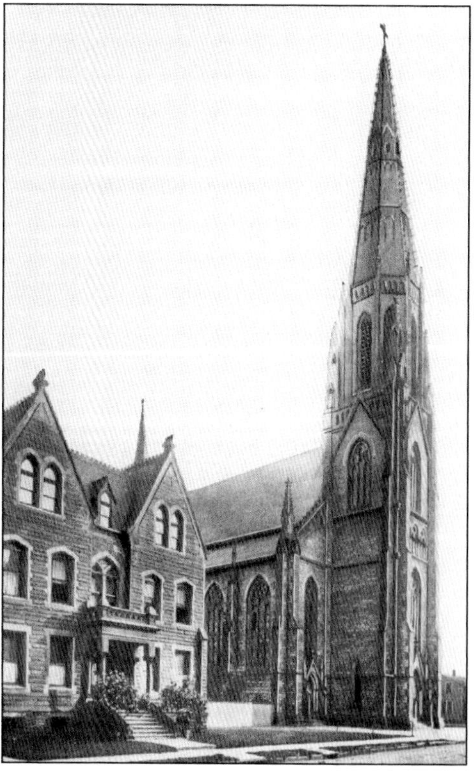

St. Joseph's Soars. At the time of its construction, the church, with its tower and spire standing nearly 200 feet high, was the tallest structure in Detroit. The tower features six bells that were cast in Baltimore. Today, the church features a Latin Mass every Sunday, and staying true to its cultural roots, a Mass is also held in German on the fourth Sunday of each month. (BHC.)

Sacred Heart Church. Sacred Heart was dedicated on July 16, 1876, and served Detroit's growing German community on the east side. Its architect was Peter Dederichs, who later designed the Ekhardt & Becker Brewery on Winder and Orleans Streets. In 1889, a small frame schoolhouse behind the church was replaced by a three-story Romanesque brick building that was used as an elementary and high school for the children of the parish. (AoD.)

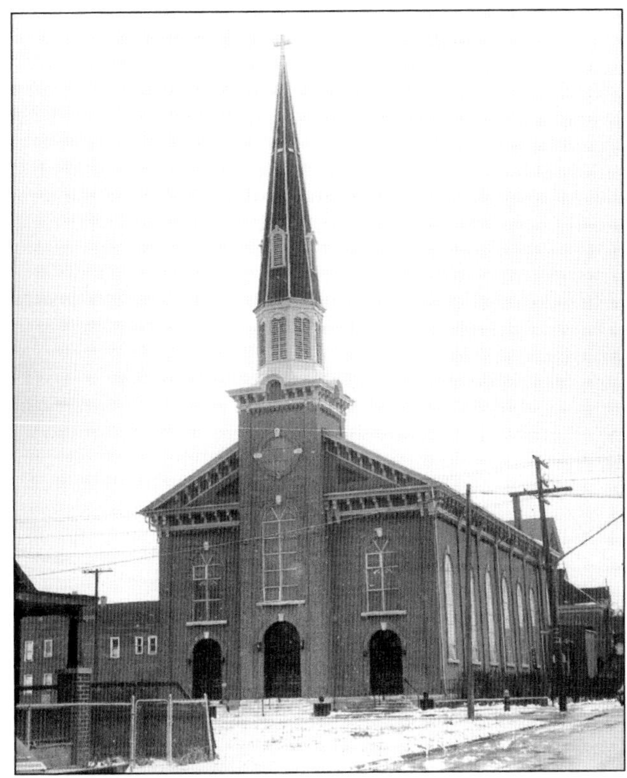

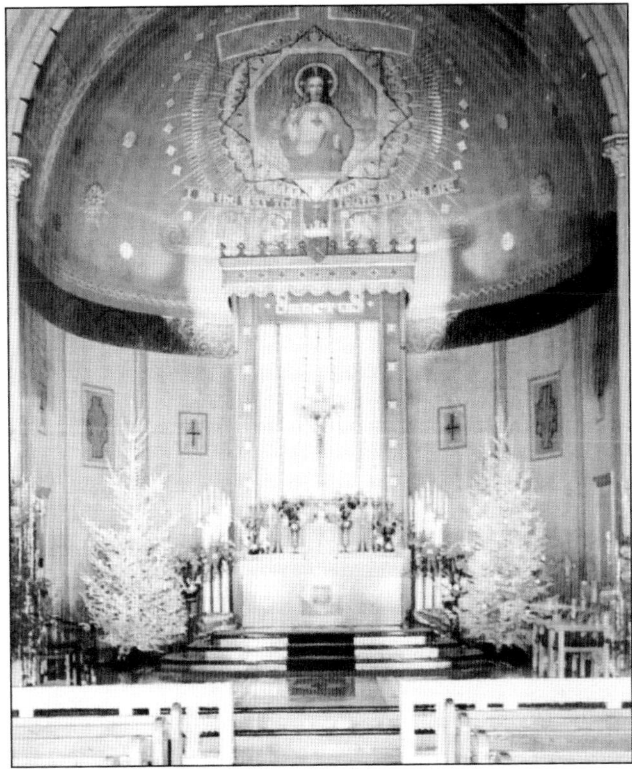

Sacred Heart's Interior. Sacred Heart features a simple and open design in contrast to the more ornate style of St. Mary's Catholic Church and St. Joseph's Catholic Church, both of which are nearby. The church seats 800 worshippers and served 275 families in the community. (AoD.)

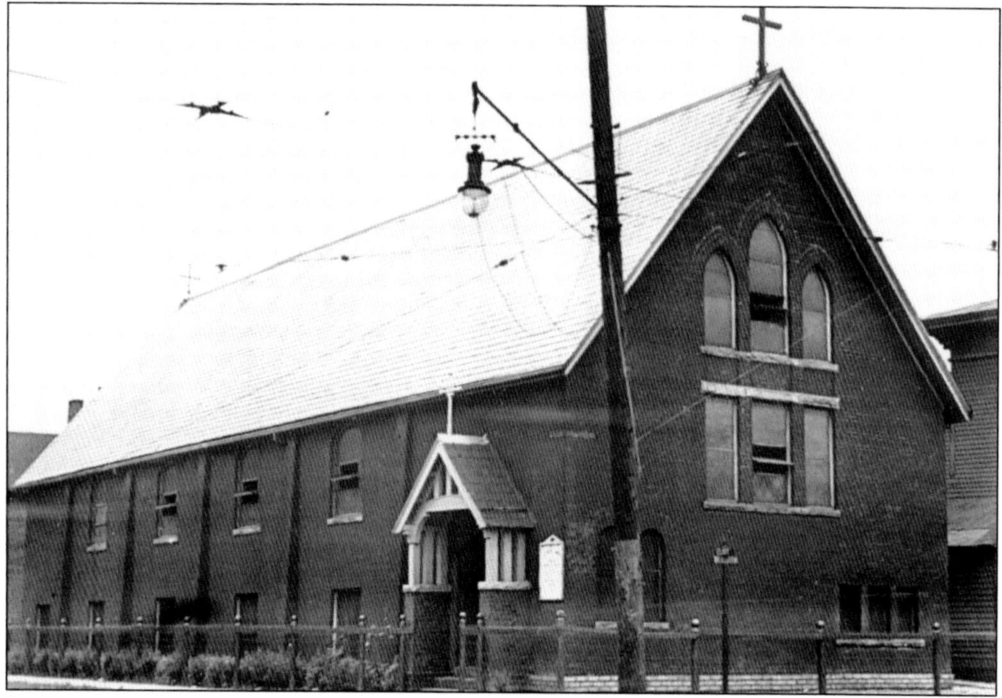

St. Peter Claver. Detroit's first African American Roman Catholic congregation was established in 1911 and moved to a small church at Eliot and Beaubien Streets in 1914. The African American population was growing in Detroit along Hastings Street (now Interstate 75, the western edge of the market), and by 1938 the church had more than 1,400 members. (AoD.)

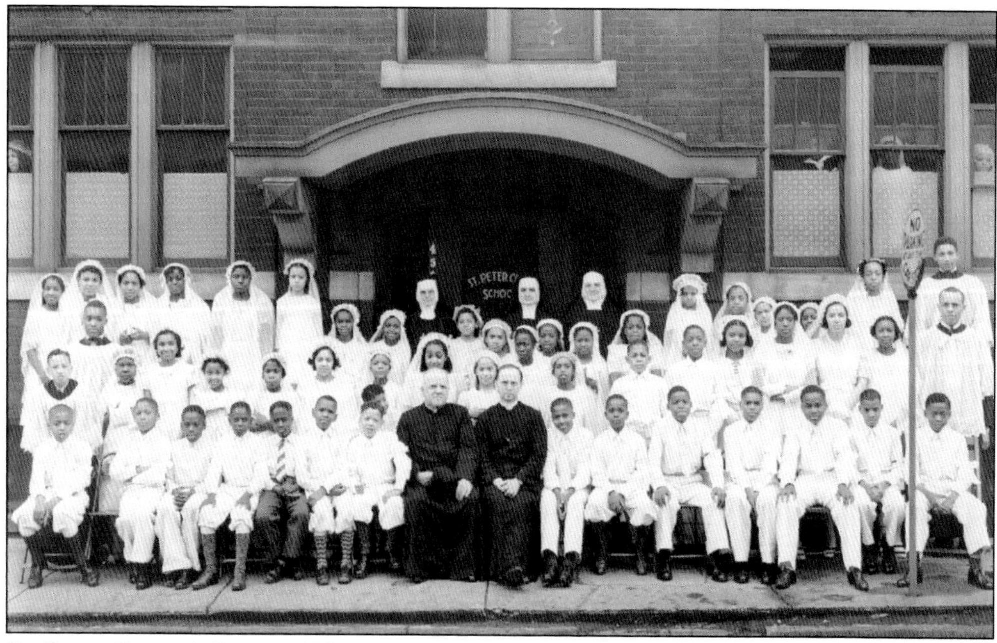

St. Peter Claver's School. Education was very important to the families of the St. Peter Claver congregation, and a school was established across from the church. The last class graduated in 1937. (AoD.)

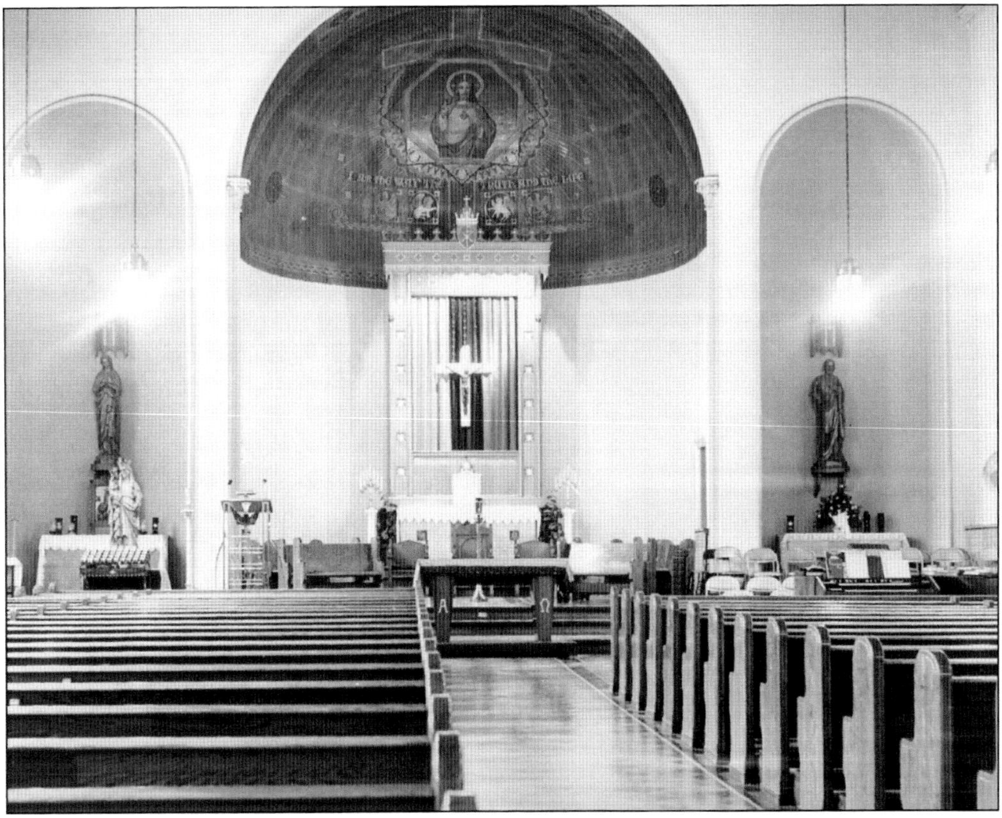

Sacred Heart is Reborn. By 1938, Detroit's German American community had largely moved farther east along Gratiot Avenue. At the same time, the St. Peter Claver congregation had outgrown its building at Eliot and Beaubien Streets, so they petitioned the archdiocese to move to the larger Sacred Heart building. On September 1, 1938, after Archbishop Edward Mooney made the historic decision to allow the move, the congregation celebrated the first Mass in their new building. (AoD.)

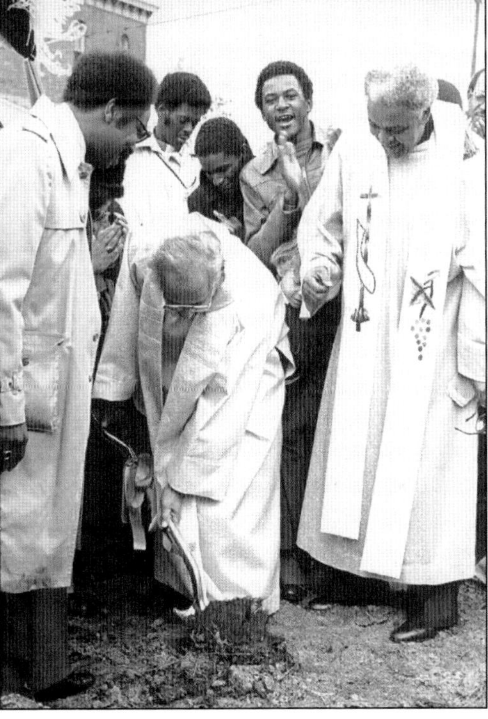

Sacred Heart's Ground-Breaking Ceremony. Sacred Heart is the center of the African American Catholic community in Detroit. The complex now features the original church and rectory, as well as an extensive activities center built in the 1980s, complete with classrooms, meeting rooms, a commercial kitchen, banquet space, and a small chapel. (AoD.)

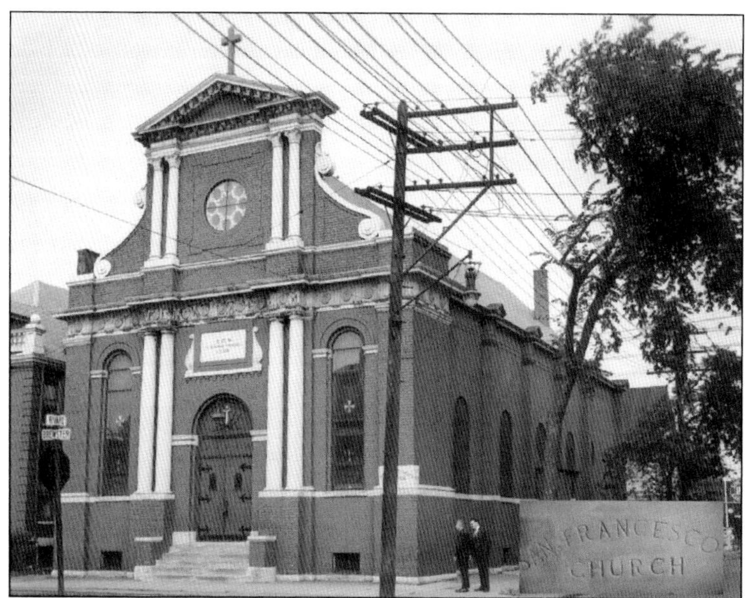

SAN FRANCESCO. By 1897, the Italian immigrant population of Detroit had grown to 207 families. Many of these northern Italian immigrants settled north along Gratiot Avenue and worked as merchants in Eastern Market. Fr. Francis Beccherini secured land for a permanent church at Brewster and Rivard Streets and commissioned architect Enrico Rill to design the new building. (AoD.)

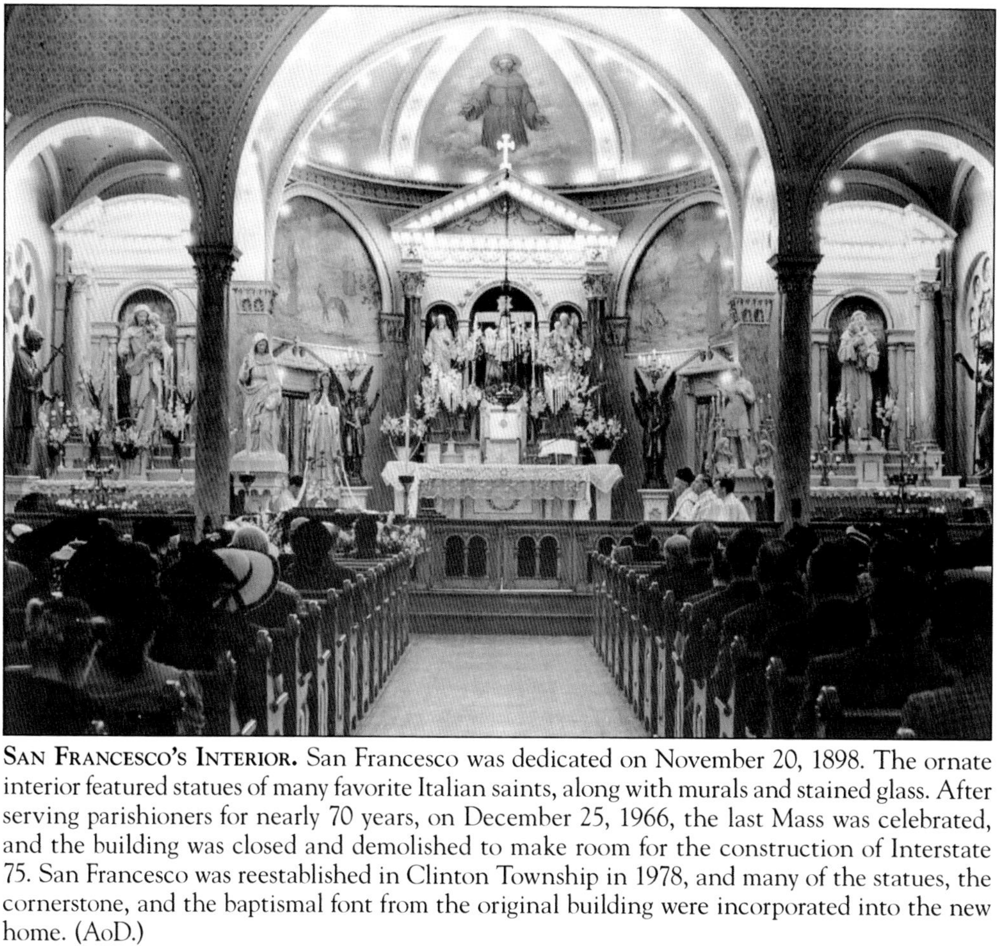

SAN FRANCESCO'S INTERIOR. San Francesco was dedicated on November 20, 1898. The ornate interior featured statues of many favorite Italian saints, along with murals and stained glass. After serving parishioners for nearly 70 years, on December 25, 1966, the last Mass was celebrated, and the building was closed and demolished to make room for the construction of Interstate 75. San Francesco was reestablished in Clinton Township in 1978, and many of the statues, the cornerstone, and the baptismal font from the original building were incorporated into the new home. (AoD.)

Four

BREWERIES

During the mid-1800s, Detroit became a destination for emigrants from Germany. These new Detroit residents brought with them their craft of beer making. Until this time, brewing in America had been primarily focused on British-style ales; soon, lighter German lagers came to dominate. With the German community being centered near the market district and having access to rail lines and supplies made Eastern Market an ideal place to situate breweries in Detroit.

From the mid-1800s until Prohibition, the number of breweries in the market grew at a rapid rate. On May 1, 1917, however, brewing in Detroit ceased when the Michigan's Damon Act took effect. The nationwide prohibition against the manufacture of alcoholic beverages did not begin until the passing of the 18th Amendment, on January 16, 1919. During Prohibition, many of Detroit's breweries closed. Others were able to remain profitable by producing other items like "near beer," malt extract syrup for home brewing, carbonated beverages, or ice cream.

Prohibition officially ended with the passage of the 21st Amendment on December 5, 1933. Breweries that had continued non-brewing operations during Prohibition were the first to reopen. They were followed by other companies that had closed, which then reopened either under original or new ownership. Between 1933 and 1985, Detroit's breweries grew, closed, or were consolidated, first locally and then nationally. Today, there is no active brewing in the Eastern Market district. However, independent microbreweries have continued to grow throughout Michigan, and there is hope that craft beers will become part of Eastern Market's unique character once again.

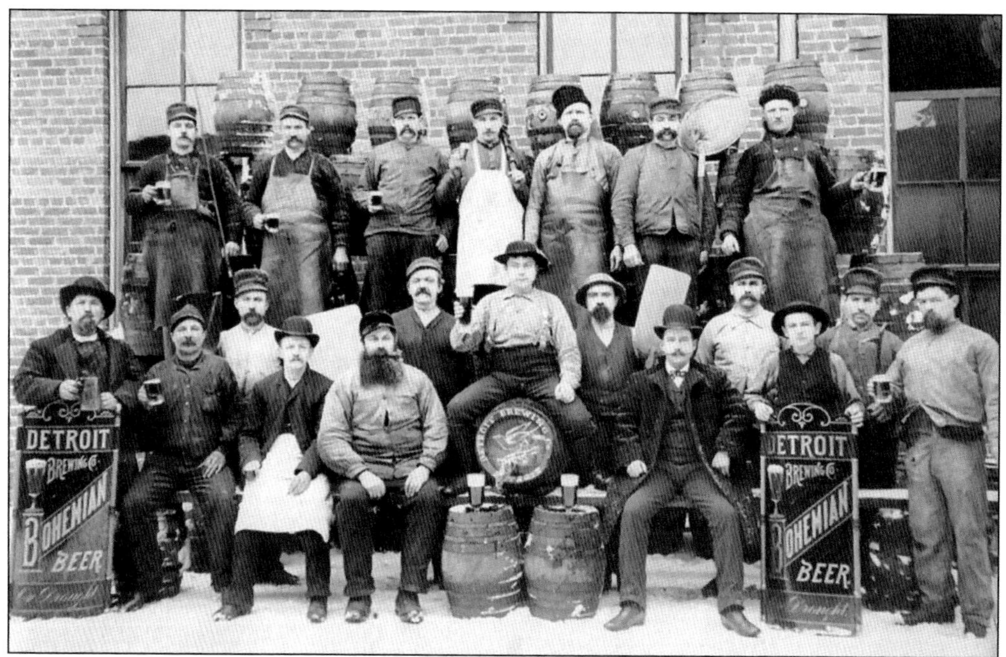

Employees of the Detroit Brewing Company. In 1868, brothers Frank and John Martz and John Steiner started the Frank Martz & Co. Brewery on Bronson (now Adelaide) Street. (MB.)

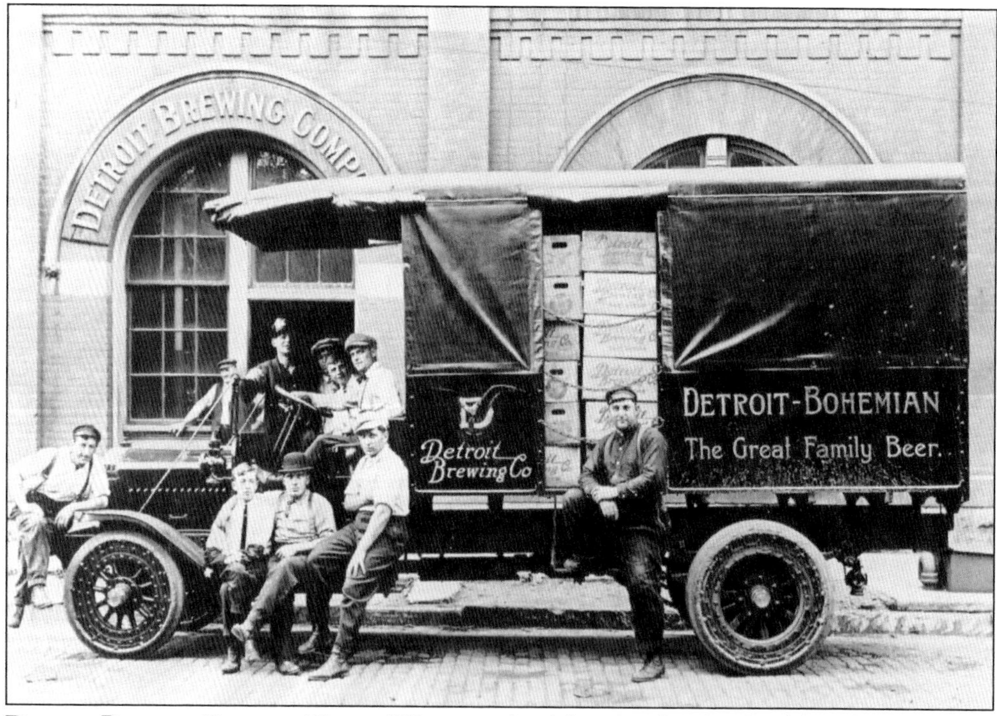

Detroit Brewing Company Truck. When another Martz brother, Michael, bought out Steiner and joined his brothers in 1884, the Detroit Brewing Company was formed. The new company expanded its operations and built a five-story brew house on Orleans Street. (Courtesy of James L. Kaiser.)

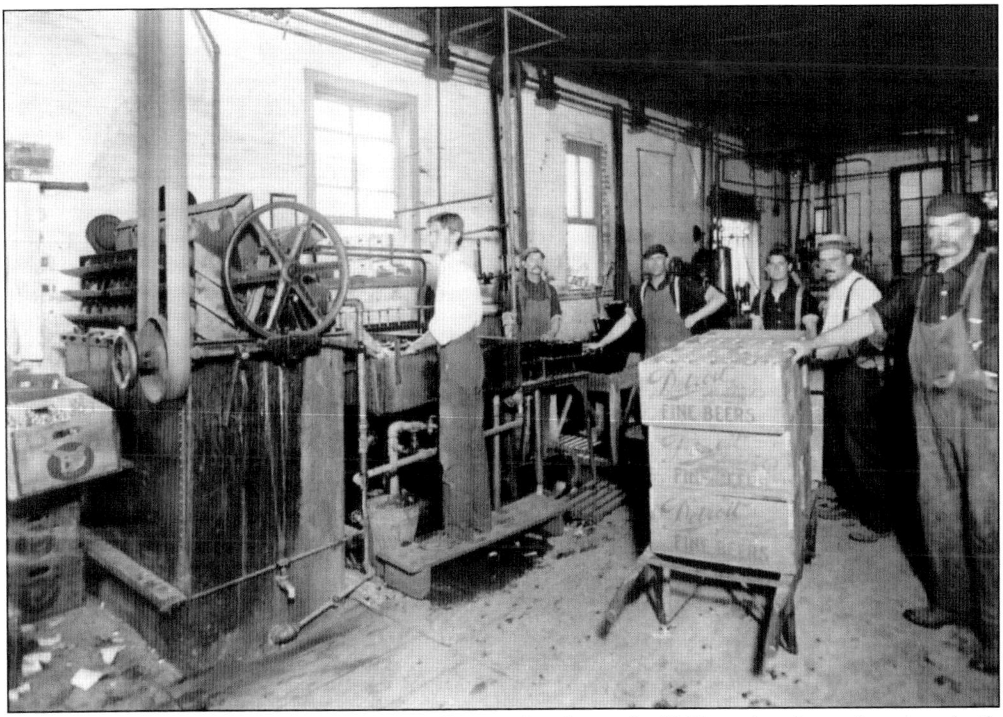

DETROIT BREWING COMPANY BOTTLING PLANT. In the early 1900s, a bottling plant was built across the street from the brew house on the corner of Adelaide and Orleans Streets. (MB.)

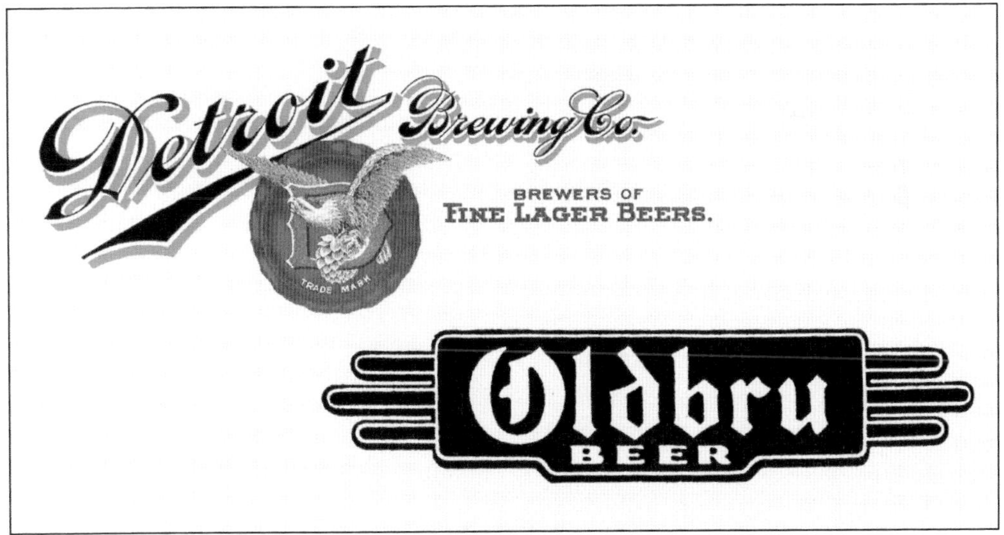

DETROIT BREWING COMPANY LOGO. During Prohibition, the Detroit Brewing Company ceased operations, and its buildings were leased to the Detroit Beverage Company, which produced soft drinks, "near beer," and home-brewing supplies. After the repeal of Prohibition in 1933, the Detroit Brewing Company once again resumed operations, producing its Bohemian Lager and Oldbru brands with their distinctive labels. (MB.)

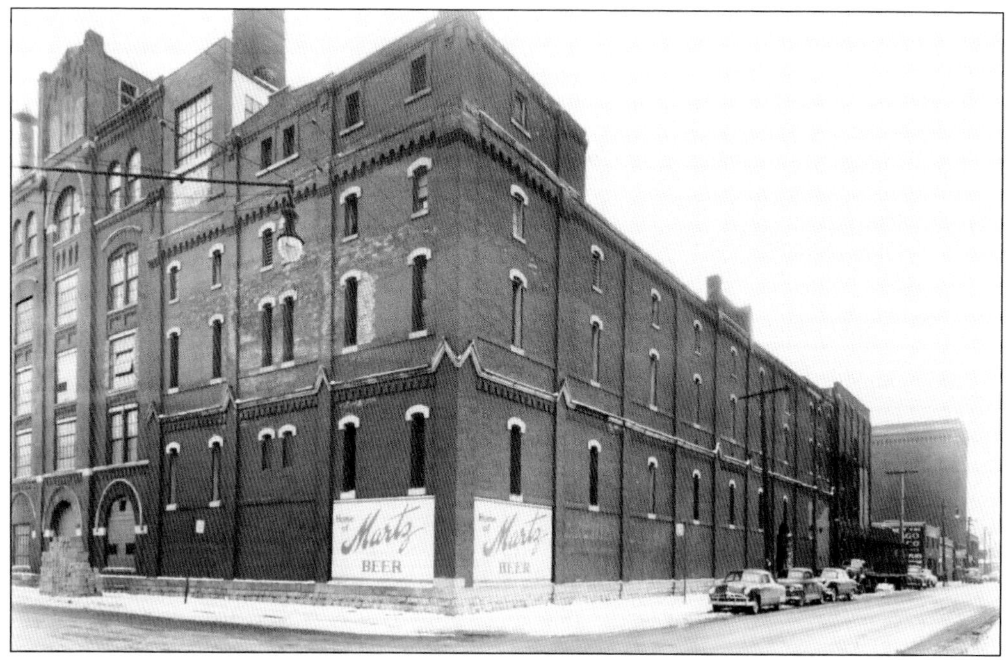

End of an Era. In 1949, after 80 years of Martz family ownership, the Detroit Brewing Company became the first of the major Detroit breweries to close. (MB.)

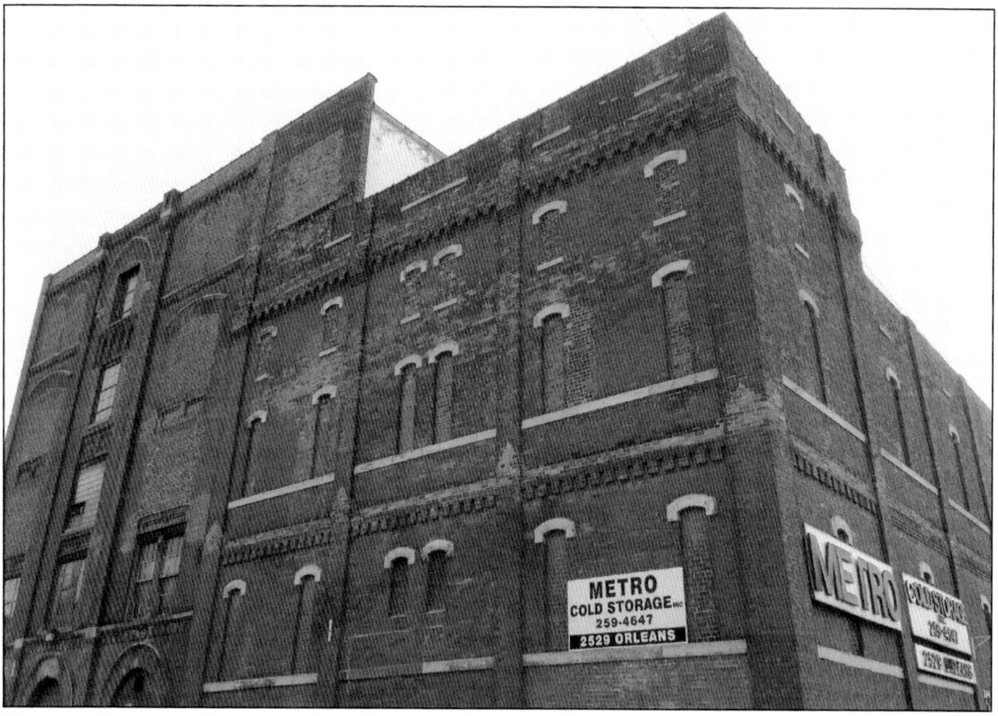

Detroit Brewing Company, 21st Century. In 1951, the main building at Adelaide and Orleans Streets was converted into a cold-storage facility (now the home of Metro Cold Storage), and the bottling facility became a slaughterhouse and sausage factory. It is now used by Mr. Sweiss Imported Foods. (EMC.)

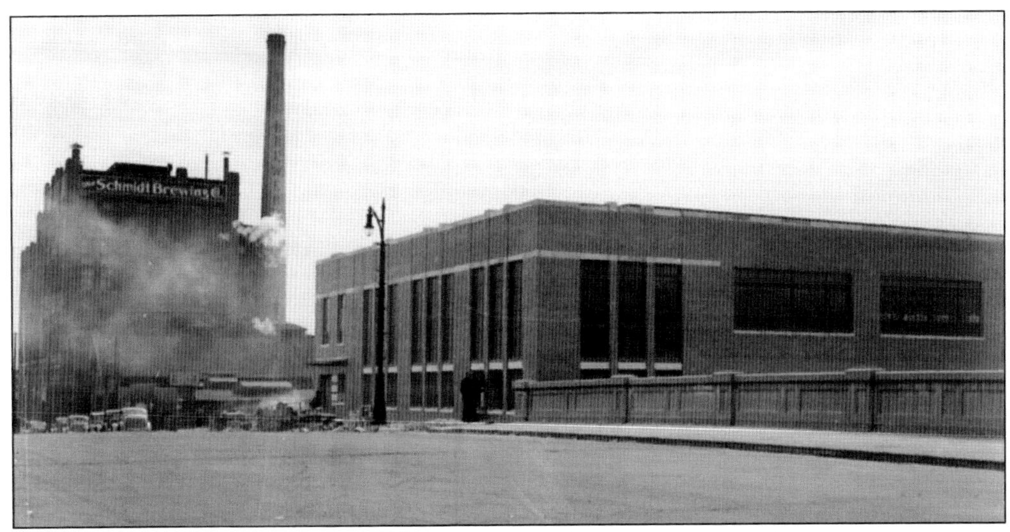

Schmidt Brewing Company. In 1895, Frank Schmidt joined with Joseph Peter Kaiser to form a company called Kaiser & Schmidt. They brewed under the name of Champion Brewery and produced the brand Old Fashion Beer. During Prohibition, the building was leased to the Acme Beverage Company, which made a hop-flavored malt syrup. In 1933, when Prohibition ended, the Schmidt Brewing Company was formed, and the men launched their Schmidt's Famous line. At the time, the brewery complex was expanded to fill the entire block of Wilkins Street between St. Aubin and Dequindre Streets. (WRL.)

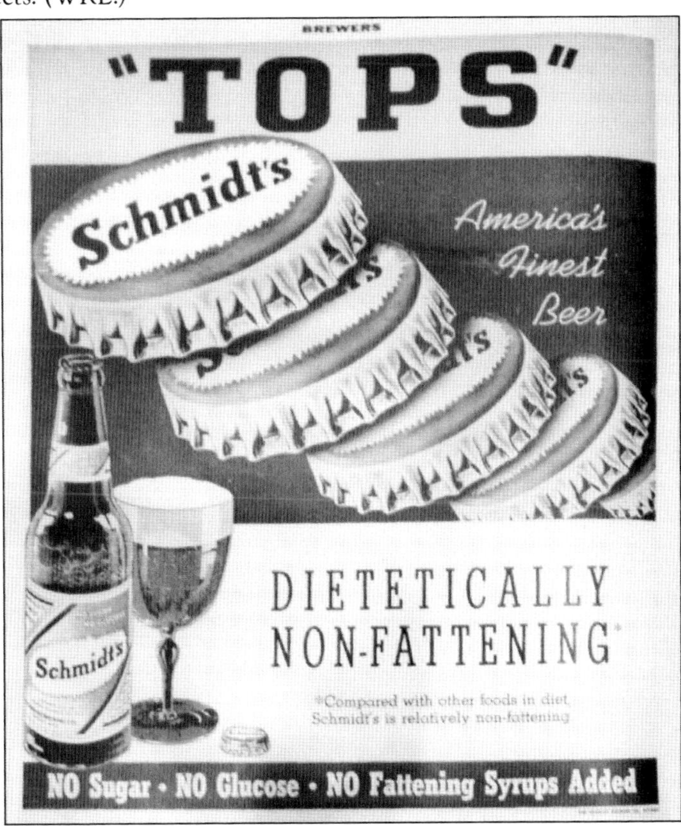

Schmidt Brewing Company Advertisement. Although Schmidt Brewing Company sold 300,000 barrels of beer annually during the World War II years, sales had dropped off by nearly two-thirds by 1950. In 1951, the company was absorbed by the nearby E&B Brewing Company, making Schmidt the second major Detroit brewery to close. The building at 1995 Wilkins Street, which served as a brewery as early as 1873, still stands today. (BHC.)

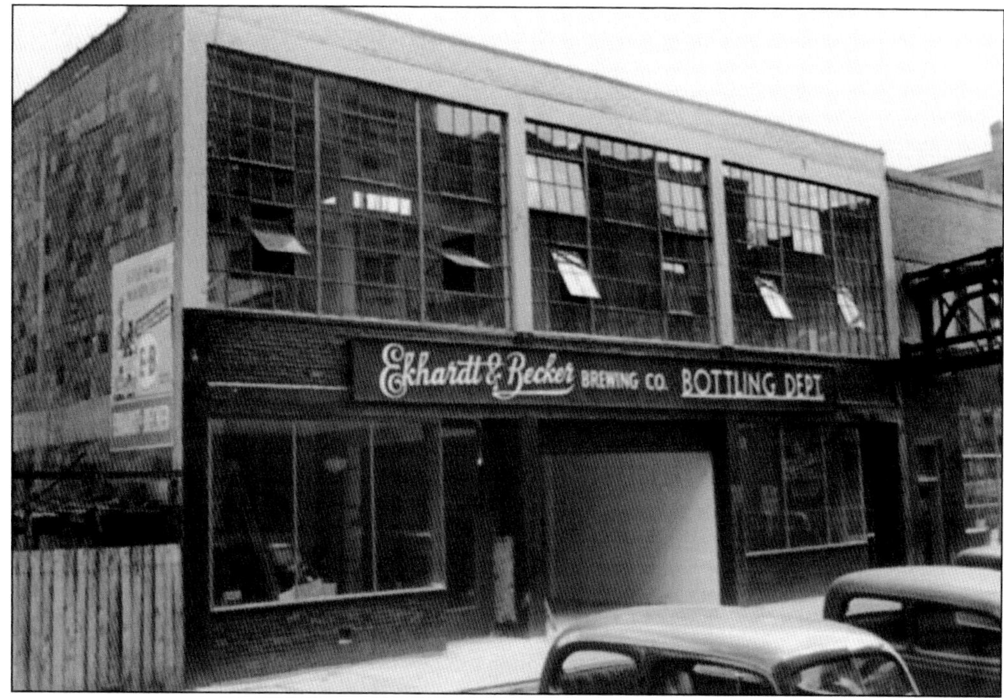

EKHARDT & BECKER BREWING COMPANY. August Ekhardt and Herman Becker began brewing operations in 1883 as the Ekhardt & Becker Brewing Company with a brewery on Russell Street, just south of Gratiot Avenue. In 1891, it merged with another brewery and hired architect Peter Dederichs to design a large Romanesque brick building at the corner of Winder and Orleans Streets. Following Prohibition, the E&B Brewing Company was reorganized by the sons of the founders. The original building was renovated, and a new bottling facility was added across the street. (WRL.)

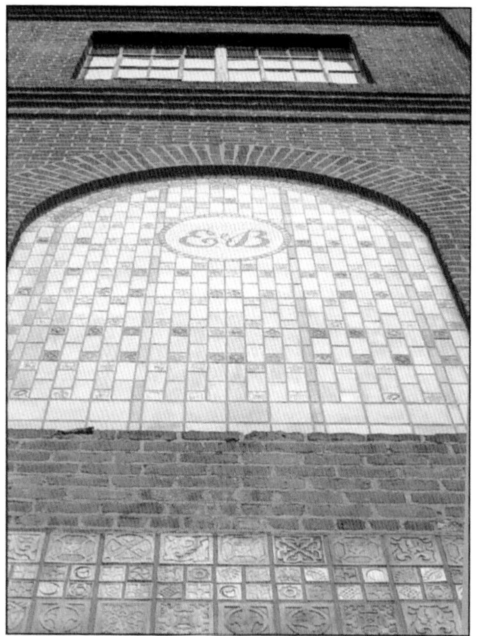

FLINT FAIENCE TILES. The renovated exterior of the building featured artistic tiles made by the Flint Faience Tile Company, a subsidiary of the AC Spark Plug Co. in Flint, Michigan. Belgian artist Carl Bergmans fired his tiles in the spark-plug kilns, utilizing excess industrial capacity for artistic purposes. In addition to the prominent E&B logo installations, the Winder Street side of the brewery featured a large sampling of the Flint Faience Tile Company's collection, including pieces from the Animals, Zodiac, Geometric, Gothic, and Drugstore series. (EMC.)

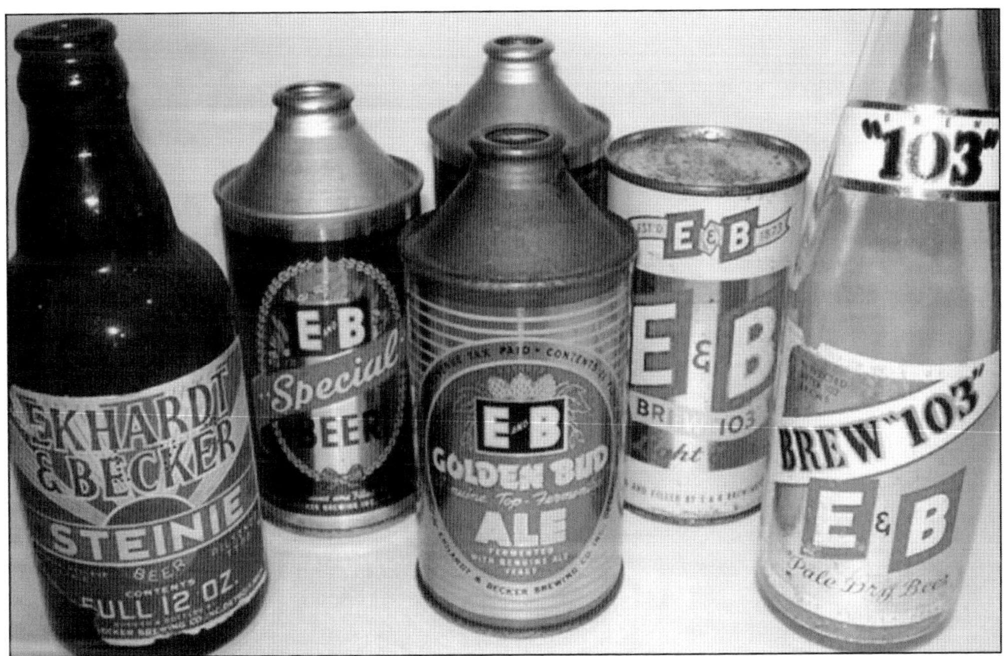

Ekhardt & Becker's Canned Beer. Always at the forefront of brewing technology, E&B was an early pioneer of canned beer and is credited with introducing the 16-ounce bottle to the Detroit market. E&B also created a smaller, lighter 12-ounce bottle known as the "Steinie." (Courtesy of Pete Cornils.)

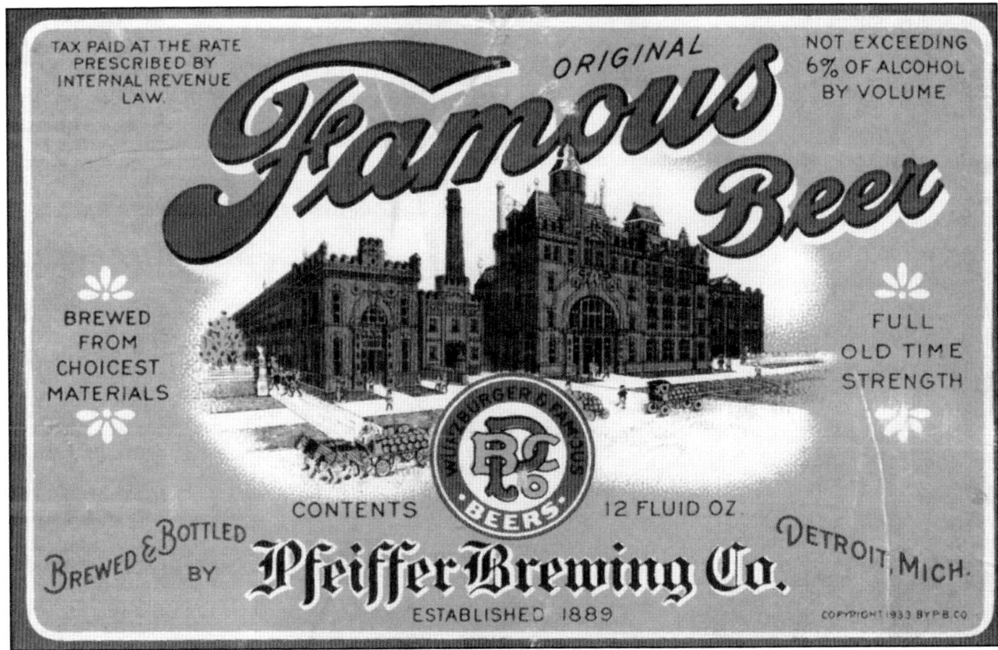

Pfeiffer Brewing Company. In 1952, E&B acquired the Schmidt Brewing Company, which increased its production by a third to 250,000 barrels annually. In 1963, the Pfeiffer Brewing Company bought E&B and moved production to the nearby Pfeiffer facility, closing the complex on Winder and Orleans Streets. (EMC.)

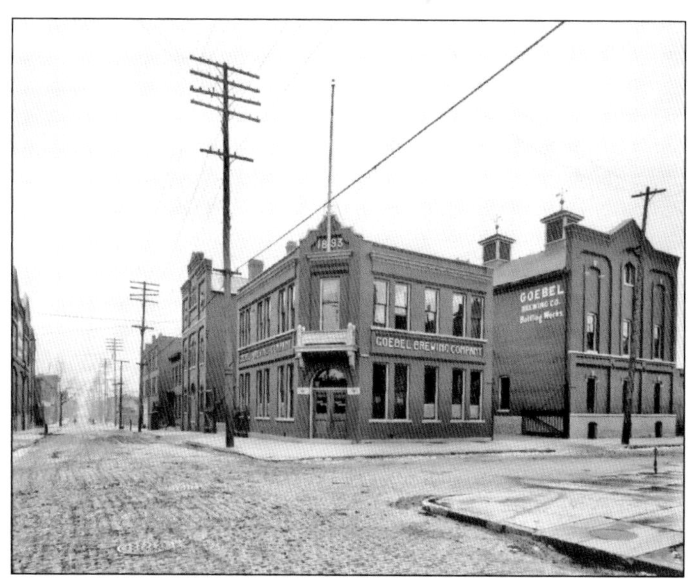

Goebel Brewing Company Exterior. The A. Goebel Company was founded in 1873 at the corner of Rivard and Maple Streets and was a fierce competitor of the nearby Stroh Brewing Company. With a large investment of British capital in 1889, the company's name was changed to Goebel Brewing Company Ltd. In 1897, a new five-story brew house was constructed next door to the original building on Rivard Street. (EMC.)

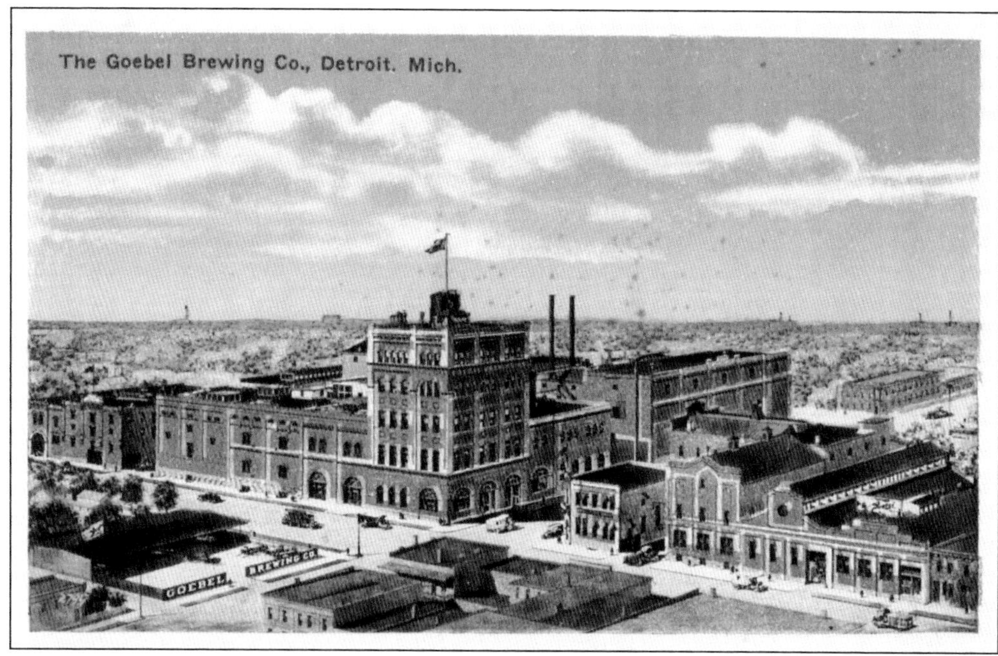

Goebel Brewing Company, Aerial View. Unfortunately, the company did not survive the Prohibition era, and the building was purchased by a group of investors who rented it out for light manufacturing. Following the repeal of Prohibition, those same investors decided to reopen the brewery and again produced beer under the Goebel name. In 1934, it managed to hire retired Stroh's brewmaster Otto Rosenbusch, the father of Stroh's brewmaster at the time, Herman A. Rosenbusch, and the rivalry reignited. (EMC.)

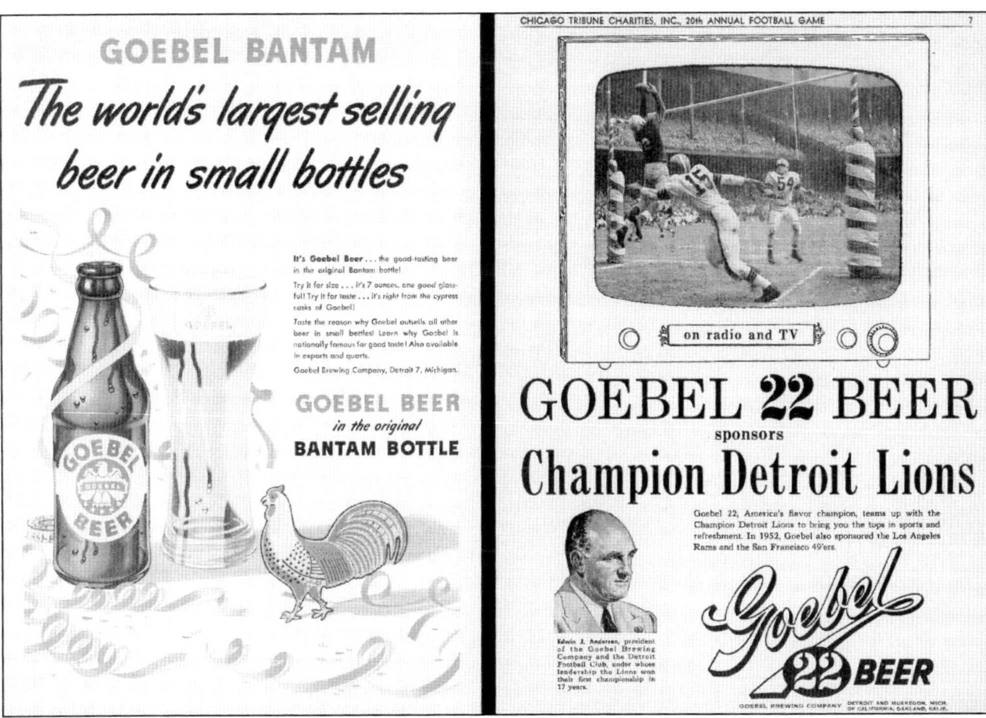

The "Brewster Rooster." Goebel was known for its seven-ounce, painted-label Bantam bottle and a marketing campaign featuring the Brewster Rooster mascot. Goebel Brewing Company was a sponsor of both Detroit Lions football and Detroit Tigers baseball. As a side note, when the Tigers switched sponsors from Goebel to Stroh's in 1959, future Baseball Hall of Fame announcer Ernie Harwell was hired as part of the new deal. (EMC.)

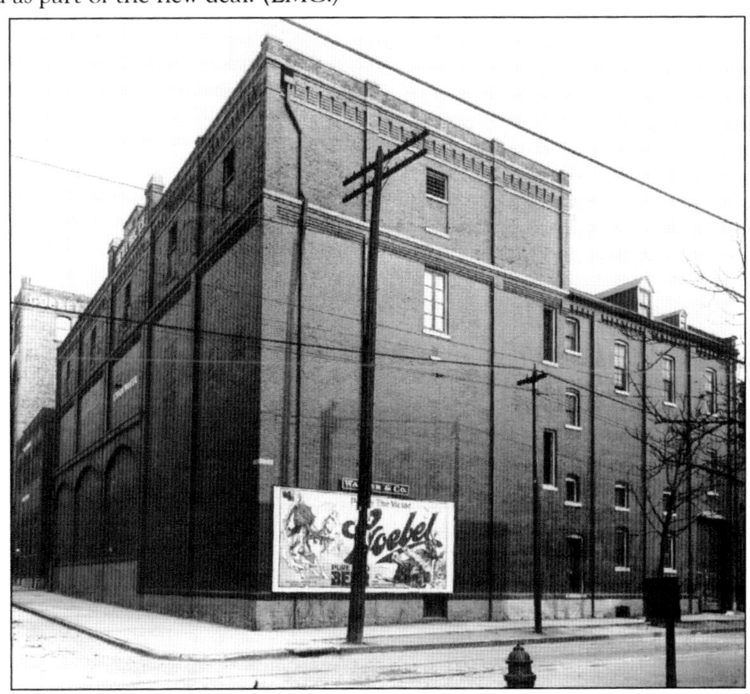

Goebel Brewing Company Closes. In 1964, Goebel closed its doors and ceased operations. The company, including the facilities and the brand name, were purchased by Stroh's, which then resurrected the Goebel brand. Six years later, the Goebel brand was discontinued for good due to diminishing sales. (BHC.)

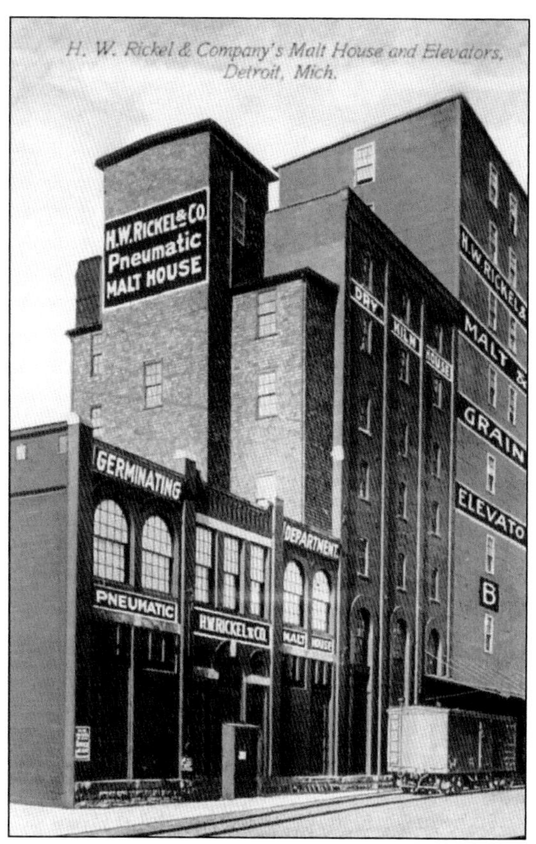

H.W. Rickel & Co. Pneumatic Malt House. H.W. Rickel founded the H.W. Rickel & Co. Malt House in 1876 at the age of 43. By 1903, the company was the largest malt house in the city, and a larger facility was built at 1824 Adelaide Street and Gratiot Avenue. The new building was situated at the cross of the Grand Trunk Railroad tracks, a good location near the many breweries and on the rail line. A landmark along Gratiot for many years, the building closed in 1971. It was demolished in June 1996. (BHC.)

331 Gratiot Avenue. Bernhard Stroh brought his family's brewing tradition from Kirn, Germany, and began the Lion Brewing Company in Detroit in 1850. About 10 years later, after outgrowing its small facilities on Catherine Street, a larger operation and a family home were built at 331 Gratiot Avenue. (BHC.)

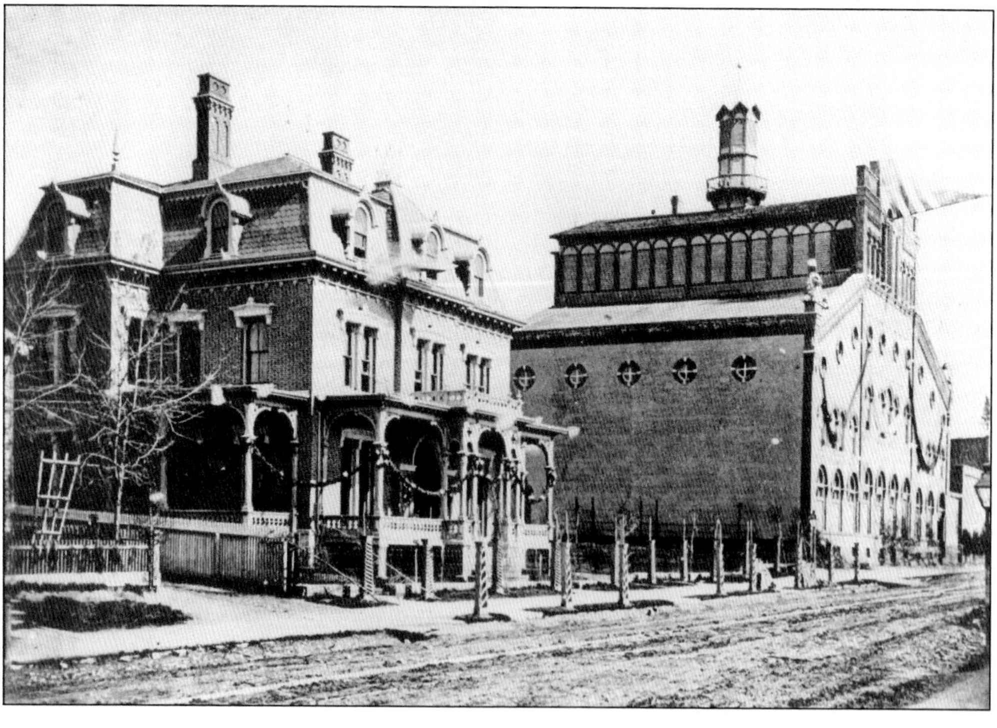

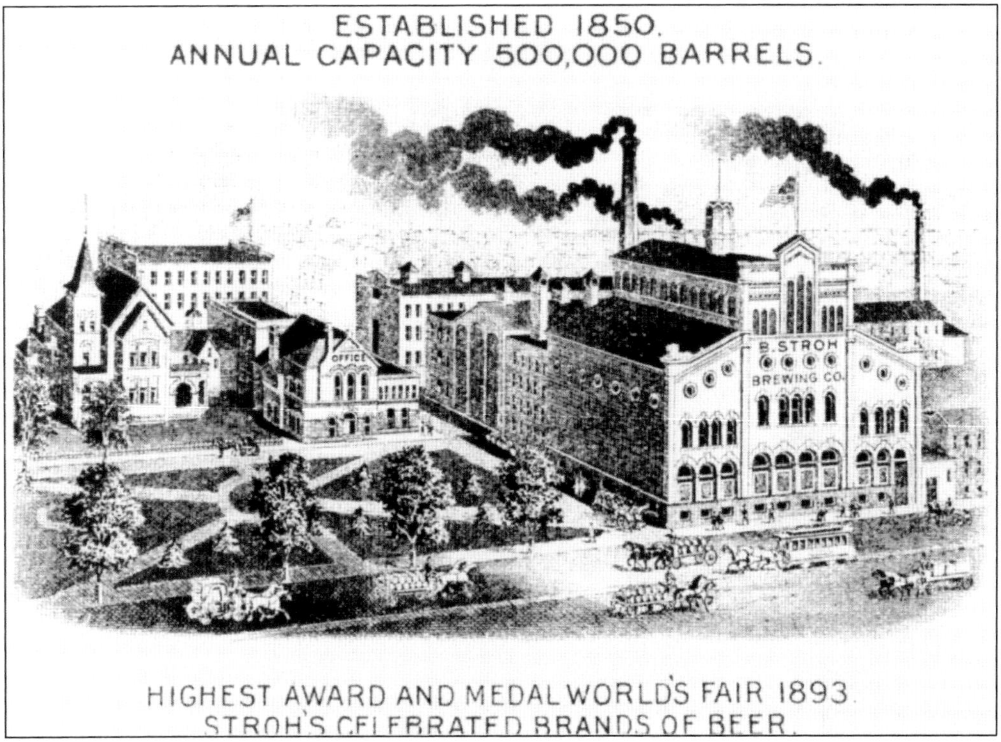

THE STROH BREWERY COMPANY, ORIGINAL FACTORY RENDERING. By 1902, the Lion Brewing Company had become the Stroh Brewery Company, and its complex at Rivard Street and Gratiot Avenue was the largest brewery in the city. (BHC.)

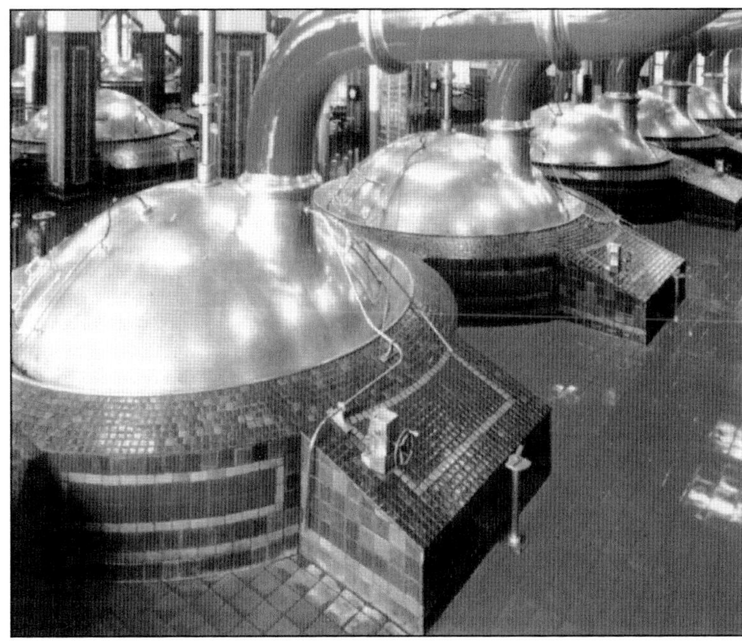

THE STROH BREWERY COPPER KETTLES. Stroh's brought fire-brewing technology from Germany in 1911, and a new eight-story brew house was built. Fire brewing was considered to produce a superior beer because the direct flames brought out more of the beer's natural flavor. Stroh's was the only fire-brewed beer in the country, and that fact played a large part in its advertising for years to come. (LR.)

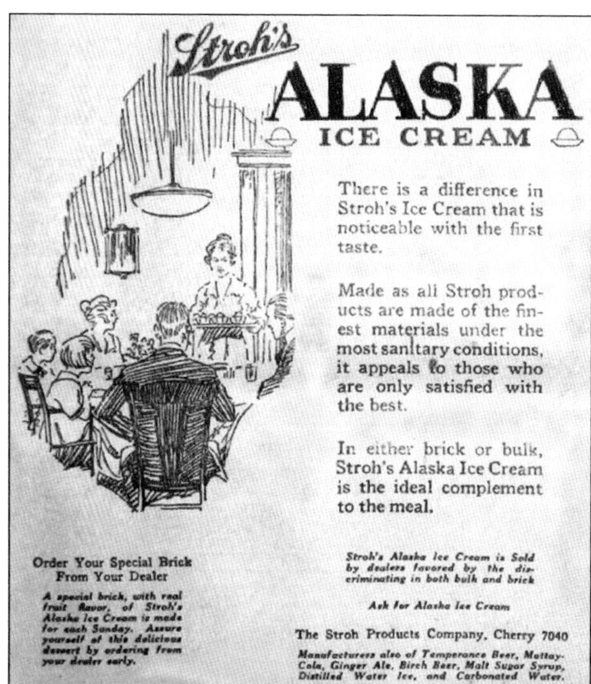

Stroh's Ice Cream. During the Prohibition years, the Stroh Brewing Company became the Stroh Products Company, making soft drinks, malt syrup, "near beer," and even ice cream under the Alaska brand name. After Prohibition ended, Stroh's returned to making beer and continued its ice cream line under the Stroh's name. (EMC.)

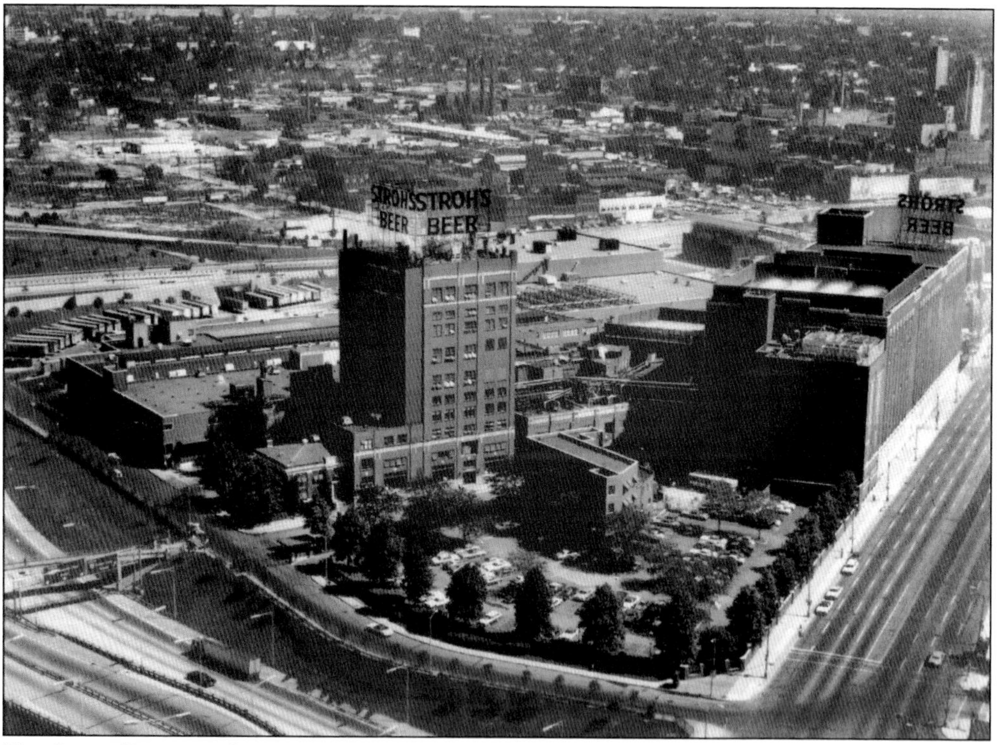

The Stroh Brewery Company, Aerial View. By the mid-1930s, Stroh's accounted for nearly one quarter of all beer production in the state of Michigan. During the next two decades, to keep up with ever-growing demand, a new stock house, fermentation plant, bottling plant, and distribution facility were added to the complex at Gratiot Avenue and Rivard Street. (EMC.)

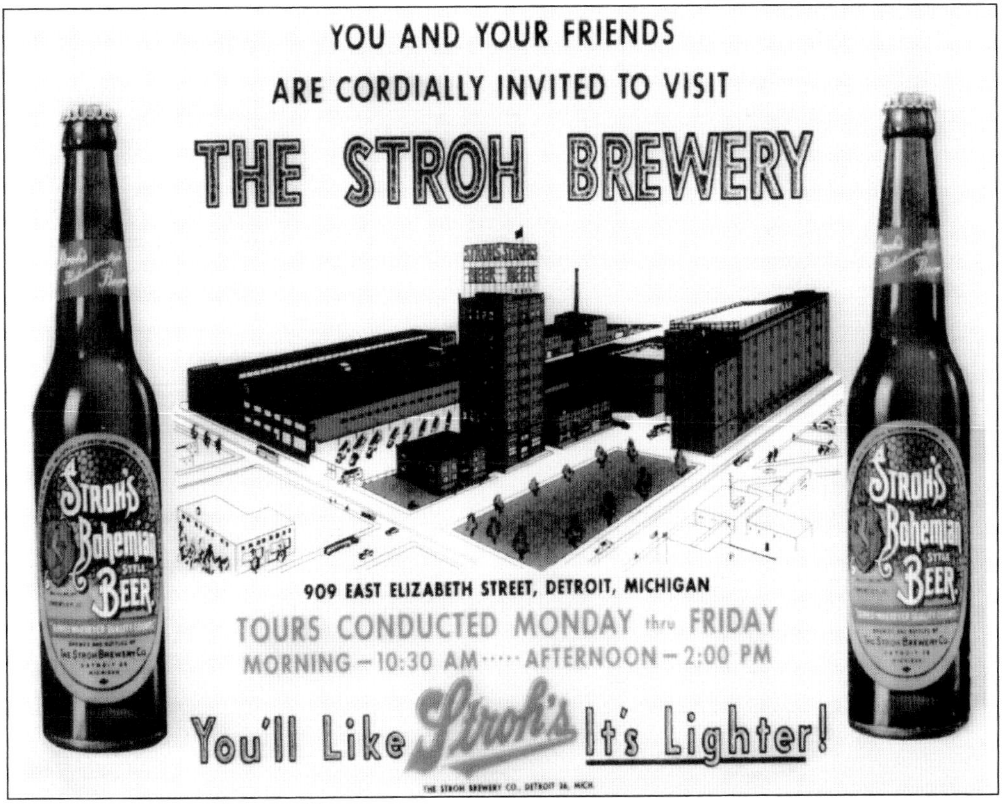

YOU AND YOUR FRIENDS
ARE CORDIALLY INVITED TO VISIT
THE STROH BREWERY

909 EAST ELIZABETH STREET, DETROIT, MICHIGAN
TOURS CONDUCTED MONDAY thru FRIDAY
MORNING – 10:30 AM ····· AFTERNOON – 2:00 PM
You'll Like Stroh's It's Lighter!
THE STROH BREWERY CO., DETROIT 26, MICH.

STROH TOURS AND TASTING ROOM. Stroh's offered tours of its complex. When completed in 1950, the bottling plant was the largest packaging plant under one roof in the country, and visitors could watch the process from viewing platforms along the balcony. At the end of the tour, visitors were treated to a cold beer in the Stroh's Strohaus. (EMC.)

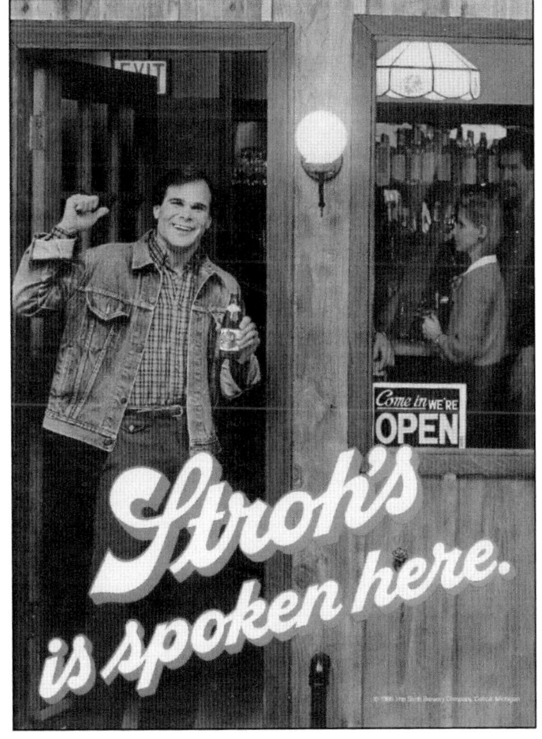

"STROH'S IS SPOKEN HERE." After acquiring Goebel in 1964, Stroh's was the only remaining local commercial brewery in Detroit. The company began an intensive acquisition strategy and emerged as a national brand. By 1982, with plants from New York to California and Michigan to Florida, Stroh's was the no. 3 brewery in the United States after Anheuser-Busch and Miller. (EMC.)

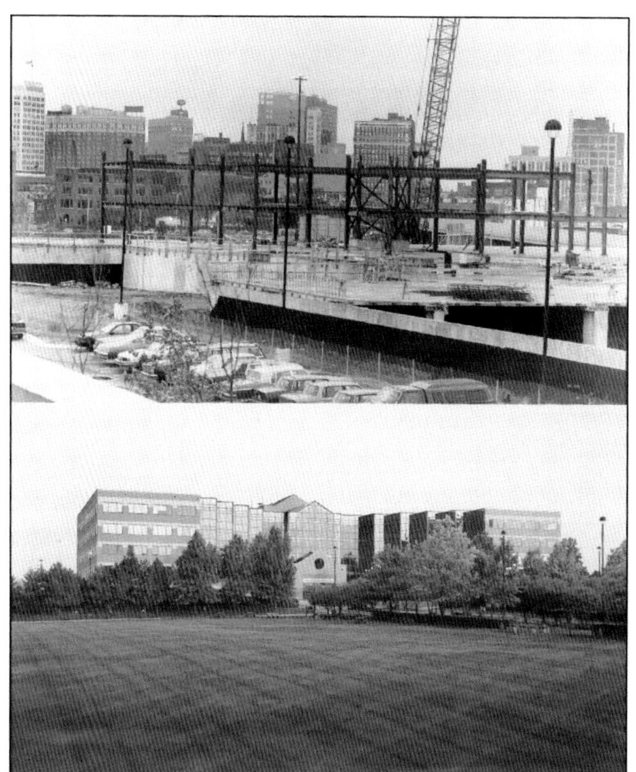

Brewery Park. By 1985, the volume of the Stroh's brand had peaked, and the smallest of their seven plants, on Gratiot Avenue, was closed on May 31. After the complex was demolished, Brewery Park, an office park, was built on the site. In 1999, Stroh's was sold to Pabst Brewing Company, ending a 150-year-old family business in Detroit. (Above, EMC; below, courtesy of Crain Communications.)

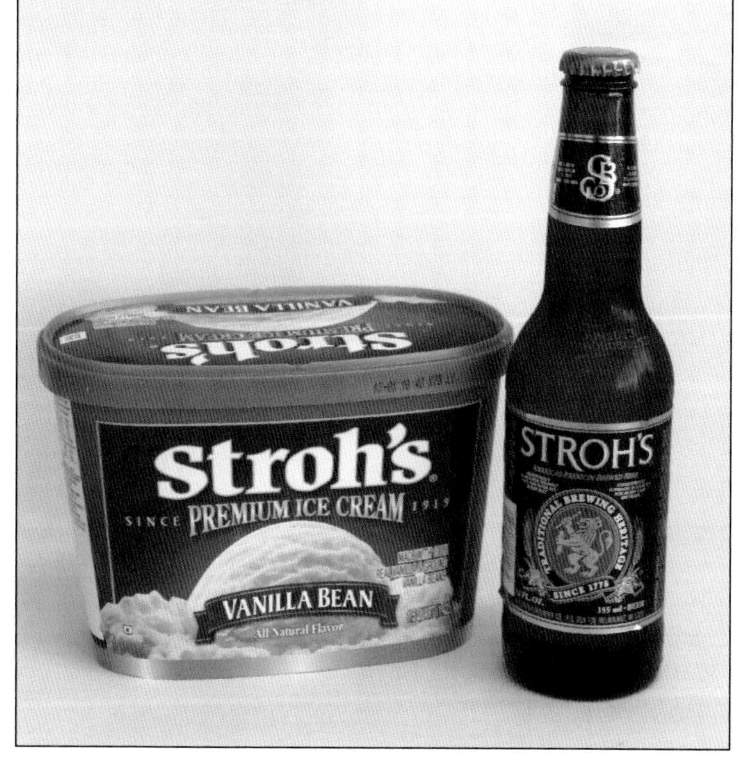

Stroh's in the 21st Century. While the Stroh Brewing Company is no more, those seeking a taste of old Detroit can still enjoy a cold Stroh's Beer, now made by Pabst Brewing Company, or a bowl of Stroh's Ice Cream, made by Dean Foods. (EMC.)

Five

Retail

Many of the retail businesses in the market district today can trace their roots back to the early days of the Eastern Market when most of the retail was there to serve farmers. Market days were "trips to the city" made to make money by selling produce and also to buy necessary supplies that were unavailable in rural towns. Those early retailers sold items that both city folk and farmers needed, such as dry goods and hardware.

Things changed after the automobile became the primary mode of transportation. From then until the advent of big-box and warehouse stores, much of the retail at the market focused on supplying mom-and-pop grocery stores in Detroit and the surrounding suburbs. Shop owners would visit the market for their produce and then stop at the surrounding retail and wholesale stores for candy, tobacco, patent medicines, spices, nuts, and more to resell at their own stores.

Many of those early warehouse stores adapted and now serve primarily retail customers with some of the same items, as well as many new ones. Shoppers have become more sophisticated over the years and are now looking for unique specialty goods like cheese, wine, meats, olives, nuts, and coffee. The retail customer may purchase less quantity than earlier grocers, but they typically spend more. More recently, retail in the market has expanded to include nonfood items, such as antique stores, print shops, art galleries, and clothing boutiques.

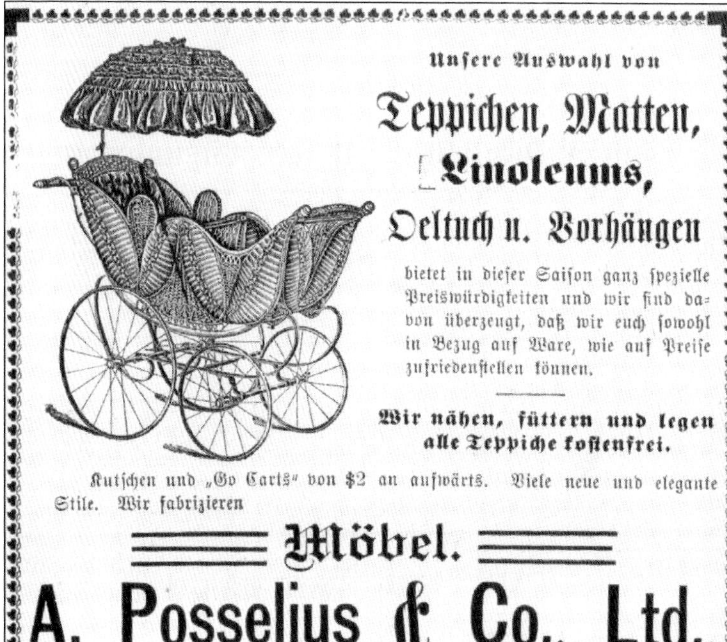

A. POSSELIUS & COMPANY. August Posselius owned several properties along Gratiot Avenue and constructed a six-story building on the south side of the street, between Russell and Jay Streets, which housed his furniture store in the early 1870s. (BHC.)

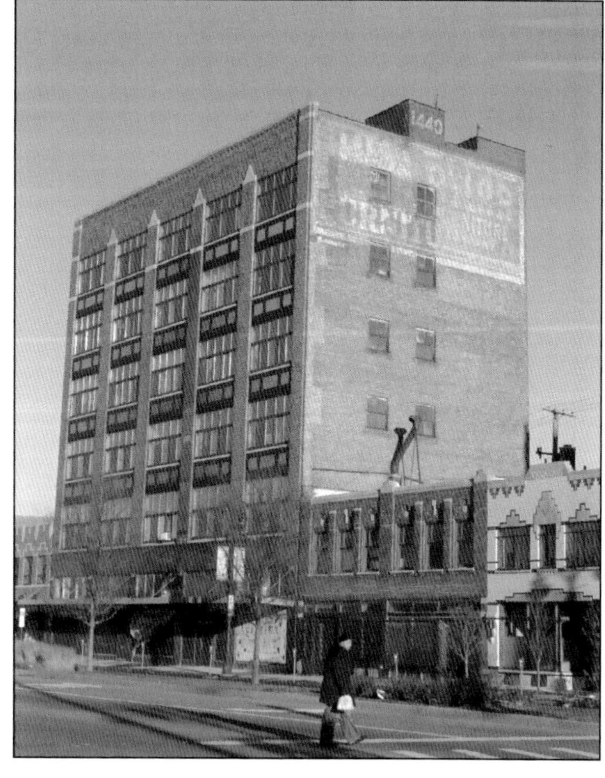

ATLAS FURNITURE BUILDING LOFTS. The Posselius building later became the home of Atlas Furniture and has since been known as the Atlas Furniture Building. After Atlas Furniture moved out in the 1970s, the building became one of the first New York–style lofts in Detroit, featuring vast open spaces that were perfect for homes and work spaces for local artists and craftspeople. (EMC.)

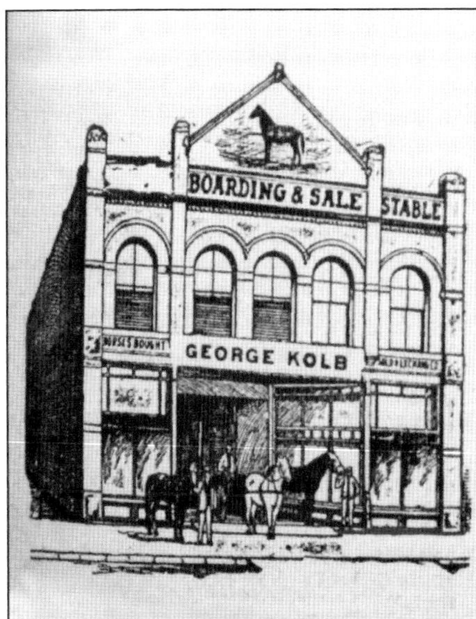

GEORGE KOLB

Gratiot Ave. Horse Market.

Boarding and Sale Stable.

BUYS, SELLS OR EXCHANGES HORSES, BUGGIES, ETC.

400 Gratiot Avenue. DETROIT, MICH.

Telephone Main 2274.

Auction Sales Every Saturday at 10 a. m.

Residence Phone, Jacob Kolb, Gratiot 17
" " Geo. Kolb, Main 1531

Parties wishing to buy, sell or exchange Horses, Carriages, Etc., will consult their own interest by calling at the above place.

GRATIOT AVENUE HORSE STABLES. Before the automobile dominated the streets of Detroit, horses and wagons were the primary form of transportation for early farmers bringing their goods from the rural areas along Gratiot Avenue to the market. George Kolb ran a horse stable for sales and boarding at the corner of Gratiot Avenue and Russell Street until just after 1900. (BHC.)

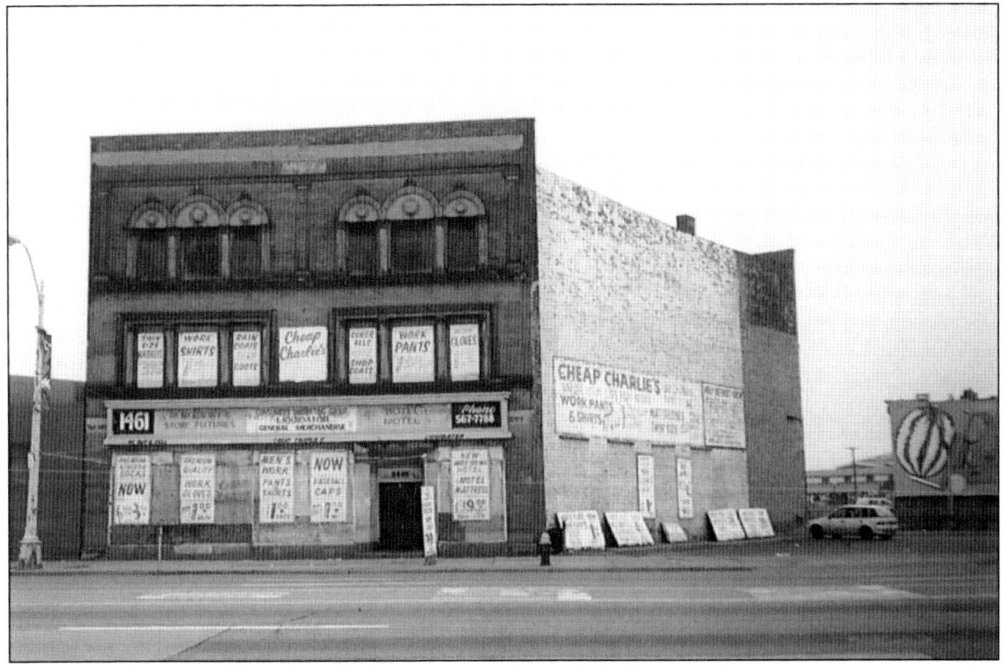

THE FAIR/KRESGE/CHEAP CHARLIES. This building, at 1461 Gratiot Avenue, was constructed in 1896 as The Fair, a general merchandise store run by proprietors Keidan and Zemon. Over the years, the building housed a Kresge store—the plaster shields on the inside walls still sport the "K"—and later Cheap Charlies. Owner Joe Garofalo, called Charlie by everyone who knew him, ran the store for more than 30 years before selling it in 2002. (LR.)

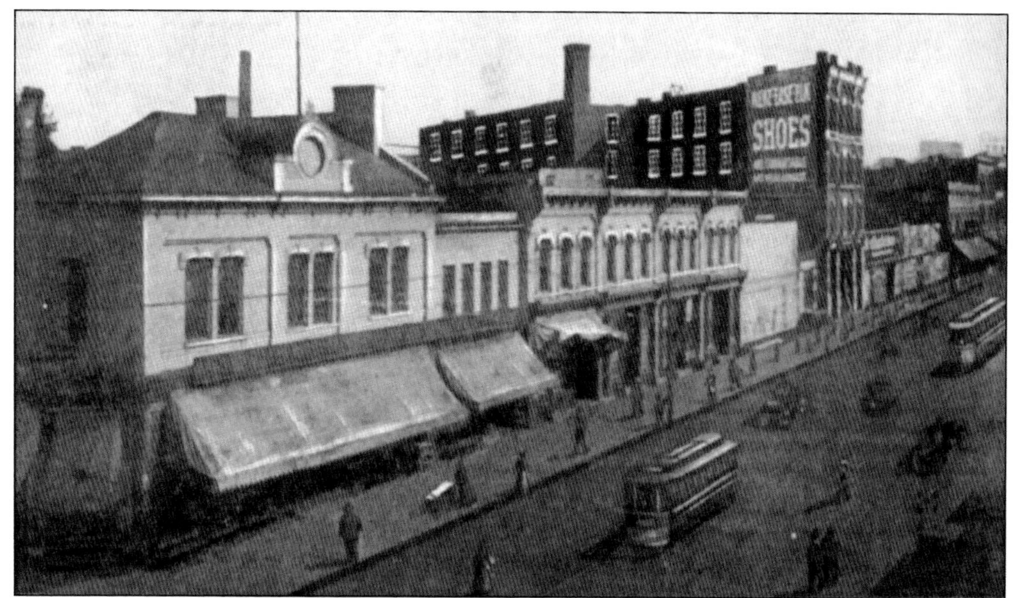

Menzies Shoe Company. This building, at 431–433 Gratiot Avenue, was home to the Menzies Shoe Company factory and sales showroom. Founded by Henry Donald Menzies in 1902, the company was well known for its American Boy and Men's Ease elk shoe brands. The Menzies Shoe site later became the location of Gratiot Central Market. (EMC.)

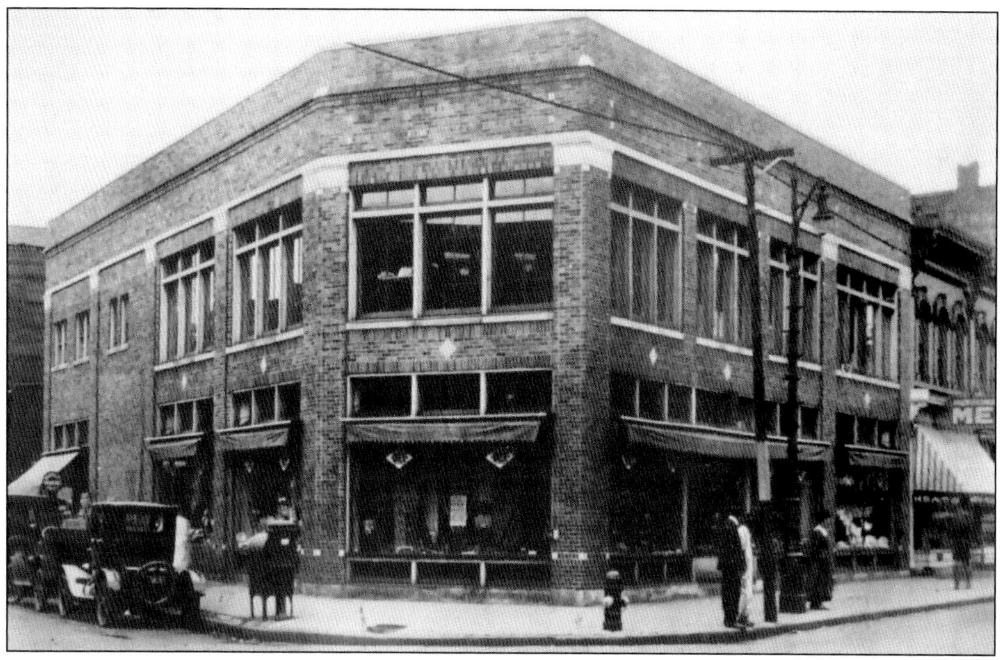

Bee Hardware/Busy Bee Hardware. Julius Berkovitz founded Bee Hardware at the corner of Gratiot Avenue and Russell Street in 1918. A few years later, Berkovitz handed down the store to his son-in-law Dan Krause and Krause's World War I buddy Herbert Crabb. They added "Busy" to the original name, and it became Busy Bee Hardware. Crabb's son Raymond operated the store from the 1940s to the 1980s, turning it over to his children Sandy (Crabb) Novak and Richard Crabb, who continue to operate the general hardware store today. (BBH.)

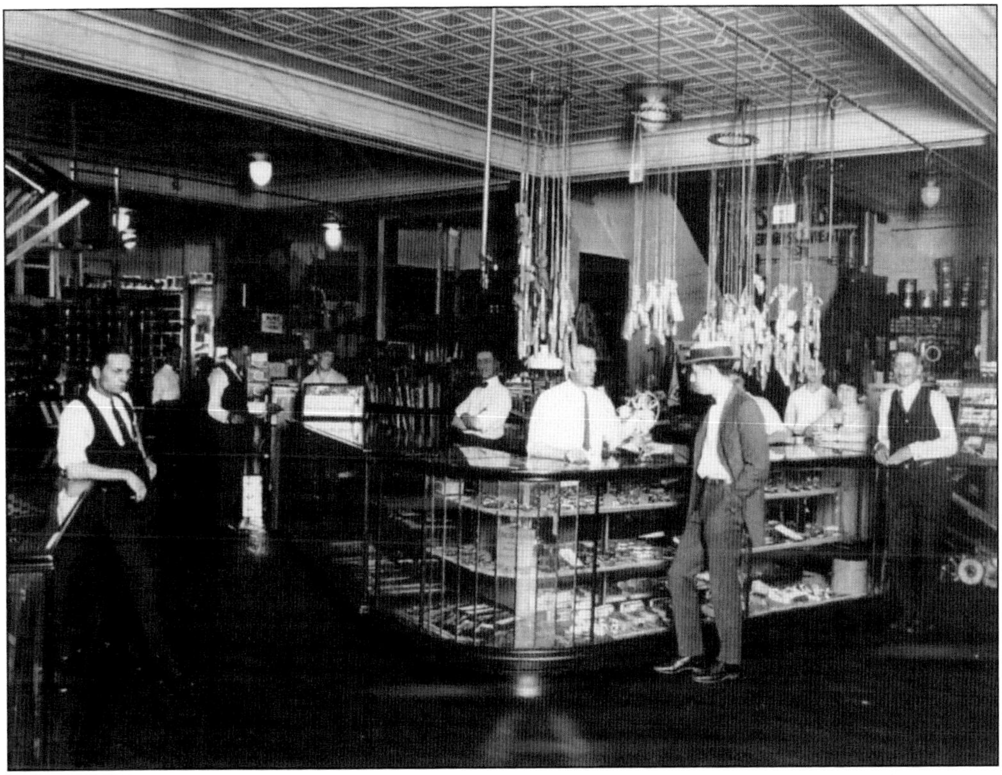

"Anything from a Mousetrap . . . to an Elephant." The motto of Busy Bee Hardware sums up the items that could be purchased or repaired at the three-story general merchandise store. Although elephants were not stocked, the store was a regular stop for repairs for the Barnum & Bailey Circus when it visited Detroit. Busy Bee also provided leather repairs and tack to the mounted division of the Detroit Police Department. (BBH.)

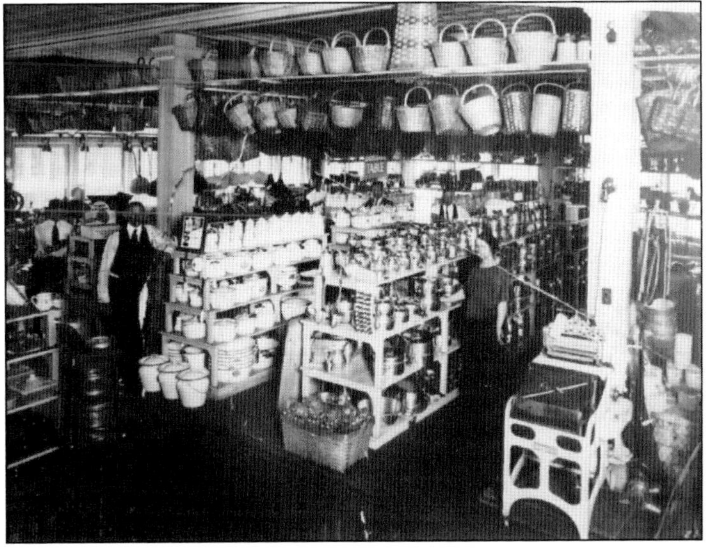

General Merchandise. The three-story building has one of Detroit's only remaining commercial, hand-cranked, nonelectric elevators. Busy Bee expanded its first floor to include the four Victorian-era buildings just east of the store along Gratiot Avenue and continues to serve the usual and unique hardware needs of Detroiters today. (BBH.)

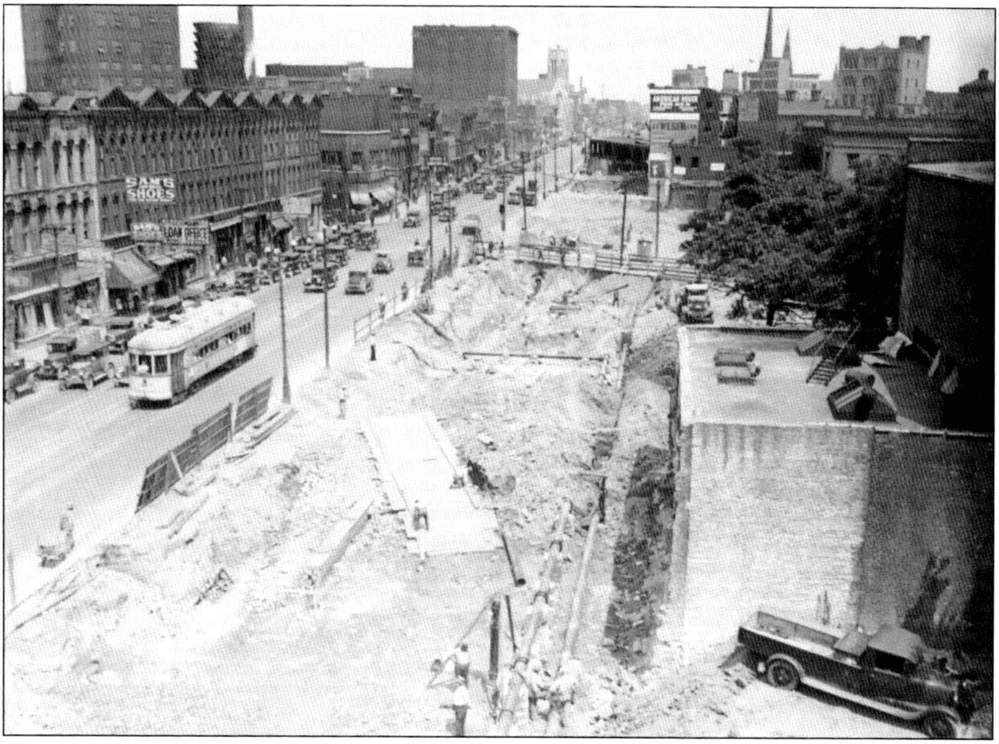

GRATIOT AVENUE EXPANDS. In the 1930s, a growing city and ever-increasing automobile traffic required a widening of Gratiot Avenue. A total of 60 feet on the south side of Gratiot Avenue was needed for the expansion. Existing Victorian-era buildings that lined the south side of Gratiot were either completely or partially demolished, with original facades and the first 60 feet of each building removed. As new buildings were constructed and new facades installed, the south side of Gratiot took on an Art Deco look, the popular architecture style at the time. (WRL.)

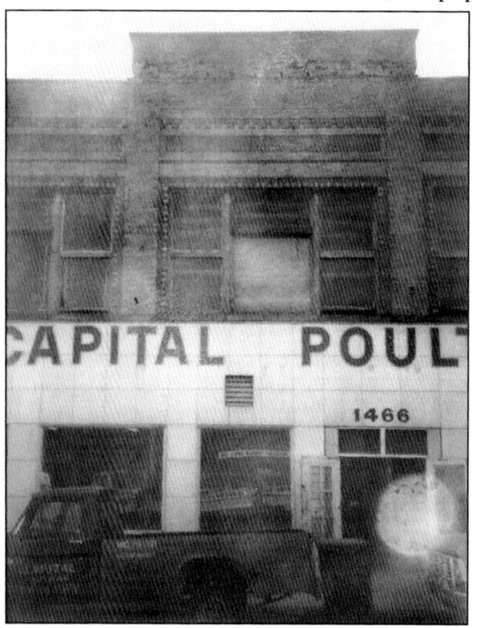

CAPITAL POULTRY. Anthony Licata came to Detroit from Sicily in 1926 and entered the poultry business. Joseph Arnone married Licata's daughter Lillian and took over the business in 1957, moving it to Gratiot Avenue, next door to Gratiot Central Market, in the early 1960s. The building fronted both Gratiot Avenue on the south and what would become the Fisher Freeway service drive on the north. Capital Poultry sold wholesale from the south entrance of the building and retail from the north entrance. The business sold live birds that were processed for customers on-site. (AP.)

Capital Poultry Fire. In August 1983, a four-alarm fire severely damaged the Capital Poultry building. Firefighters were seen wheeling cages of live birds out of the building, while others worked to extinguish the flames. The building was soon reconstructed and the business reopened, but because of changing consumer grocery habits and increased regulations, live processing was prohibited, and the retail operation closed in 2006. The wholesale operations were moved to the other side of the Fisher Freeway, at 2456 Riopelle Street. (EMC.)

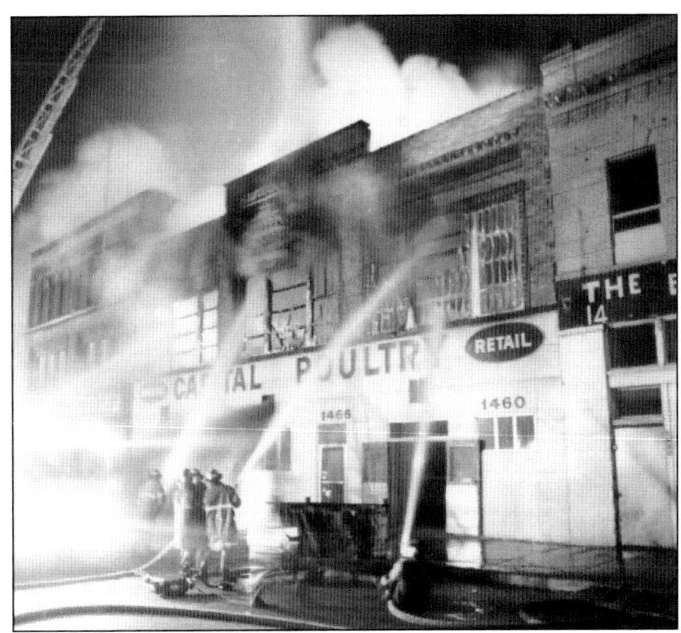

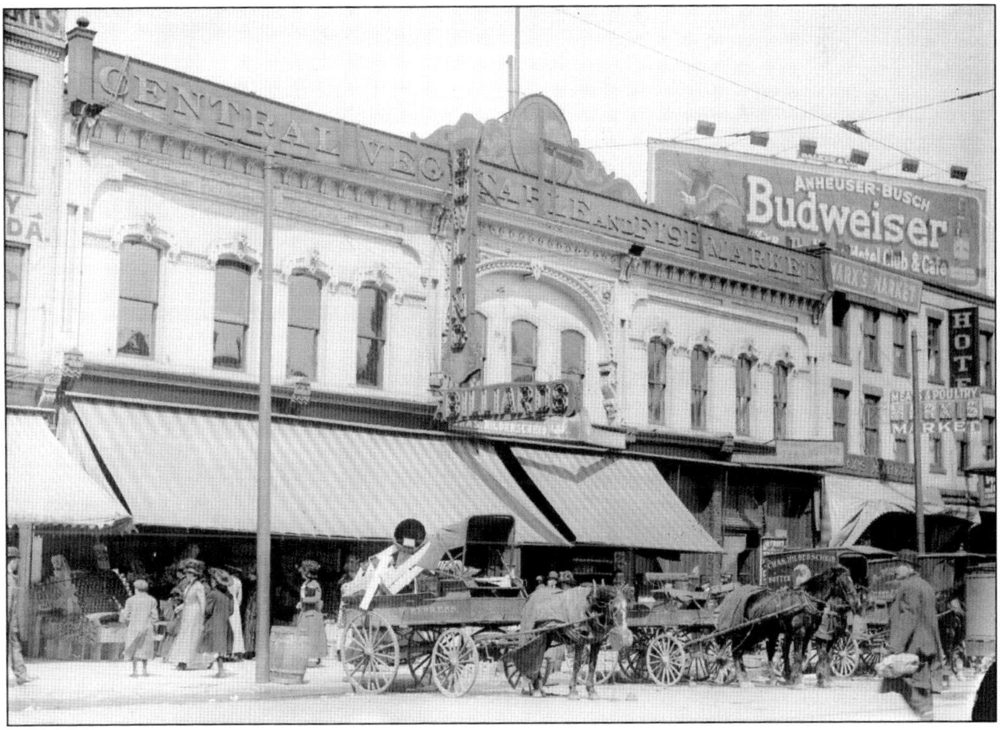

Gratiot Central Market. With its main entrance on Vernor Highway, now the Fisher Freeway service drive, Gratiot Central Market was built in 1915 as a market hall, with open stalls featuring mostly meat sellers. The prominent Detroit architectural firm of Smith, Hinchman & Grylls designed the white-glazed terra-cotta building with interior white ceramic tiles, and it was constructed at a cost of $50,000. (WRL.)

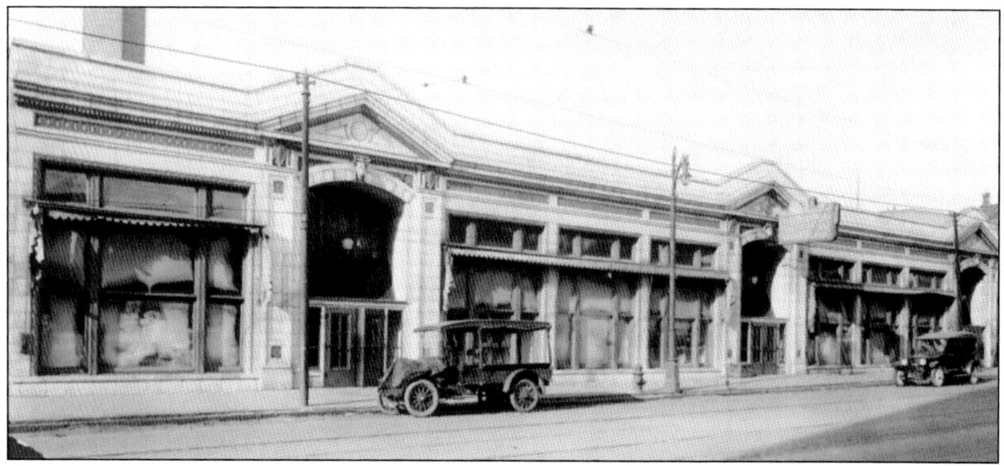

GRATIOT CENTRAL MARKET ALONG GRATIOT AVENUE. A much more plain entrance along Gratiot Avenue allowed shoppers to enter from the Gratiot streetcars. Over each doorway was a terra-cotta bull head, indicative of what was sold inside. The first floor served as a public market, and the second floor of the building featured a bowling alley. (DO.)

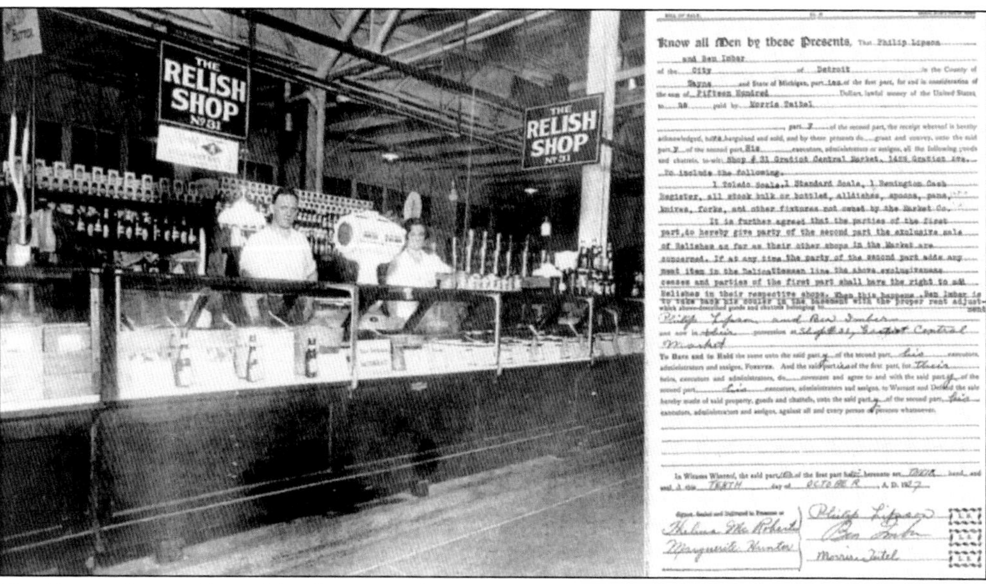

THE RELISH SHOP. Morris Teitel came to Detroit as a teenager. In 1927, he borrowed money from his cousin to lease space in Gratiot Central Market. Teitel and his wife, Bessie, sold European specialty foods and a wide variety of delicatessen items and sweets. (GC.)

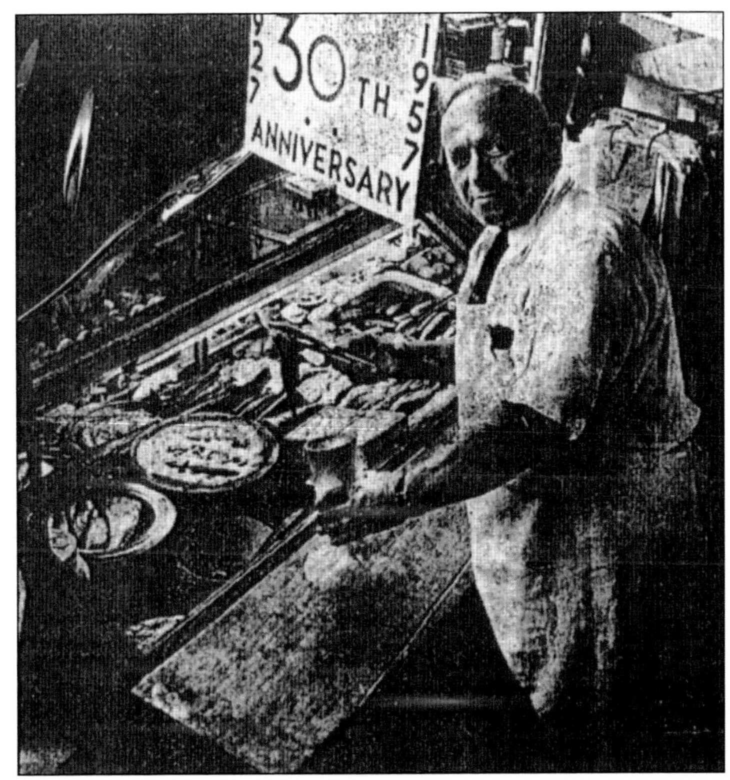

The Relish Shop in Later Years. After World War II, the Teitels' son-in-law Oscar Cook joined them at the Relish Shop and developed a wholesale business that supplied local restaurants. Morris Teitel passed away in 1962, and Cook later sold the company to longtime employee Johnny Ardelyan. Ardelyan moved it to Mittleman's pickle warehouse after the Gratiot Central Market fire in 1966. (GC.)

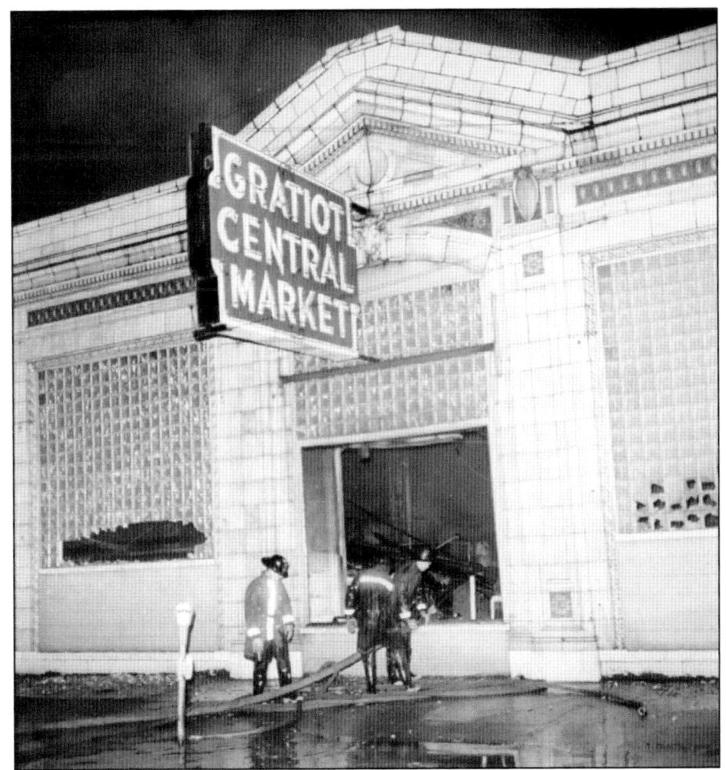

Gratiot Central Market Fire, 1966. An interior fire caused damage to the roof framing and the interior in 1966. Customers reported that they could smell the corned beef being "cooked" by the fire. The exterior wall on the Gratiot Avenue side and the facade on the east service drive of the Fisher Freeway remained intact. After many months of repairs at a cost of $75,000, Gratiot Central Market reopened in late 1968 to enthusiastic returning shoppers. Many of the longtime merchants had decided to retire, leaving several stalls open for new merchants. (WRL.)

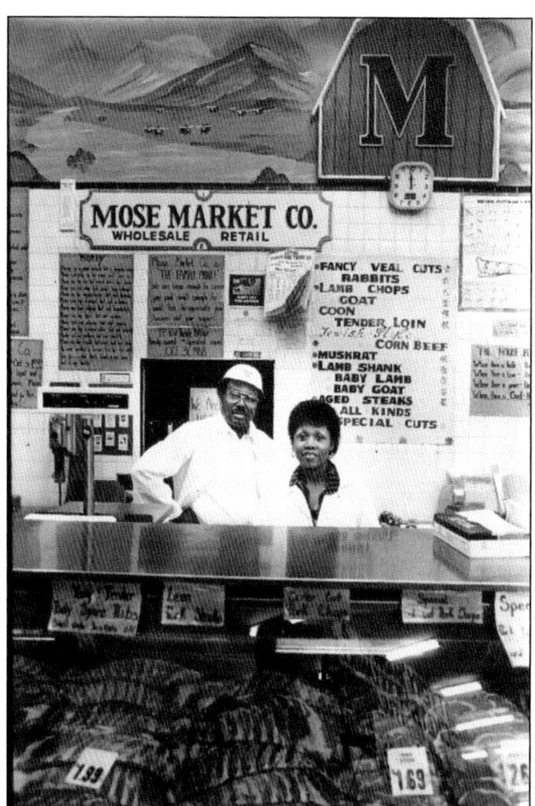

Mose Quality Meats. Mose Primus had been working at nearby K&L Meats when he decided to open a stall in the newly renovated Gratiot Central Market, selling a variety of meats—from muskrat to corned beef. Primus and his wife, Marie, continued selling into the 1990s with the slogan, "When you've seen the rest, come back to Mose and get the best." (EMC.)

Wigley's Corned Beef. Job Wigley came from England to Detroit by way of Toronto and opened a store in Gratiot Central Market in 1924. Wigley's Corned Beef has remained a family-owned corned beef producer in Eastern Market ever since. (MSN.)

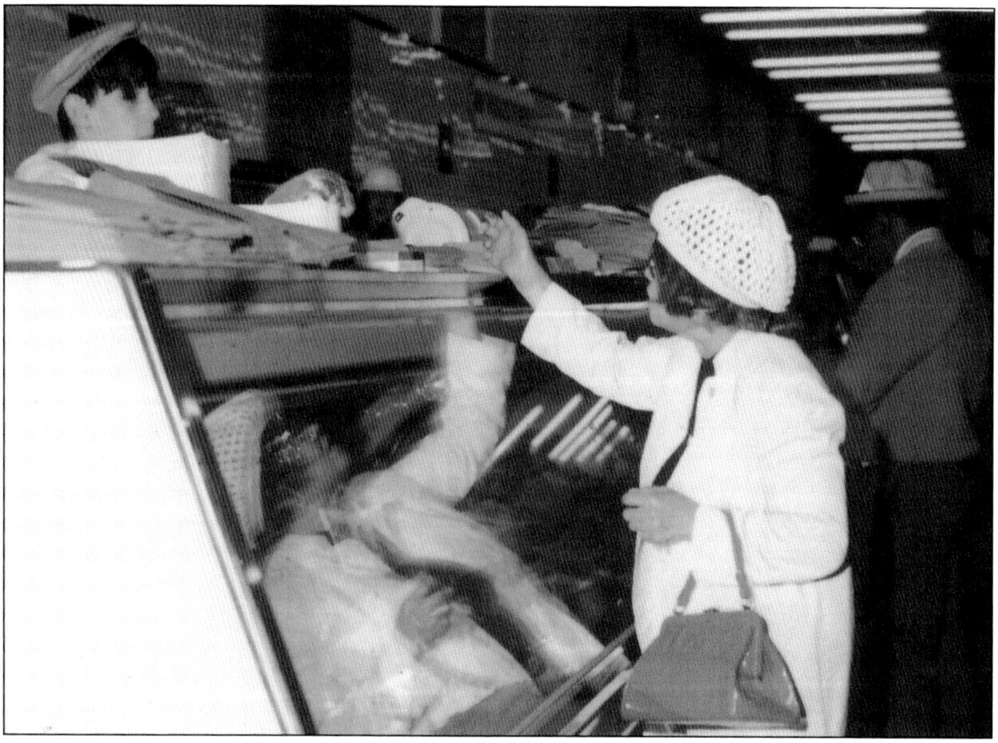

RONNIE'S MEATS. Ronnie Bedway started working in Gratiot Central Market at Zack Meats when he was just 10 years old. After the 1966 fire, the owners of the building recruited new merchants to occupy the repaired facility. Bedway, who was working for the A&P grocery store chain at the time, seized the opportunity to open his own venture in a location he knew very well. (EMC.)

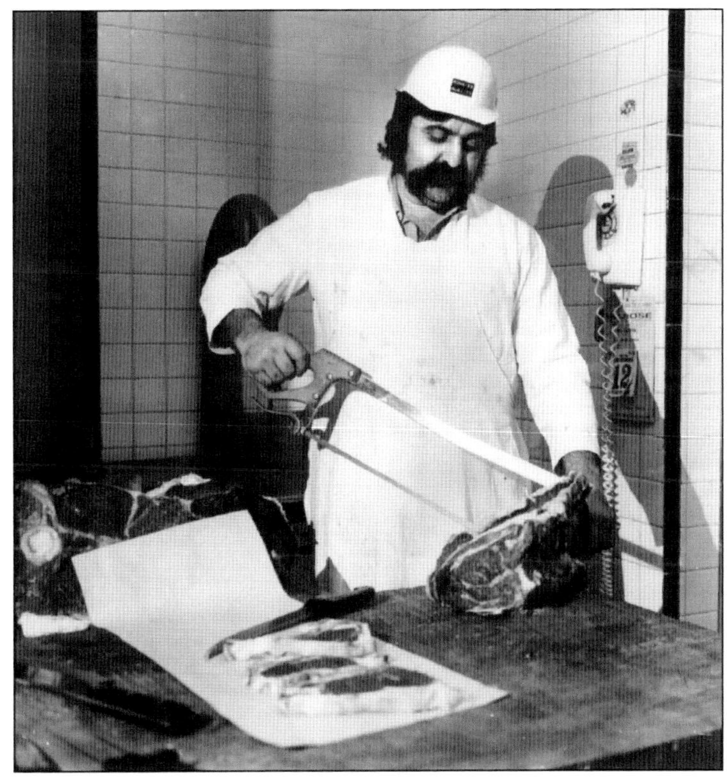

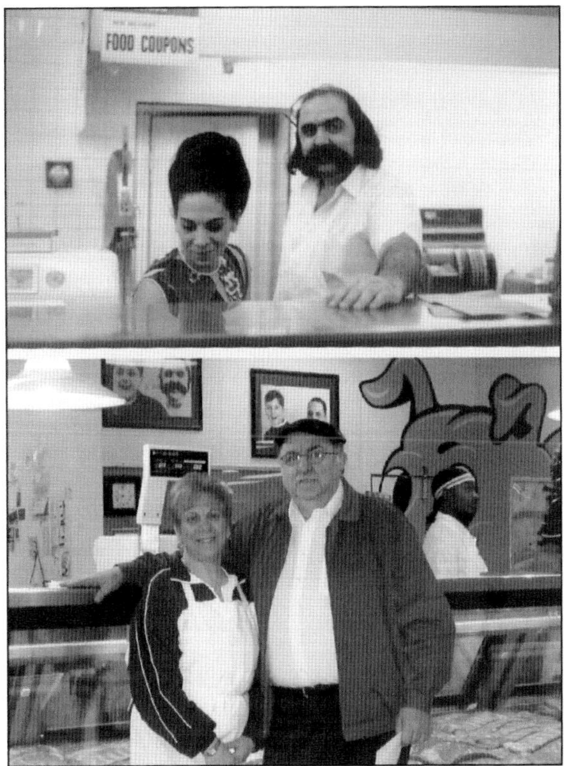

RONNIE'S MEATS, THEN AND NOW. Bedway and his wife, Rosemary, borrowed $200 from her parents, who were also in the meat business, established a small line of credit with a local packinghouse, and opened for business as Ronnie's Meats. They had very little equipment at first, even foregoing a cash register because they could not afford one. (BF.)

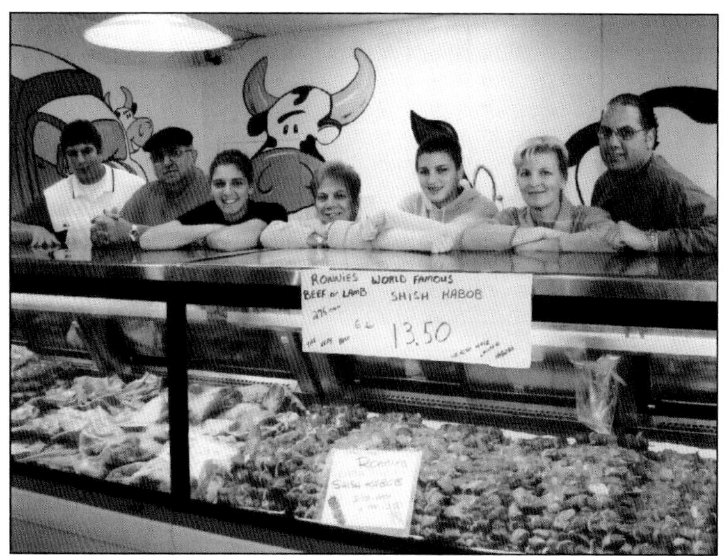

Ronnie's Meats, behind the Counter. Ronnie Bedway's son Tommy came on board full-time in 1979. Today, family members from three generations of the Bedway family can often be found working side by side behind the counter on busy days. In 2013, Tommy and two partners purchased the entire Gratiot Central Market building. (Courtesy of John Schrage.)

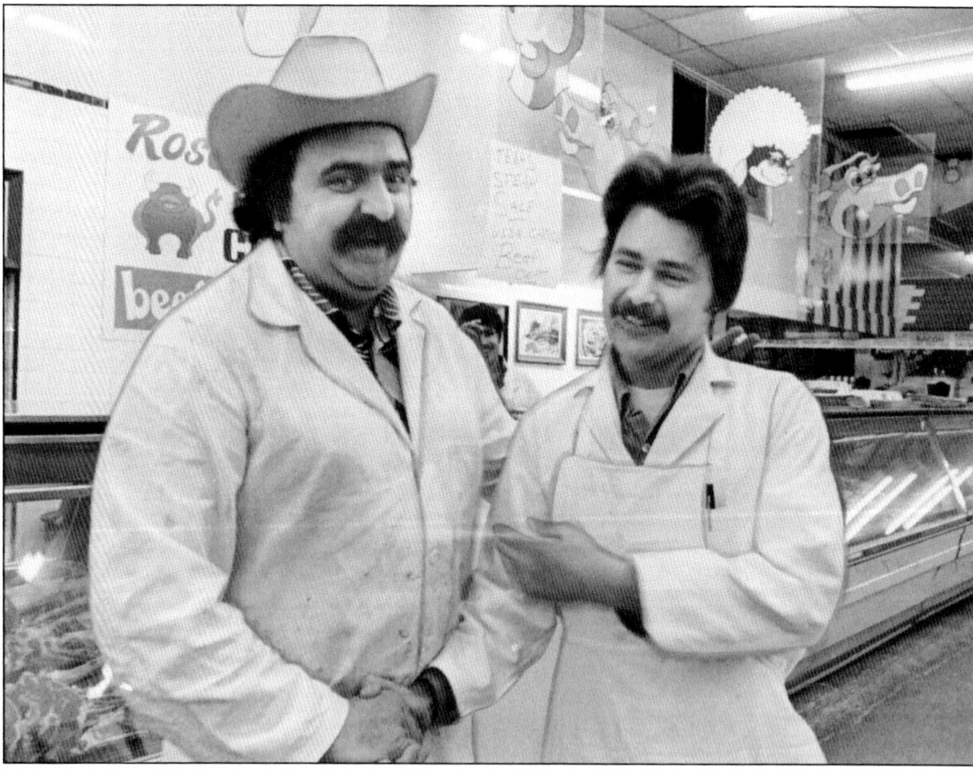

The Corned Beef War. In early 1977, Ronnie's Meats and Wigley's Meats began a corned beef price war that attracted much media attention. The "Corned Beef War" was even featured on an *NBC News* broadcast on February 25, 1977, showing Detroiters waiting in long lines at Gratiot Central Market to pay 49¢ per pound. The war's real winner was a third merchant, John Lepko, who sold his corned beef at regular prices after Ronnie's and Wigley's stocks sold out for the day. (EMC.)

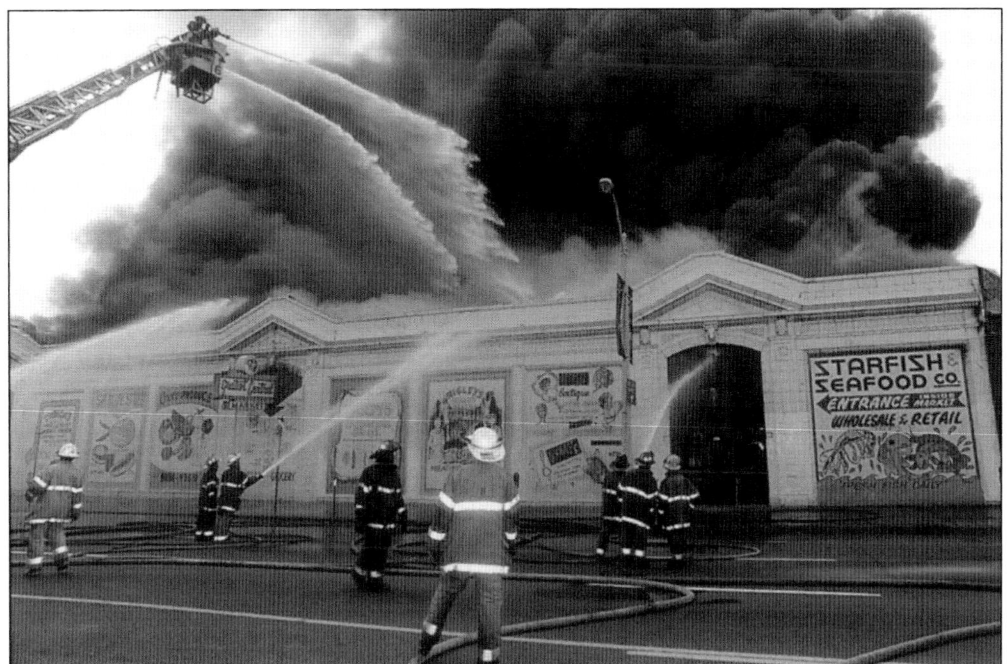

GRATIOT CENTRAL MARKET'S SECOND FIRE. On Thursday, June 22, 1995, a three-alarm fire completely gutted the historic Gratiot Central Market, leaving only the Gratiot Avenue facade. Many merchants retired or closed, while others found temporary locations while the building was revamped into a one-story, open-plan facility. Brothers Richard Ruzumna and Donald Ross, who had inherited the building from their father, hired local builder Bernie Glieberman to construct a new Gratiot Central Market that reused the historic terra-cotta facade on Gratiot Avenue. (BF.)

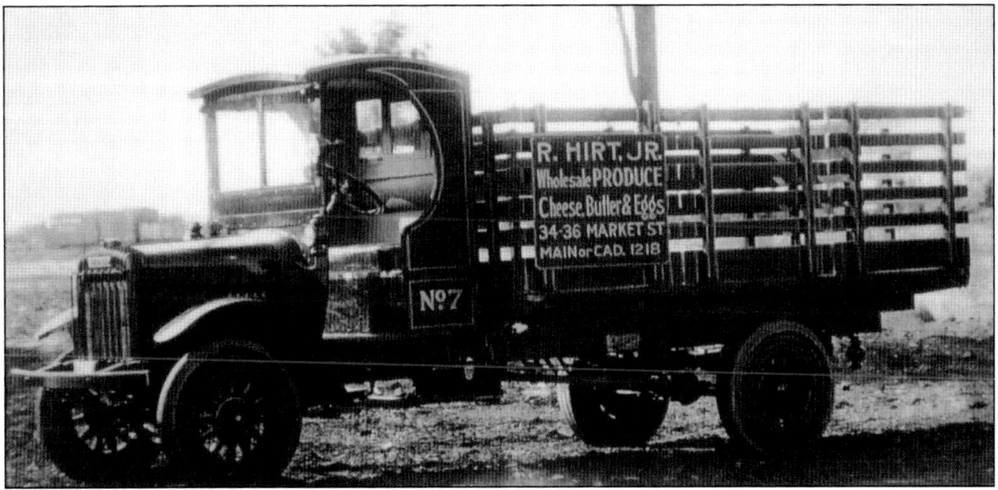

R. HIRT JR. CO. Rudolph Hirt immigrated to Detroit from Switzerland in 1880 and worked as a stove-maker until 1887, when he opened a small business selling butter, eggs, and cheese at Central Market. The family moved to 2468 Market Street in 1889, anticipating that a city market would soon develop in the area of Gratiot Avenue and Russell Street. The building featured the business on the first floor and the family residence above. In 1892, a fire destroyed the original building. It was reconstructed in 1893, and the building and the business have remained in the Hirt family ever since. (Courtesy of Dianne and John Little.)

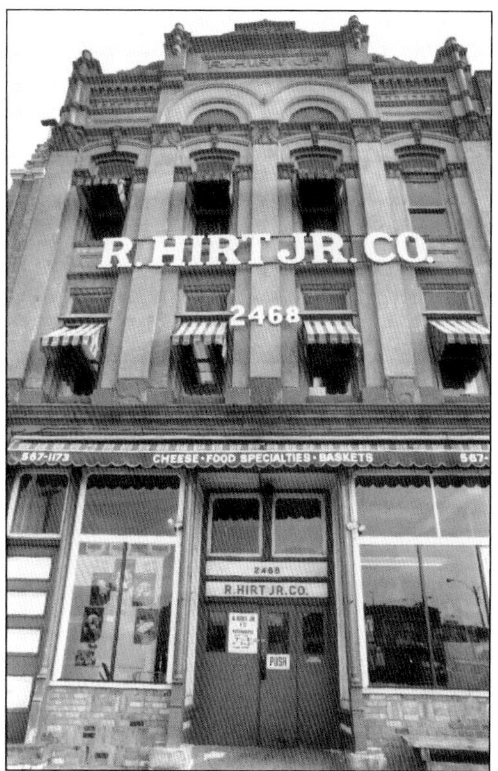

CHEESE PIONEERS. R. Hirt Jr. Co. sold produce as well as butter, eggs, and cheese. Much of the cheese was imported from Hirt's native Switzerland. In 1963, the produce portion of the business was phased out, and cheese, meat, and specialty foods became the main focus. R. Hirt Jr. Co. became well known as Eastern Market's "cheese store." (EMC.)

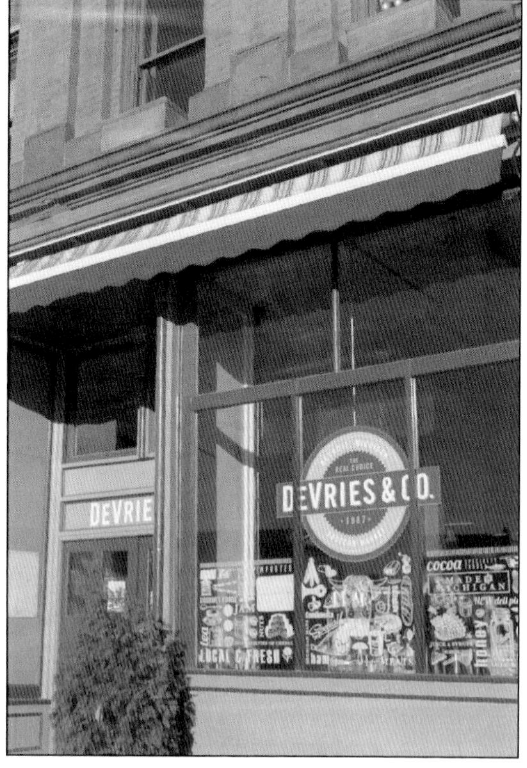

DEVRIES & CO. 1887. Since its founding in 1887, R. Hirt Jr. Co. has remained a family-owned business. Over the years, the business grew to include a cheese and specialty-food distribution business, located in the district on Wilkins Street, in addition to the ever-growing retail operation on Market Street. The Market Street address was the original Hirt building, and the company occupied all three floors, selling gift baskets, lawn ornaments, shopping carts, and more. In 2011, the large, white R. Hirt Jr. Co. letters were removed from the facade of the historical building as the company shifted its focus. The name remained on their wholesale distribution business. After an extensive renovation, David DeVries, the grandson of Rudolph Hirt and the longtime operator of the retail division of the company, reopened the store in May 2012 as DeVries & Co. 1887. (EMC.)

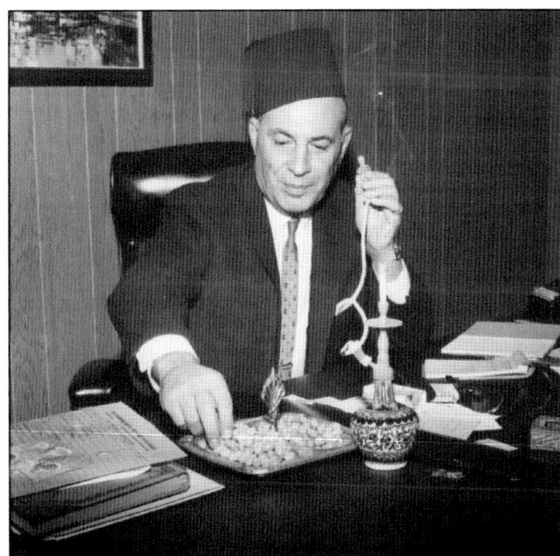

Germack Pistachio Company. Frank Germack Sr. and his brother John arrived in Detroit from Brooklyn in 1924 to expand their growing food-import business. After a few years, John returned to New York, leaving Frank Sr. to run the business at 1346 East Vernor Highway. Frank Sr. introduced the pistachio to Detroit consumers during the Depression and used marketing techniques such as dyeing the shells red. (WRL.)

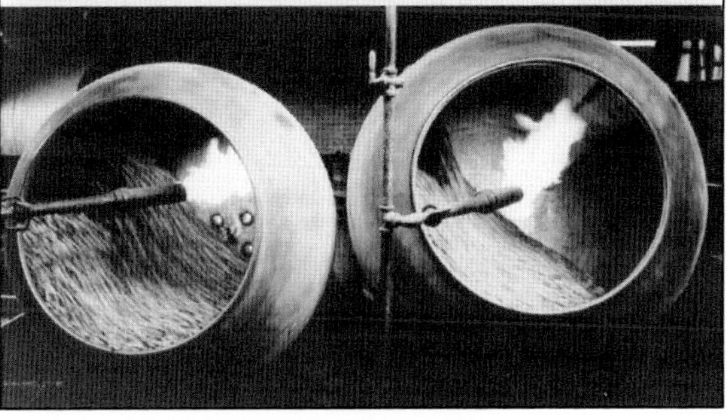

Germack Pistachios. In March 2012, the company, now led by third-generation owner Frank Germack III and his wife, Elyse, moved its retail operations to the former home of the Rafal Spice Company on the corner of Russell and Adelaide Streets. They renovated the space to house the Germack Pistachio Company and the Germack Coffee Roasting Company. (EMC.)

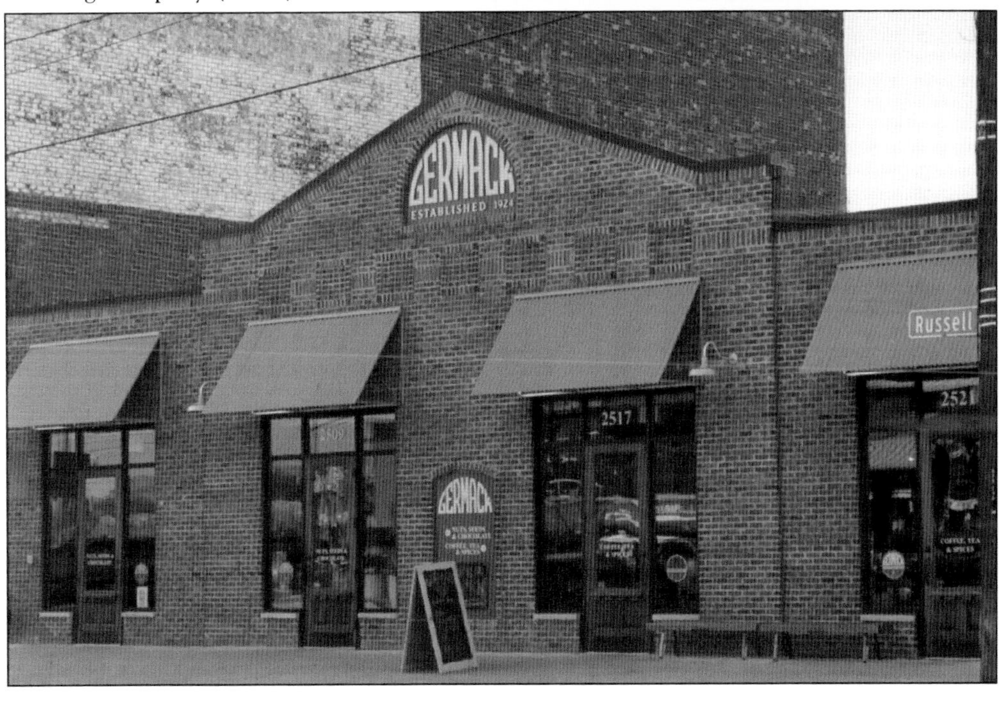

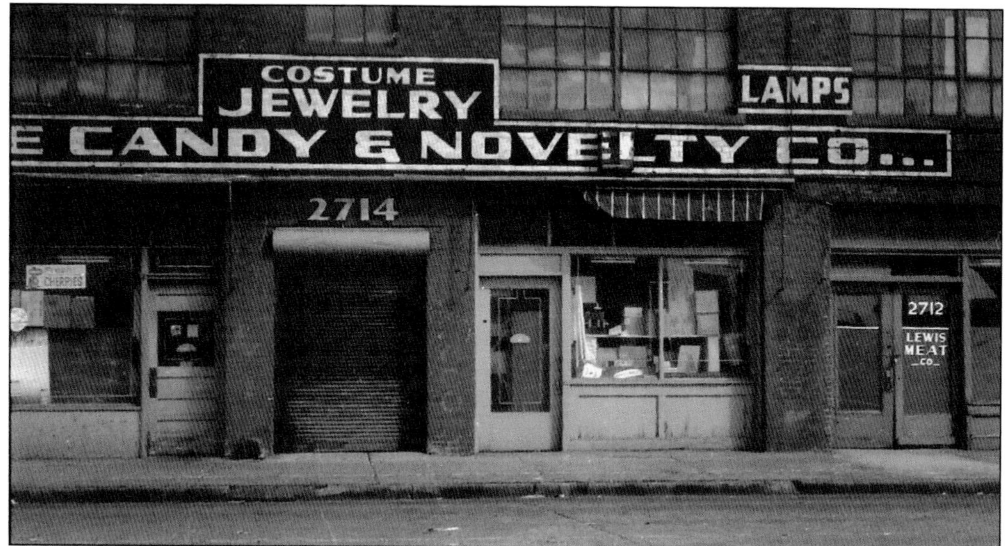

SUPREME NOVELTY/SAVVY CHIC. This building, at 2714 Riopelle Street, was built in 1933 and housed Lee & Cady, a grocery supplier and wholesale butter dealer. After World War II, Supreme Novelty was one of several stores in Eastern Market that sold novelties such as candy, tobacco products, small trinkets, and toys to mom-and-pop grocery stores all over the city. In 2004, local entrepreneur Karen Brown opened Savvy Chic in the space, an eclectic boutique featuring items with a French flair. (MSN.)

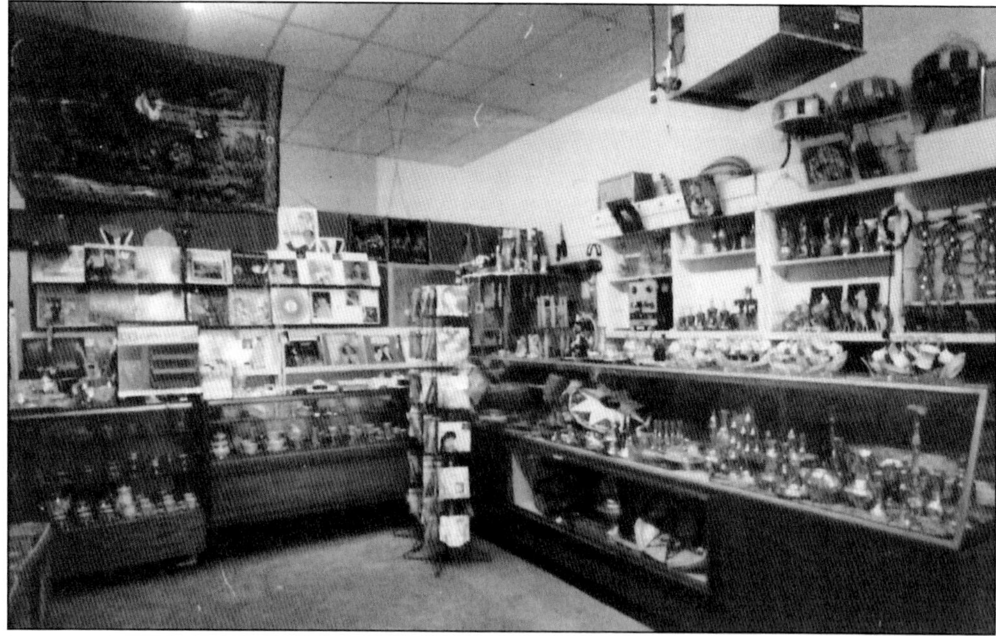

GABRIEL IMPORTING COMPANY. Gabriel Importing Company has been selling homemade and imported Middle Eastern specialty foods since 1945, when current owner Michael Sandros's parents began the business. The small space at 2534 Market Street is a few blocks away from the original store on Russell Street and is packed with varieties of olives, feta cheese, hummus, tabouli, breads, nuts, coffees, and more. An item unique to Gabriel Importing is shankleesh, a homemade yogurt cheese ball rolled in cumin-heavy spices and herbs. (MSN.)

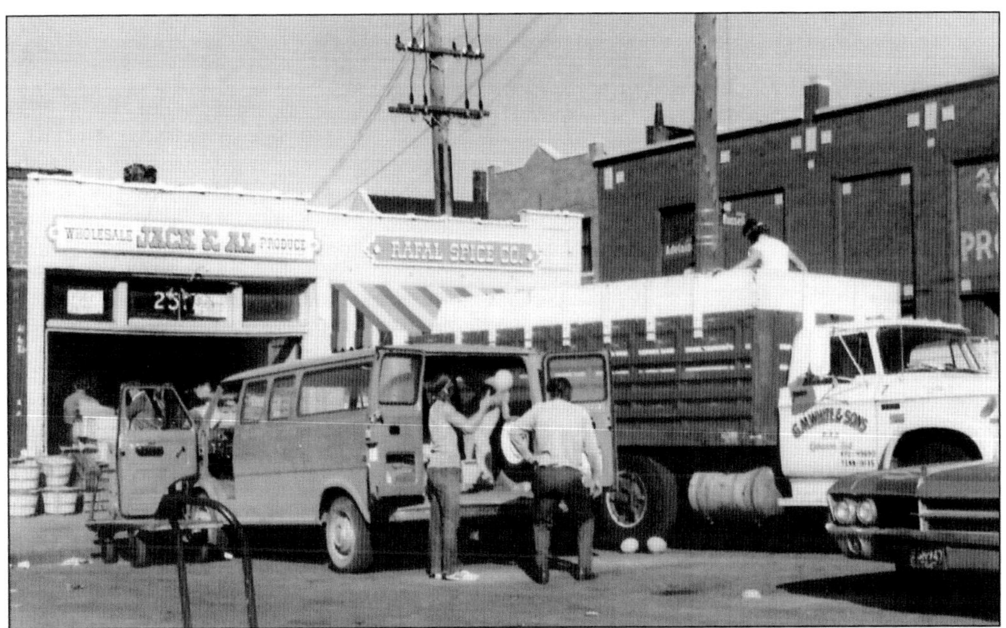

Rafal Spice Company: the Beginning. Marty Rafal was a young World War II veteran and grocer from Norfolk, Virginia, who moved to Detroit to be closer to his wife's family. In 1949, he opened a grocery on Hastings Street that was eventually demolished for the construction of Interstate 75. After that, Rafal started selling bulk spices, mostly for making sausage, to Detroit-area butchers. In the early 1960s, he took over his father-in-law's former produce house on Russell Street and opened Rafal Spice Company. (MSN.)

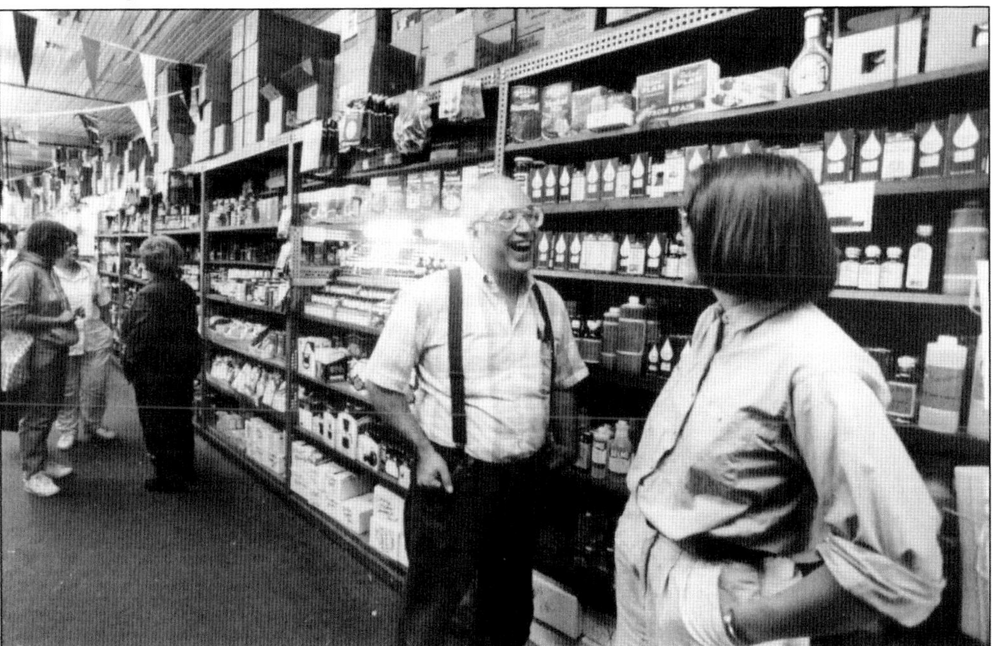

Rafal Spice Company. Marty Rafal's son Donald joined his father's business in 1973. Rafal Spice Company sourced spices and herbs directly from importers and was a market mainstay until closing in 2008. (EMC.)

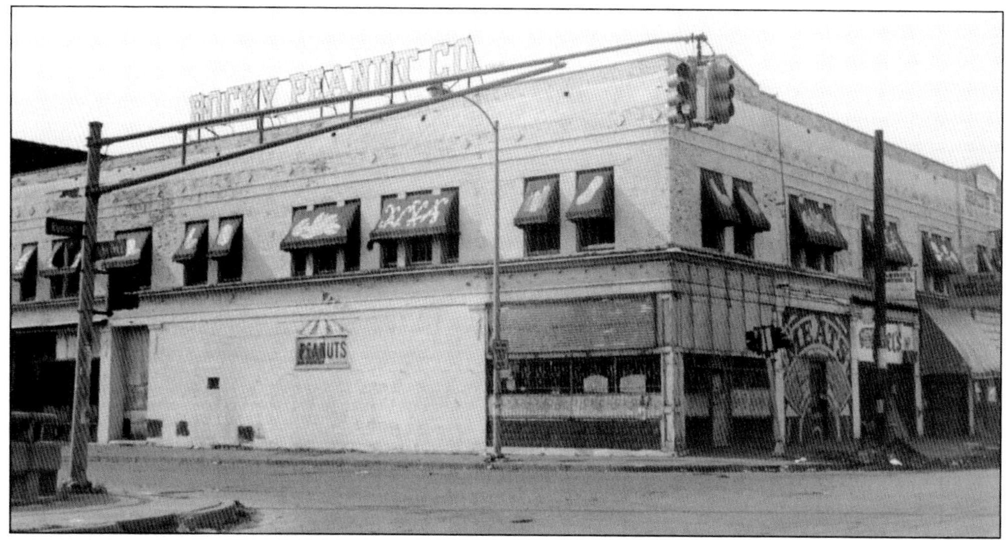

Rocky Produce and Rocky Peanut Company. Jack Russo began selling produce at Eastern Market in 1931. After returning from the Korean War, Jack's son Rocco "Rocky" Russo took the helm of the family business. In 1969, Rocky purchased a small peanut-roasting business, and in 1971 he opened a store on the corner of Russell Street and the Fisher Freeway service drive. (DHS.)

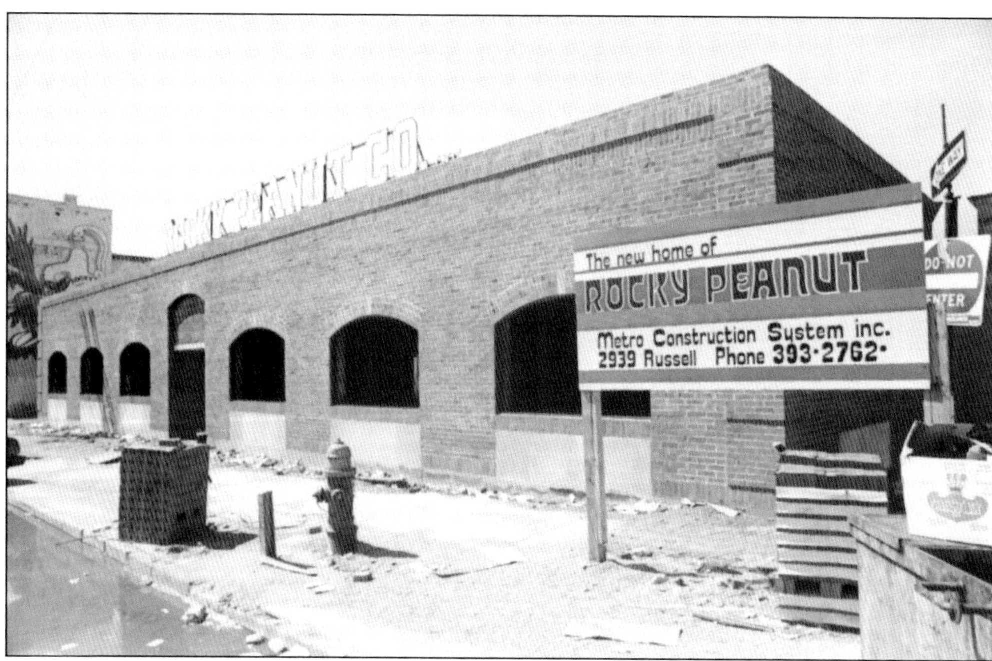

Rocky Peanut Company. In 1981, the younger Russo constructed a much larger retail building featuring a deli counter, specialty foods, dried fruits, and bulk candy, as well as their famous peanuts on the site of the family's original produce house on Russell Street. The business continues in the family today, with Rocky Russo's daughter Patty (Russo) Gianetti, along with a couple of Rocky's grandchildren, running the retail shop and Rocky's son heading up the wholesale business, now located in nearby Ferndale. (WRL.)

Six

Produce Houses and Meat Processors

"Produce houses" and "commission houses" refer to the produce-related businesses that surrounded the market core from its earliest days in the 1890s. They were mostly congregated on Russell and Market Streets around Sheds 1 and 2. Many of these brick-and-mortar businesses were the result of the hard work and perseverance in pursuit of the American dream by many young, unskilled immigrants, mostly from Eastern Europe and Italy, who worked long and hard hours, first as peddlers in the market and then in their own businesses.

Early commission merchants were the forerunners of today's wholesalers, buying produce from farmers or at the produce auction to resell to their customers. Some commission merchants would sell their goods by wagon or truck through Detroit's neighborhoods. Other commission merchants established commission houses where goods were stored and delivered from. Many of the current produce businesses that serve both retail and wholesale customers, as well as those that deliver to local grocery stores and restaurants, can trace their roots to these early businesses, which were started by a determined group of young immigrants.

Eastern Market is also the longtime hub of Detroit's meat-processing industry. Prior to 1891, Detroit's slaughterhouses were located mainly along the railroad lines near Michigan Avenue. Due to the growing Eastern Market and access to the railroad along Dequindre Street, within a few years many of the national brands, such as Hammond-Standish, Armour, and Swift, had established meatpacking facilities or branch stores in the area. The livestock was mostly shipped by rail from the Chicago stockyards, Kansas, Nebraska, and Montana. By 1930, meatpacking was Detroit's second-largest industry, after automobile manufacturing, and was bringing in revenues of over $50 million per year.

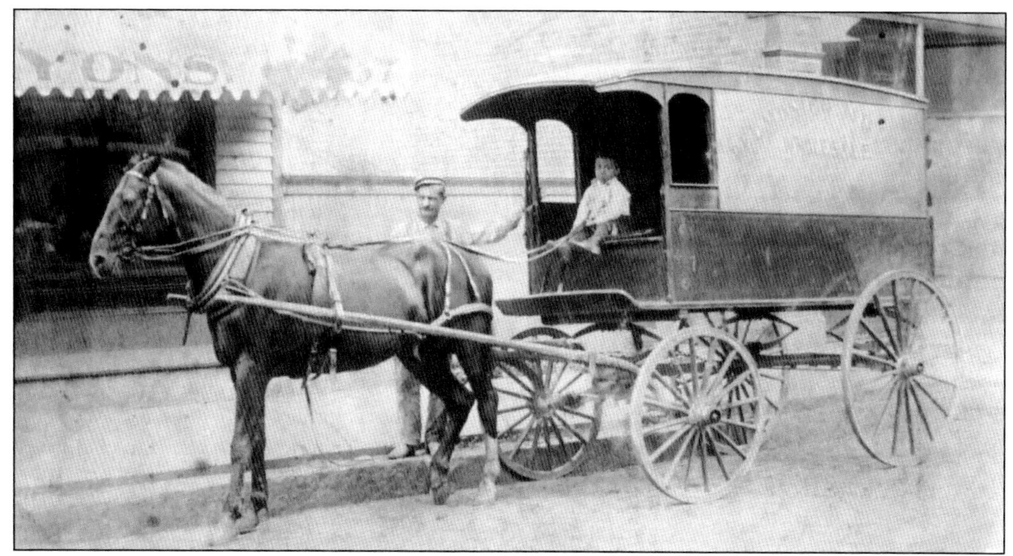

Moceri Produce. Domenico Moceri was born in Sicily in 1865 and came to Detroit in 1890. Three years later, he started his produce business by selling from a horse and wagon. Blessed with an unusually large number of sons eager to enter the family business, the Moceri family expanded in Eastern Market from the 1920s through the 1940s. The last Moceri business in Eastern Market, Jim Moceri & Sons on Orleans Street, closed in the early 2000s, but Moceri Produce, in San Diego, was begun by Domenico's son Dominic after a vacation to California and still traces its roots back to Domenico Moceri's early days in Eastern Market. (Courtesy of Mary Moceri Hoehner.)

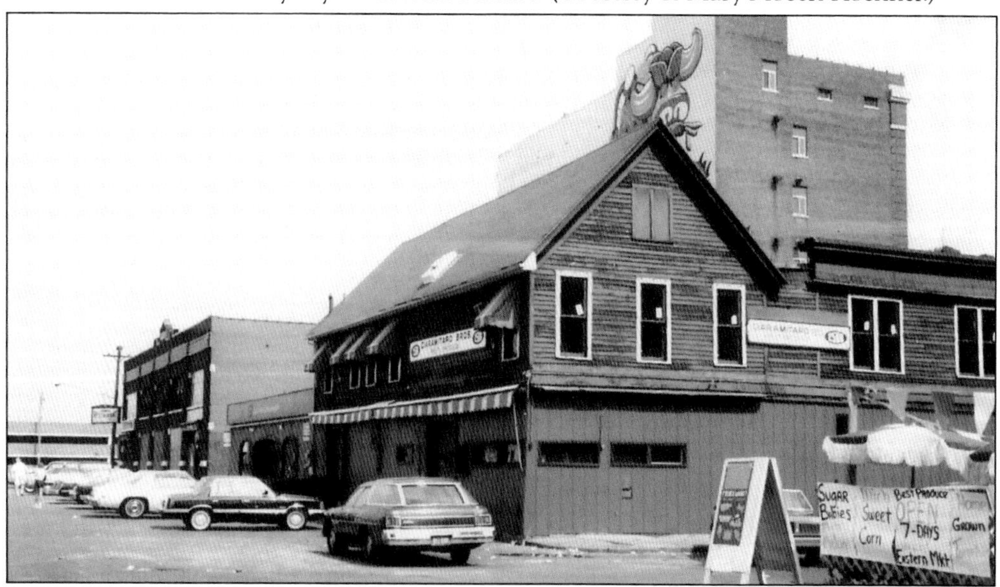

Ciaramitaro Bros. Wholesale Produce-Commission House. In 1914, Anthony Ciaramitaro opened the first commission house in Eastern Market and brought his brothers into the business. By 1930, the business was located at 2506 Market Street, where it remained for the next 73 years. Anthony's grandson Sal Ciaramitaro began working there as a child and eventually became the third-generation owner until his retirement in 2003. An active member of the Eastern Market community, Ciaramitaro was an unflagging champion of the preservation and improvement of the district as a true gem of Detroit. (MSN.)

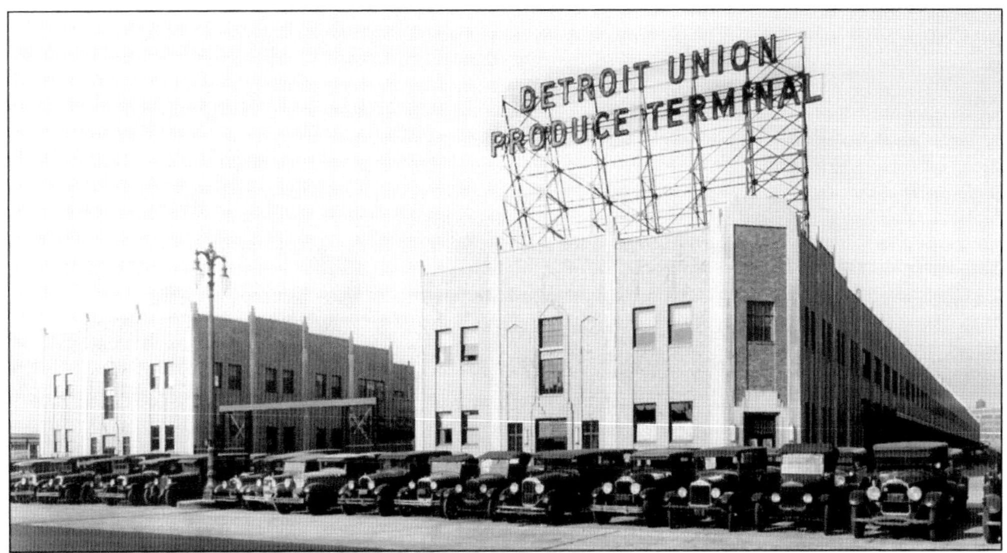

Produce Terminal. With the growing population of Detroit in the 1920s, a new and larger produce terminal was built by the Pennsylvania Railroad Company on Fort Street in 1929. The building was designed for five rail lines, but only two were constructed. Fruits and vegetables were brought in by railcars from all over the country and the world. The terminal was the point of entry in the city for what were then considered "exotic" fruits like bananas and pineapples. (EMC.)

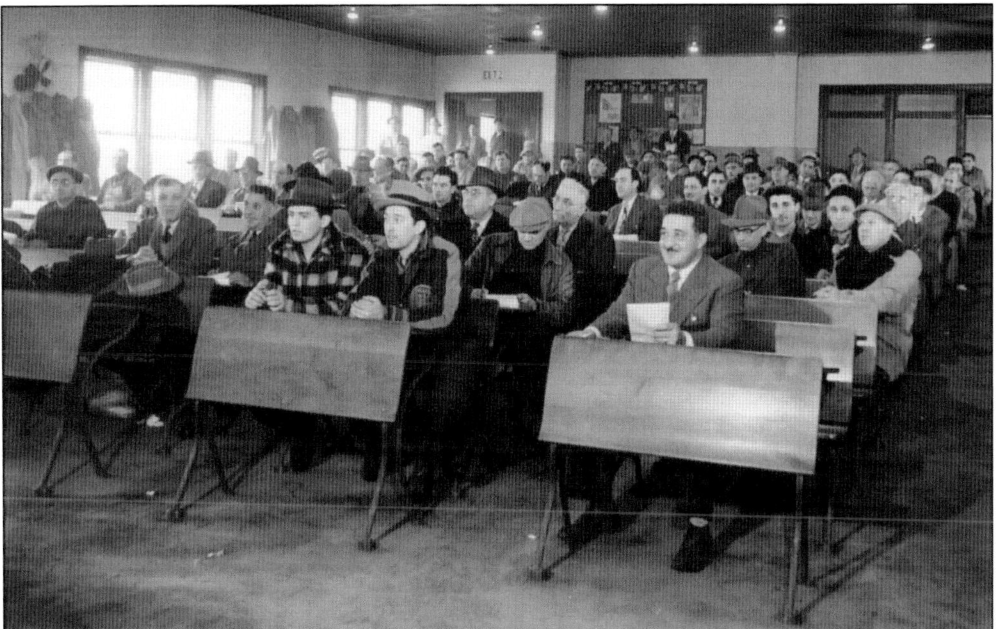

Produce Auction. The main activity in the produce terminal was the auction, held on the second floor of the building. Sellers brought samples to the boardroom for quality assurance and to be approved for sale. Merchant buyers from Eastern Market made their bids from the 252-seat auction room, filled by two-person, school-style desks. All buyers had an assigned seat with their name, and each had a coffee mug stored on a shelf on the wall. Sales by auction ceased in the 1980s, but wholesalers continue to transact business at the terminal in the early-morning hours. (Courtesy of Don Schneider.)

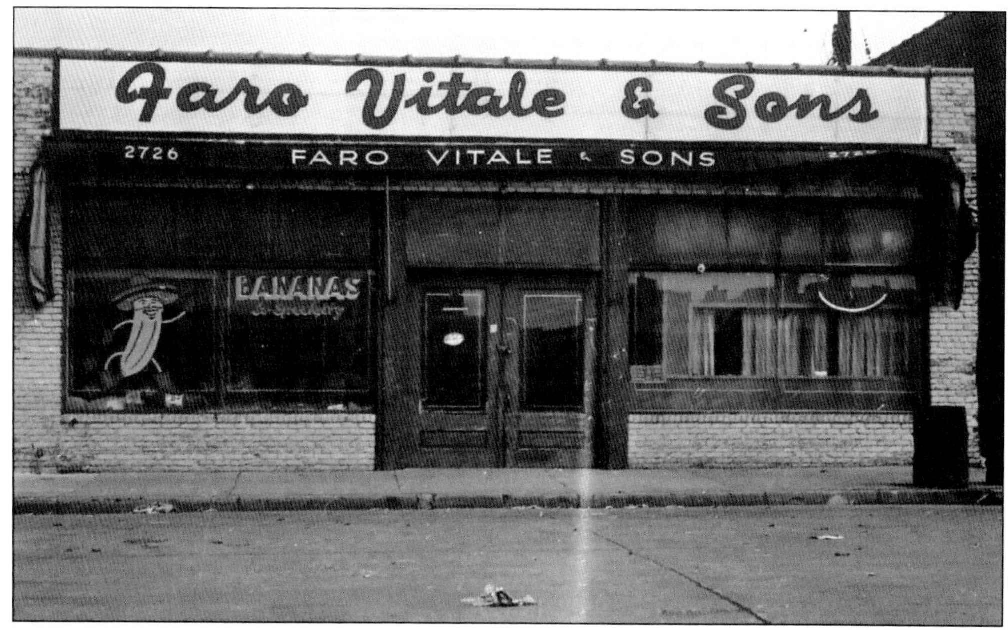

Faro Vitale & Sons. Faro Vitale immigrated to Detroit from Sicily in 1924 and opened a fish store on Hastings Street. In the 1940s, he moved his business, by then transitioning into produce, to Eastern Market. Faro's sons Vincent "Jim" Vitale and Faro "Frank" Vitale Jr. joined the business after serving in World War II. Faro Vitale & Sons was located at 2726 Riopelle Street and quickly gained a reputation for its quality watermelons and bananas. Jim Vitale came to be known as "the Watermelon Man." By the 1980s, he was selling over 24 million pounds of watermelon a year. (MSN.)

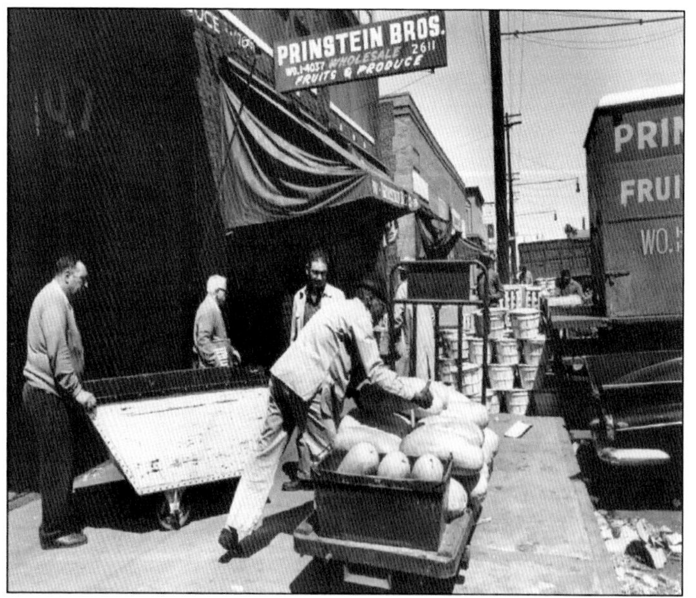

Prinstein Brothers. Another multigenerational family business, Prinstein Brothers, was founded by Meyer Prinstein, who came to America in 1914. His sons and daughter sold produce in the sheds and from a store on Russell Street, and Meyer's grandson Steve ran the business until 1987. (EMC.)

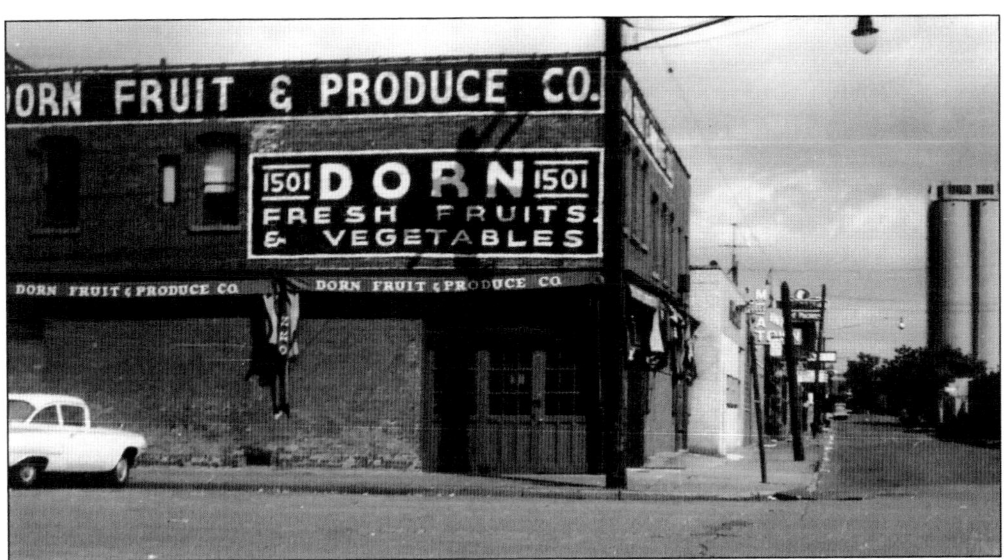

Dorn Fruit and Produce Company. Built in 1880 for grocer John Spielman, the property at 1501 Division Street originally housed a grocery store on the first floor and residential quarters on the second. Later, the building was home to the Dorn Fruit & Produce Company and then United Specialty Produce. Since March 2010, it has been home to OmniCorp Detroit. Referred to as a "hacker space," OmniCorp is a community-operated collaborative studio that offers space to creative entrepreneurs. (MSN.)

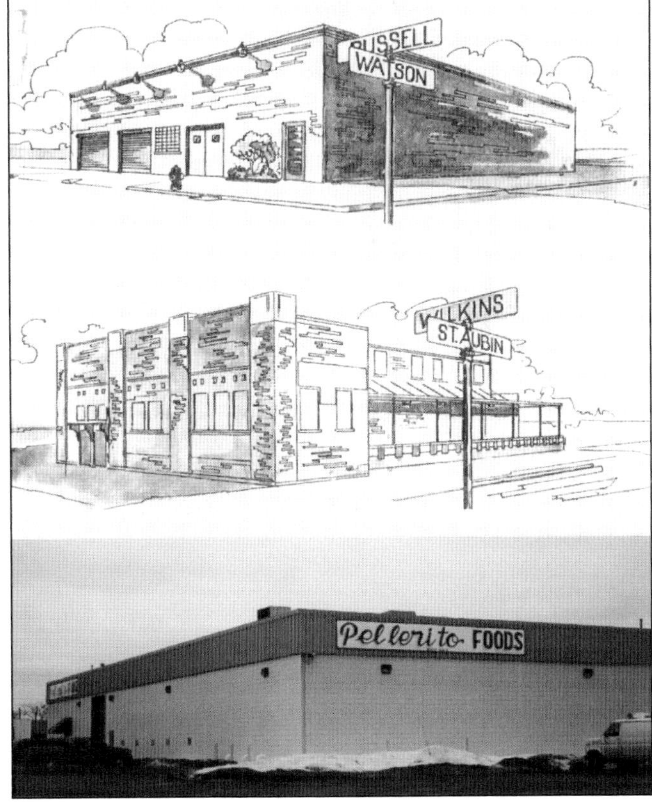

Pellerito Foods. Currently located on Mack Avenue, Pellerito Foods traces its origins back three generations. John Bolone, the grandfather of current owner Jim Pellerito, started with a banana house in the early 1900s. John's son Carmen left his father's business and teamed with his brother-in-law John Pellerito to open the Carmen Bolone Company in 1943, focusing on fresh-cut vegetables and peeled potatoes. Together, the younger Bolone and Pellerito ran the business for over 30 years. In the late 1970s, Pellerito's son Jim joined the family business, which became Pellerito Foods in 1980. Currently, it employs more than 100 people and processes fresh-cut vegetables in a state-of-the-art processing plant under the Vita Pac label. (Courtesy of Jim Pellerito.)

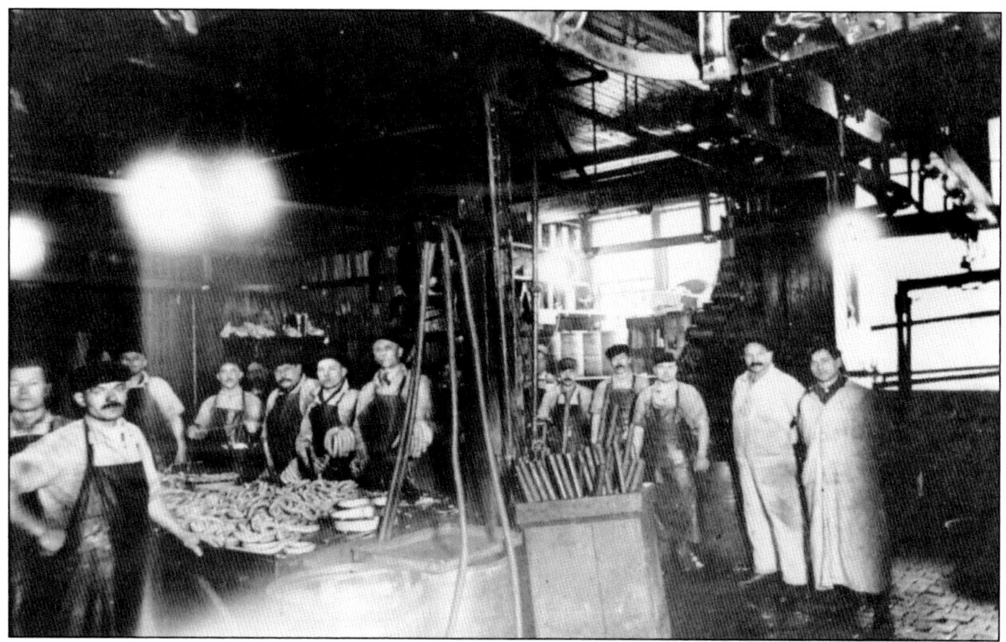

"PACKERS AND JOBBERS OF PROVISIONS, PORK AND BEEF." Local Detroit business Parker, Webb & Company was an early manufacturer of sausages. Its main offices were near Cadillac Square, and it had a branch office in Eastern Market at 394 High Street. By 1930, Parker, Webb & Company had become a branch of Hygrade Foods, which later branded Ball Park Franks. (BHC.)

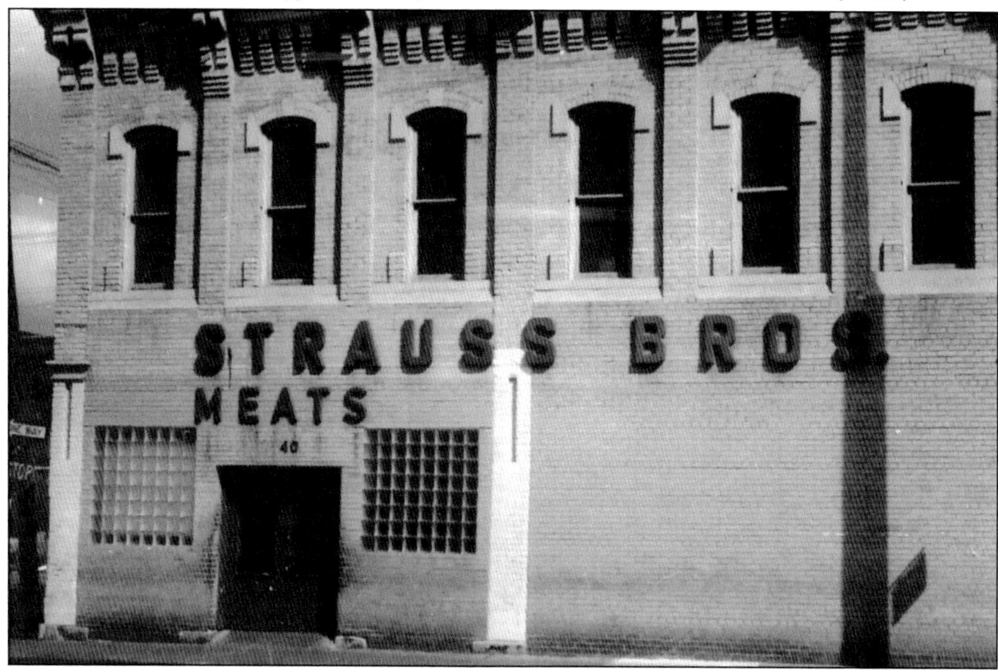

STRAUSS BROTHERS MEATS. In 1873, Joseph Bieke opened Bieke Bros. Grocery at 2738 Orleans Street in what was then a residential community. The structure was rebuilt in 1892 as a two-story store with a dwelling upstairs. After World War II, the grocery closed, and Strauss Brothers converted the building into a meat-processing facility. (MSN.)

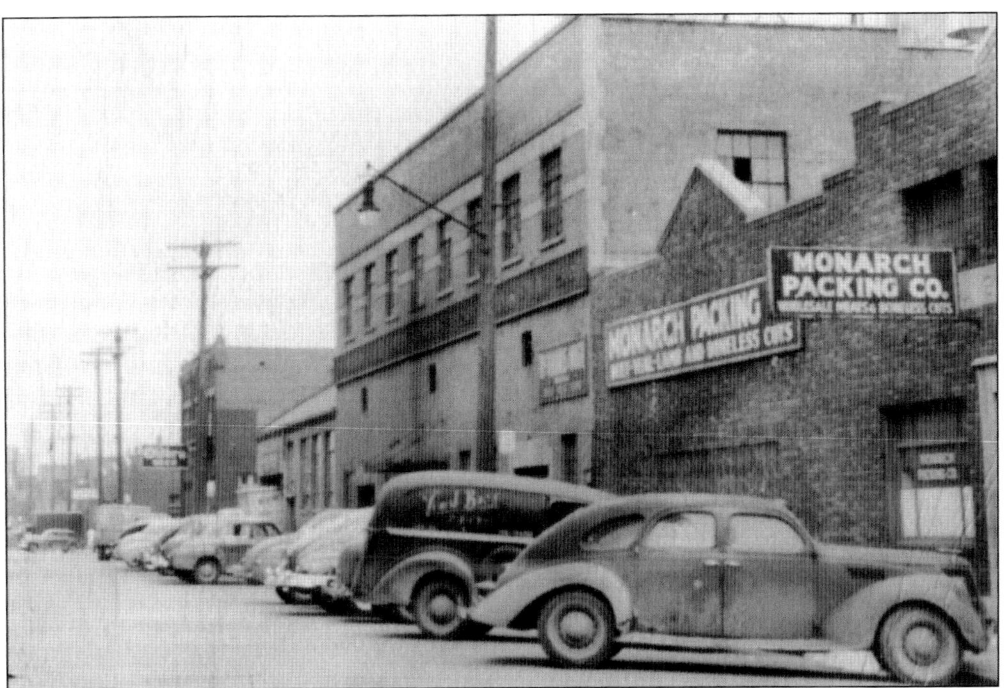

Louis Fineman/Monarch Packing. This building, at 2496 Orleans Street, was constructed in 1936 as a slaughterhouse for Louis Fineman, whose name can still be seen above the doorway. By 1940, Monarch Packing had opened a slaughterhouse there that operated for the next 30 years. (JM.)

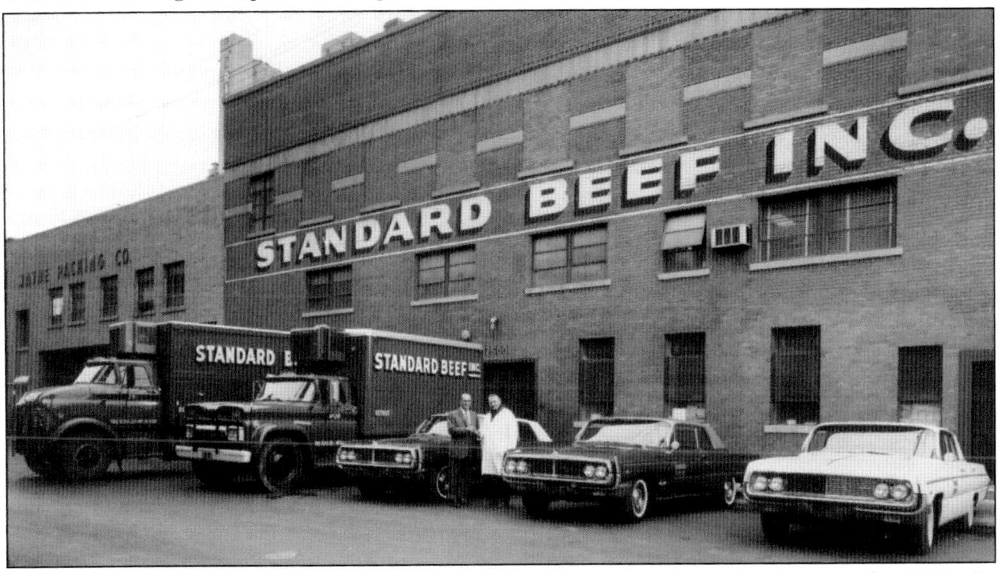

Standard Beef. Joe Palmer started out as a Michigan Avenue meat merchant in the 1940s. In 1947, he and his wife, Phyllis, set up Standard Beef at 2500 Orleans Street, where they operated a slaughterhouse for cattle. The business continued to grow along Orleans Street, and within a decade it was slaughtering between 800 and 900 head of cattle per day. In the mid-1970s, the Palmers made plans to consolidate Standard Beef's various components into a large tract of land on the west side. Unfortunately, these plans were halted by Joe's untimely death, and the Standard Beef businesses closed a few years later. (JM.)

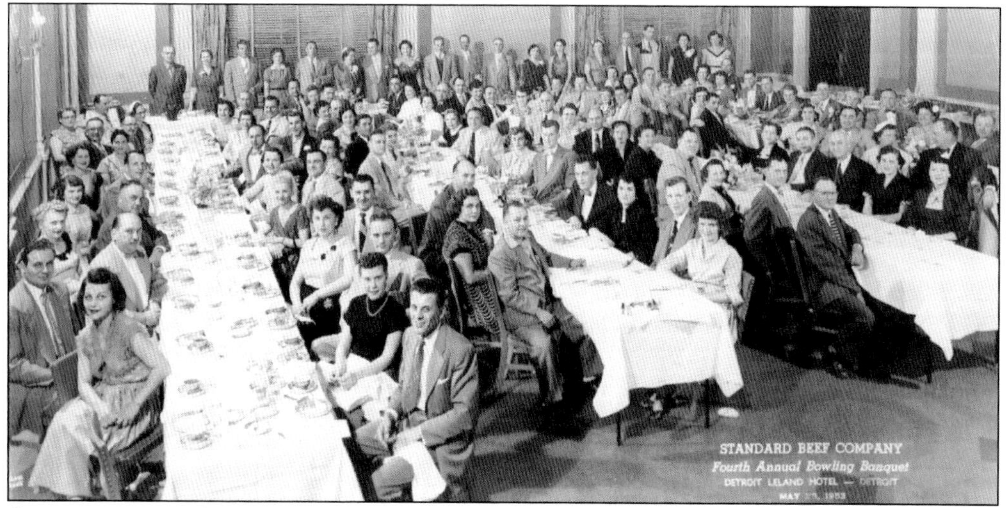

Cutters. Meatpacking was a difficult job, but the pay was good, and it attracted unskilled laborers from home and abroad. After the cattle were killed, at first with a revolver and then with a stun gun, to keep the head intact the carcass was sent to the freezer, where a team of six to eight cutters would debone the cow in 30 minutes. Workers were paid by how many cows they could debone per day. The tough conditions bred a camaraderie that carried over to after-work socializing with activities like company-sponsored bowling leagues. (JM.)

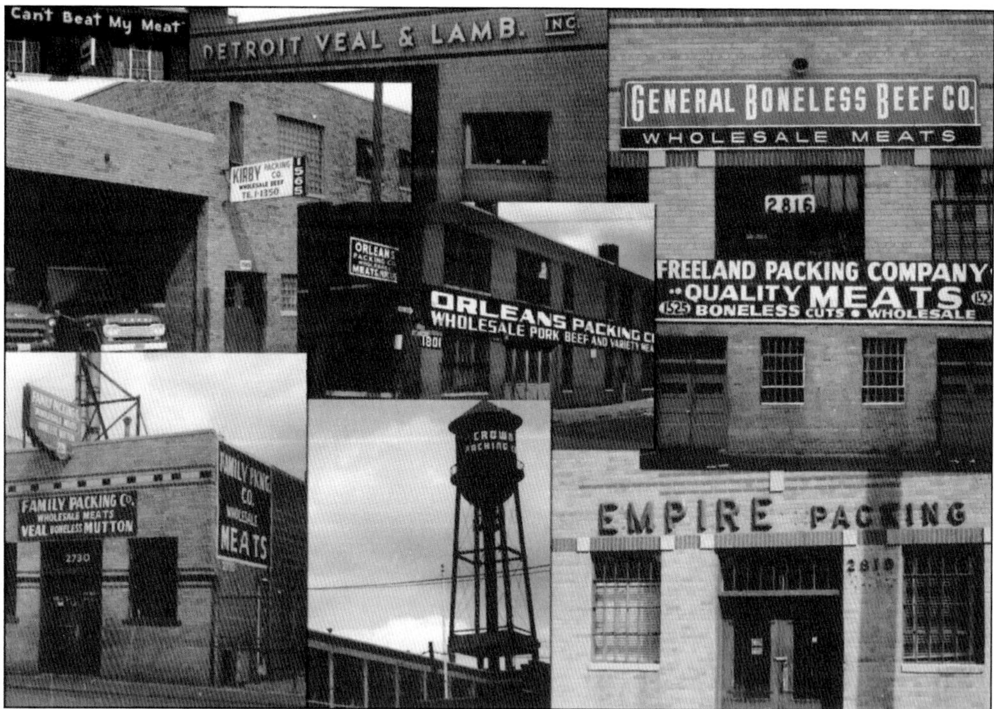

Packinghouses. The meatpacking industry in Detroit began with small family-run enterprises in Eastern Market, but few survived to the second generation. Some meat processing still takes place in the Eastern Market district today, but on a much different scale. There are also now a few halal meat processors that abide by special religious guidelines and serve metropolitan Detroit's sizable Muslim community. (MSN.)

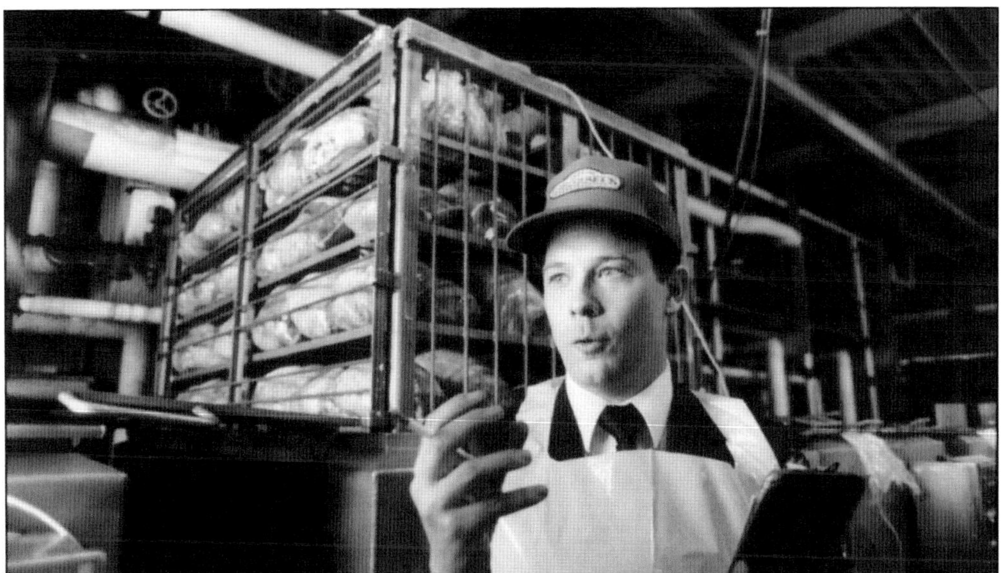

E. W. Grobbel Sons. E.W. Grobbel Sons traces its roots back to 1883, when young Emil Grobbel arrived from Germany and established a business at the Central Market selling ham, veal, beef, and other meats. In 1925, Grobbel, who by then had been joined by his three sons, moved the business to 1807 Adelaide Street. In the 1940s, it began to specialize in cured meats, primarily corned beef. Outgrowing the facilities on Adelaide Street, the business moved to 2500 Orleans Street in 1980. Emil's great-grandson Jason Grobbel assumed ownership in 1987, continuing the legacy of "America's Oldest Corned Beef Specialist." (EMC.)

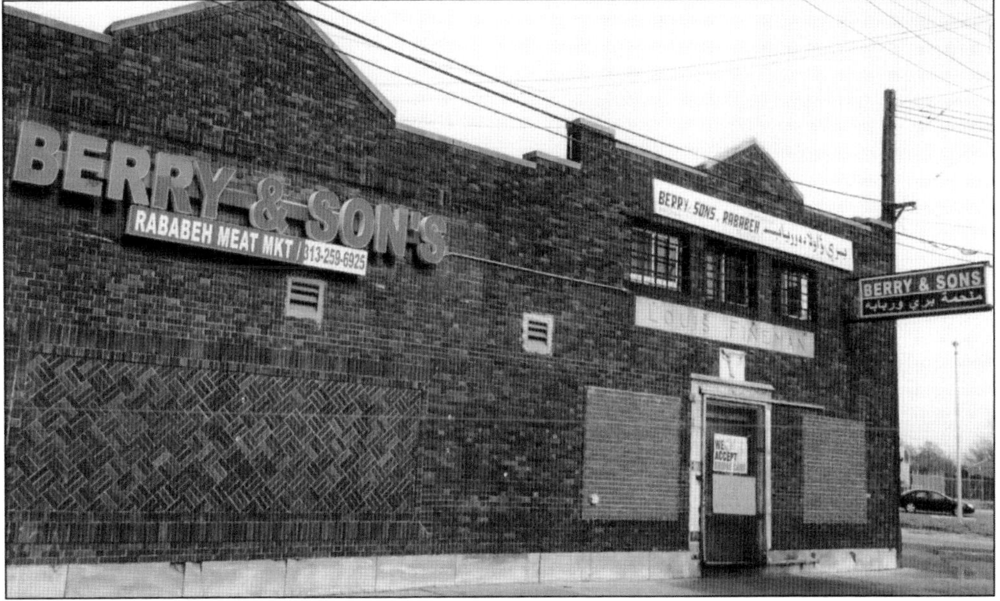

Berry & Sons Islamic Slaughterhouse. Since 1973, Sam Berry and his four sons have operated an Islamic slaughterhouse at 2496 Orleans Street, which previously housed Monarch Packing. The USDA-certified slaughterhouse processes sheep, lamb, and goat according to halal guidelines. In addition to the halal processing, a rabbi visits Berry & Sons two days a week for kosher slaughter of meats sold to Jewish businesses and consumers. (EMC.)

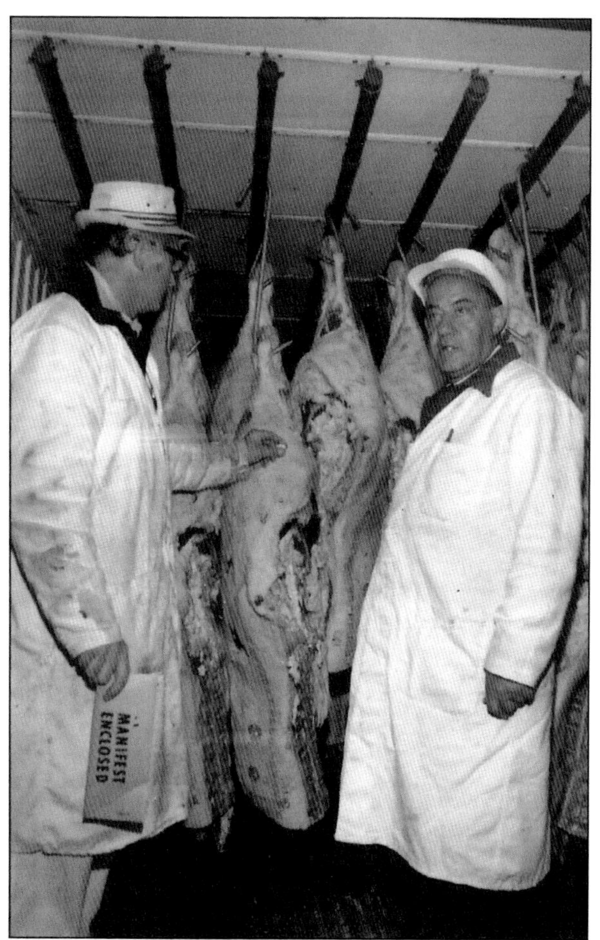

Wolverine Packing. Founded by Al Bonahoom in 1937 as a processor of lamb and veal, the company has grown to become a nationally recognized distributor of beef, pork, poultry, lamb, veal, seafood, and more. From its beginnings at 1340 Winder Street, Wolverine Packing has adapted to various changes in the meatpacking industry, including portion control for retail and food service, beef breaking (breaking down cattle into "primal cuts"), and most recently steak cutting and gourmet burger fabrication for national grocery stores and restaurant chains. (MSN.)

Wolverine Packing Today. Wolverine Packing's yellow trucks are a common sight in the market area. Now employing over 400 full-time workers, Wolverine Packing has expanded into multiple buildings along Rivard Street. Al Bonahoom's sons Jim and Roger have run the business since 1970. In 1995, they were joined by Jim's son Jay. (LR.)

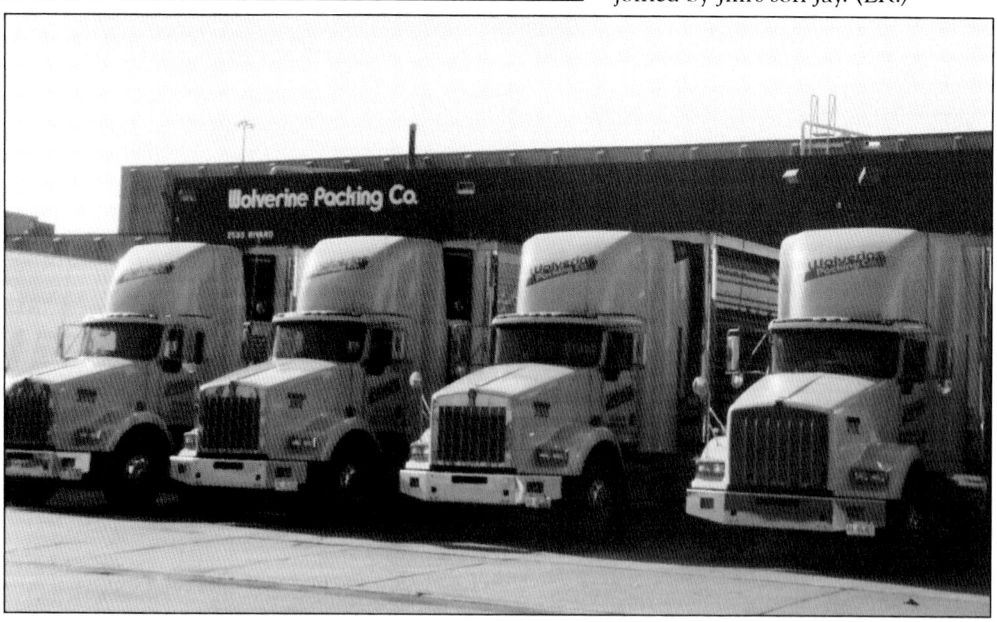

Seven

Restaurants and Bars

Early restaurants, like retail establishments, were there to serve the farmers who traveled long distances to sell at the market. The oldest restaurant in Detroit is Roma Café, which began its life as a boardinghouse for Italian immigrants working in the market. Word spread quickly about the great food, and the boardinghouse was soon closed to make room for more restaurant space. Joe Muer did not intend to get into the restaurant business until Prohibition nearly closed down his cigar factory on the south side of the market. He then opened a restaurant in the cigar factory, and Joe Muer Seafood eventually became one of Detroit's premier steak and seafood restaurants.

The majority of Eastern Market's many small restaurants catered to local workers and shoppers, serving large portions of home-cooked food at reasonable prices. One with a great following was Samuels Bros. Cafeteria, which was well known for its traditional Jewish fare. On and around Orleans Street, there were a number of bars, traditionally serving the butchers and meatpackers working nearby. Market Center Bar was another longtime drinking establishment on nearby Market Street; it later became Vivio's and is now known for its Bloody Marys and mussels. Bert's Marketplace, on Russell Street, features live jazz entertainment and serves traditional Southern-style fare.

Taken as a whole, Eastern Market is home to a very eclectic mix of dining establishments. Although most are small, customers can be found waiting patiently in line on busy days, passing the time chatting with fellow shoppers and enjoying the convivial atmosphere at the Eastern Market.

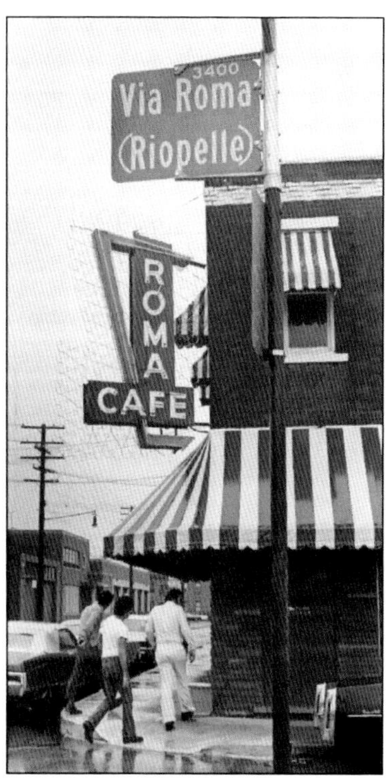

LA VIA ROMA. Roma Café, located at 3401 Riopelle Street, is the oldest restaurant in Detroit and one of the classic Italian-cuisine landmarks of the region. Mrs. Marazza opened her boardinghouse in 1888 to serve the farmers that often traveled a full day by horse-drawn wagon to sell their goods at the market, and she quickly gained a reputation as an excellent cook. Her Roma Café opened in 1890 and expanded over the years into adjacent buildings, the oldest of which predates 1885. (EMC.)

ROMA CAFÉ. The Marazza family sold the restaurant to Morris Sossi and John Battaglia in 1918. Battaglia died within a few years, and Sossi bought out his late partner's share from the Battaglia family. (WRL.)

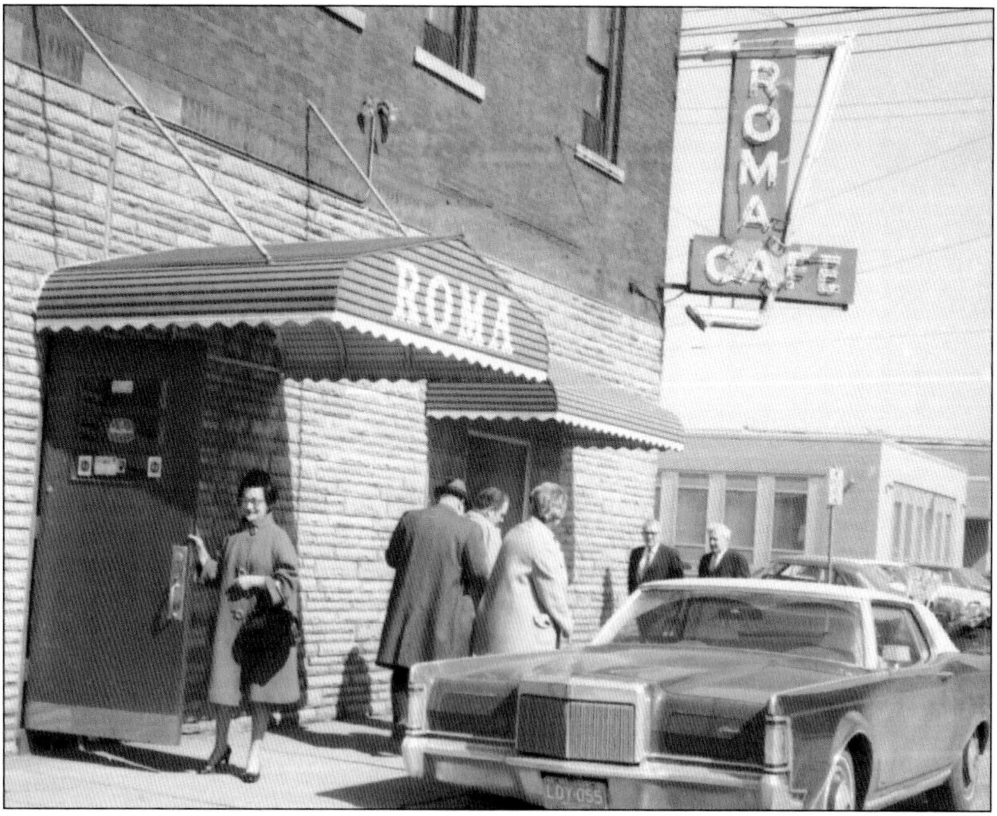

Roma Café's Next Generation. Hector Sossi, the nephew of Morris Sossi, began washing dishes at the restaurant in 1940 and then took over in the early 1950s after Morris returned to Italy. In 1965, Hector purchased the business from his uncle. (EMC.)

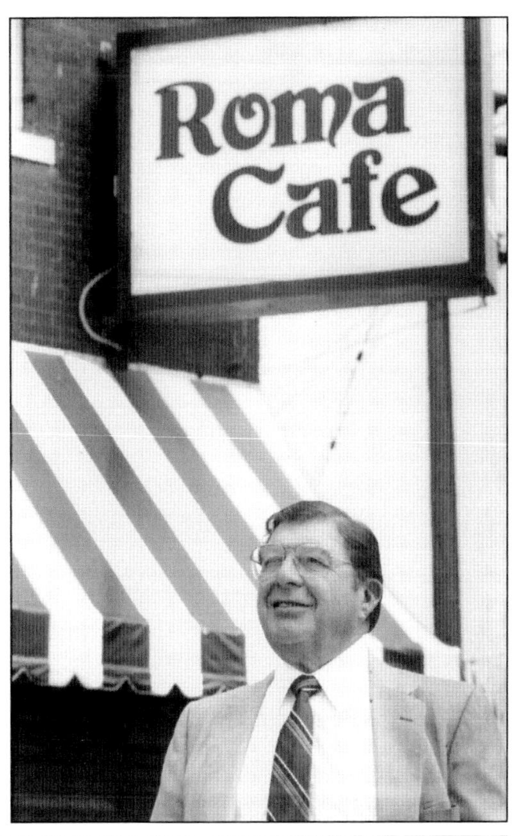

The Famous Roma Café. Known for its fine food and tuxedoed waiters, Roma Café has always been the gathering spot for Detroit's sports, political, and business elite. Janet Sossi Belcoure, the daughter of Hector, began working at the restaurant as a youngster and took over ownership after her father retired. In 2010, Roma Café celebrated its 120th year in business. (Courtesy of Janet Sossi Belcoure.)

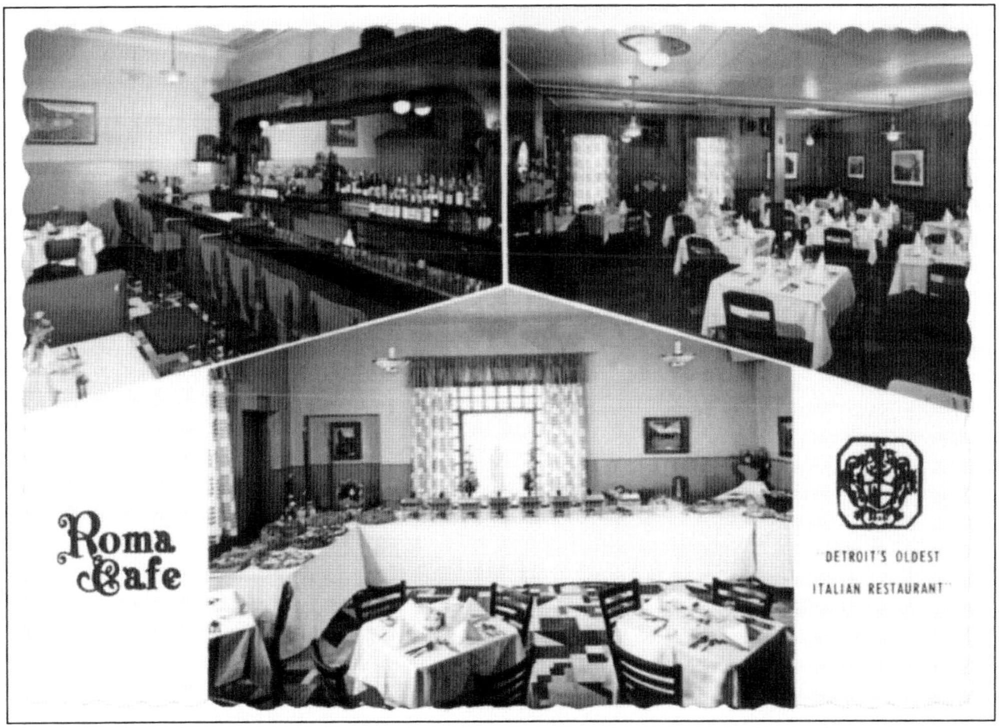

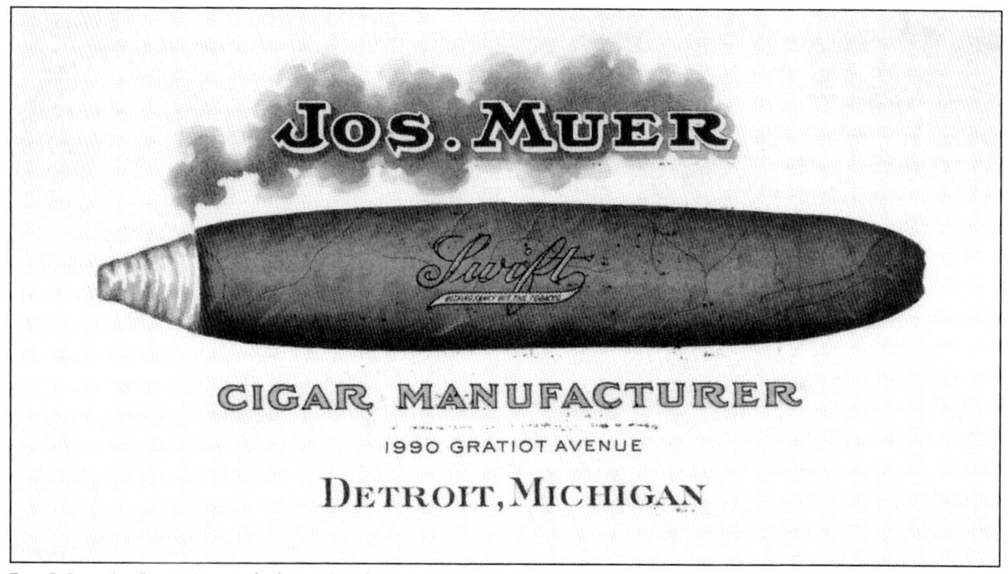

JOE MUER'S. Joe Muer's father, Anthony "Tony" Muer, began a cigar business at 34 Jay Street, just south of Gratiot Avenue, in the 1870s. In 1906, after Tony's death, Joe moved the cigar business to the 1880s-era building at 1996 Gratiot Avenue, which was owned by his father-in-law. Muer started his Swift Cigar Company with the goal of selling a quality 5¢ cigar. "Nothing fine but the tobacco" was one of Swift's clever advertising slogans. (JMIII.)

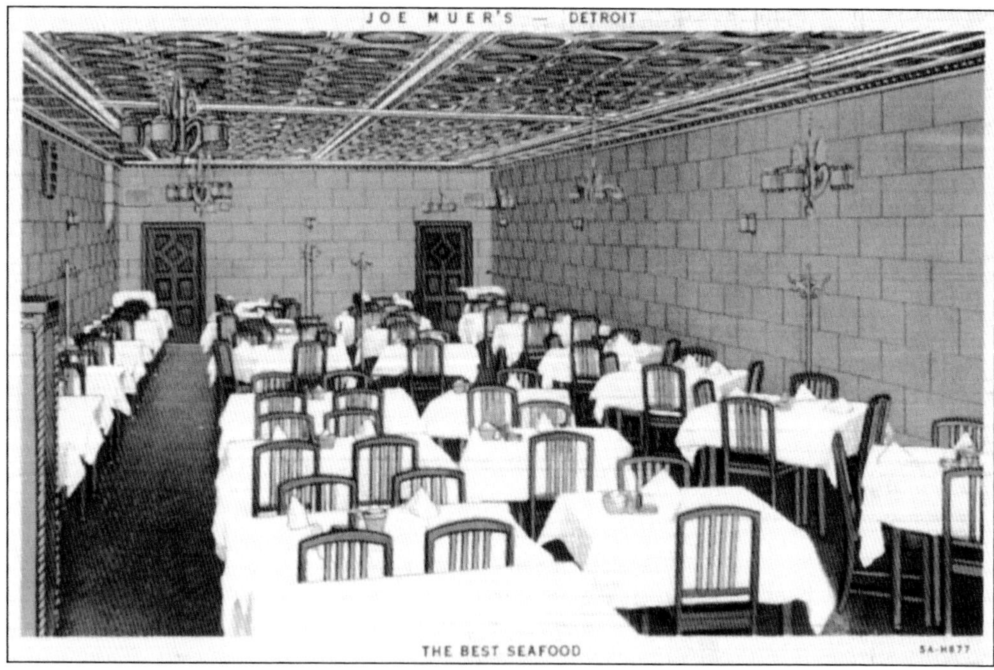

MUER MOVES TO ADAPT. By 1920, Detroit was the cigar-manufacturing center of the Midwest, but the industry declined during Prohibition. Muer then converted the former cigar factory into a restaurant and opened on October 28, 1929, the day before the Wall Street stock market crash. (JMIII.)

Joe Muer's Stood Firm. Joe Muer's restaurant became one of the city's premier dining establishments. Bill Muer, Joe's son, took over the business and was succeeded by his nephew Joe Muer III. The Muer family closed the restaurant in 1998, and the building was razed in 2002. In 2011, Joe Muer III collaborated with Andiamo Restaurant Group owner Joe Vicari to open a new Joe Muer Seafood in the Renaissance Center. (EMC.)

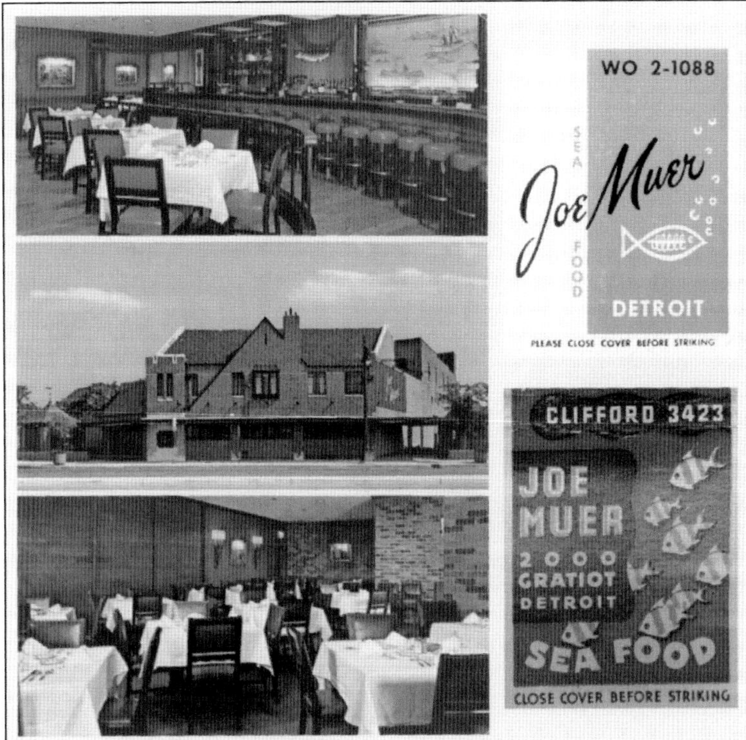

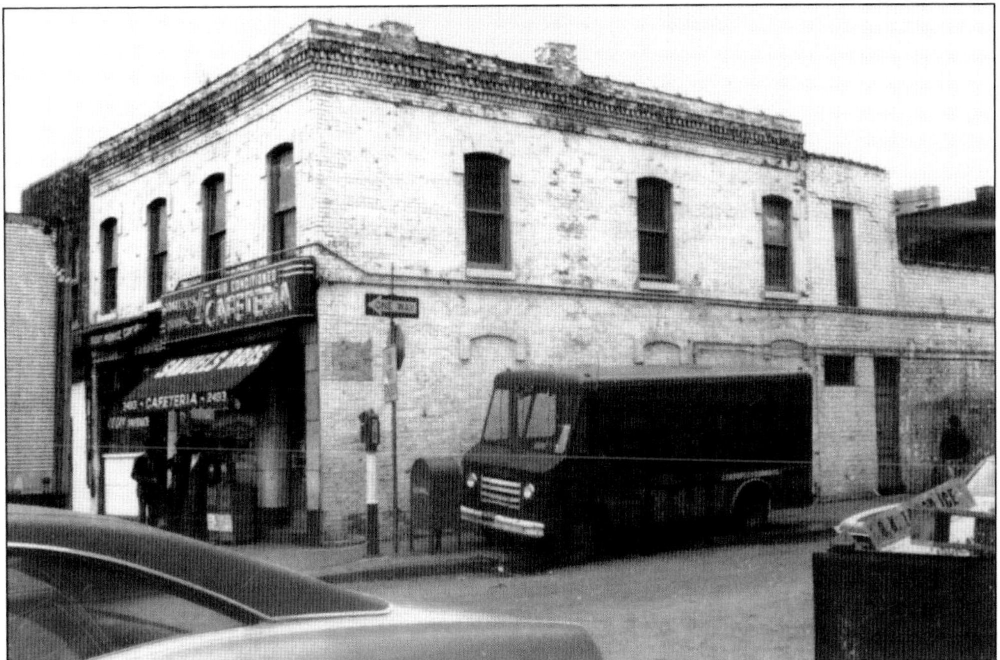

Samuels Bros. Cafeteria. Brothers Morris and Alex Samuels came to the United States from Poland in 1922 and worked as busboys. In 1927, they opened Reliable Lunch with a partner at 2439 Russell Street. A few years later, they bought out their partner and renamed the restaurant Samuels Bros. Cafeteria. (AP.)

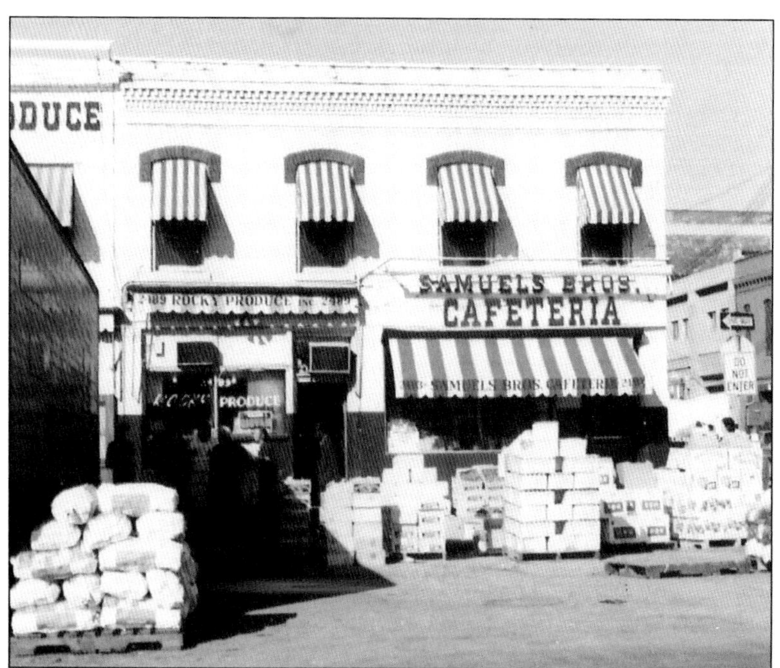

SAMUELS BROS.' NEW CAFETERIA. Samuels Bros. Cafeteria was rebuilt after a 1940 fire. The new space was strictly a cafeteria and specialized in corned beef sandwiches and traditional Jewish fare, such as gefilte fish, herring, and brisket. (MSN.)

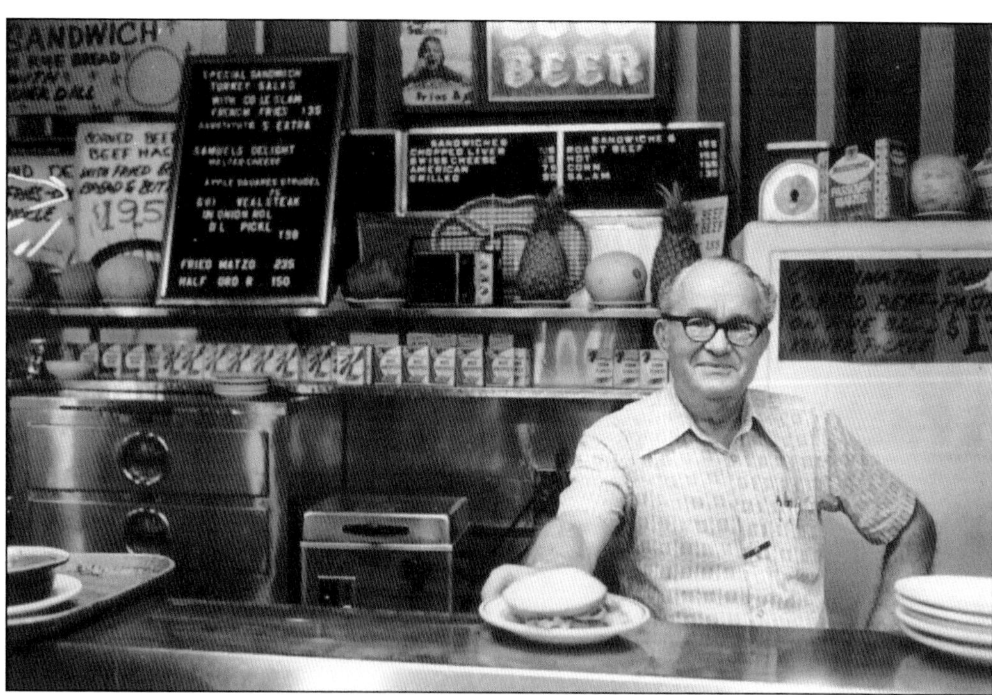

SAMUELS BROS. CAFETERIA. Samuels Bros. was a popular destination for people from all walks of life, including the farmers and vendors at the market and local celebrities. Alex left the business in 1966. Morris's son Ira took his place and ran "the store," as it was affectionately called, with his father until the restaurant closed in 1977. (EMC.)

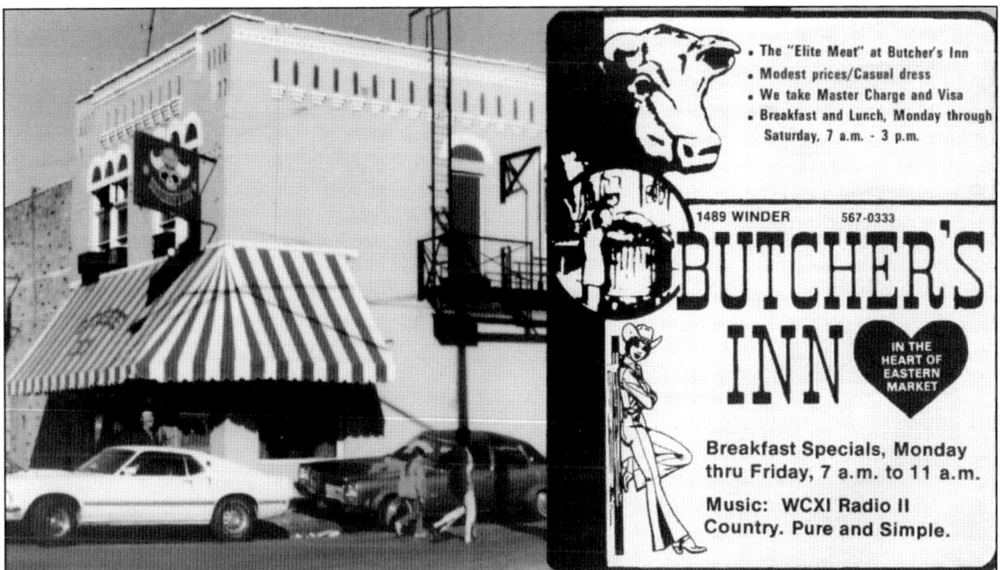

Butcher's Inn. This structure, at 1489 Winder Street, dates back to 1890, when it was built as a residence and a saloon for William Wiedmaier. The building has a storied past and was rumored to have housed a brothel and a bookmaking operation. It also hosted high-stakes poker games. The business officially became Butcher's Inn in 1940. (Left, MSN; right, EMC.)

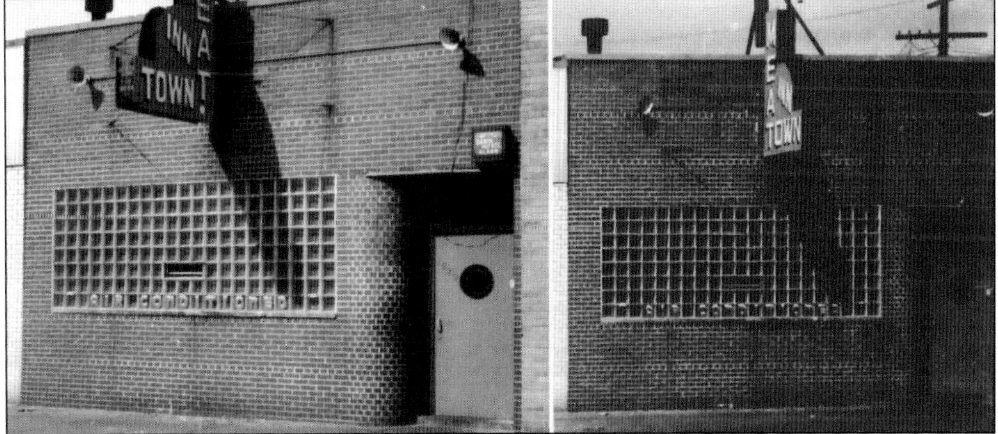

Meat Town Inn. Along and near Orleans Street, a number of bars and restaurants were frequented by local meat cutters working in the packing factories in the market district. Beginning work early in the day and putting in long hours in freezer-like conditions, the meat cutters would often stop in for a drink and conversation after work, oftentimes still wearing their stained aprons. (MSN.)

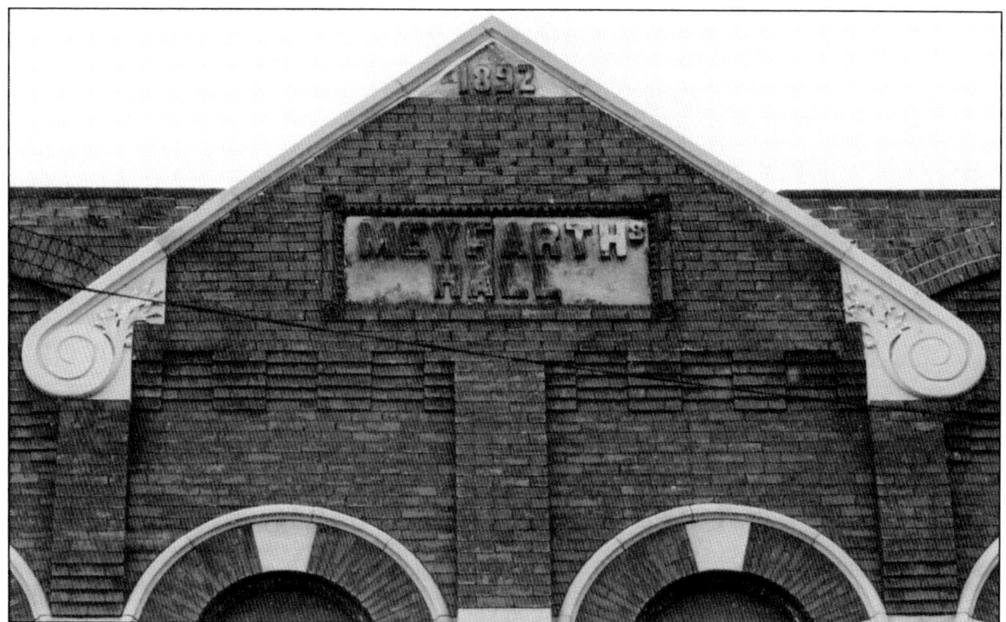

MEYFARTH HALL. In 1891, Henry Meyfarth built his residence, a saloon, and a community meeting hall at 2460 Market Street. During Prohibition, it took in temporary boarders—the wholesale fruit and produce sellers who came to the market—in order to stay in business, but it has been an eating and drinking establishment since its original construction. It is reportedly the oldest site in Detroit to have continually operated as a tavern and was originally known simply as the Market Center Bar. (EMC.)

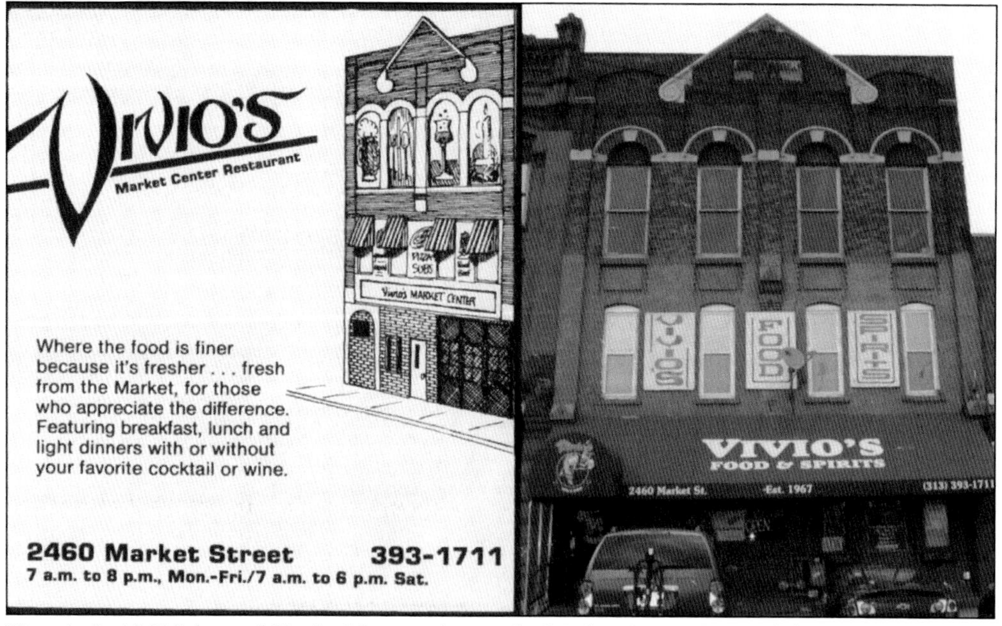

VIVIO'S. In 1967, John and Shirley Vivio took over the Market Center Bar and changed the name to Vivio's. Now run by their son Vince and his brother-in-law Mijo, Vivio's is a popular spot for pregame outings and famous for its Bloody Marys, served with a pickle and a shot of beer. Its signature Bloody Mary mix is bottled and sold on-site and in stores across metropolitan Detroit. (EMC.)

Farmer's Restaurant. This building, at 2630–2642 Market Street, was built in 1914 by Adolph Padelt to house his dairy business. In 1958, the building was converted into a restaurant. On November 15, 1975, Gerry and Dora Fermanis took over what was then called the T.P. Restaurant and renamed it Farmer's Restaurant. An Eastern Market breakfast favorite, the 140-seat restaurant opens its doors to farmers and visitors at 5:00 a.m. six days a week. (EMC.)

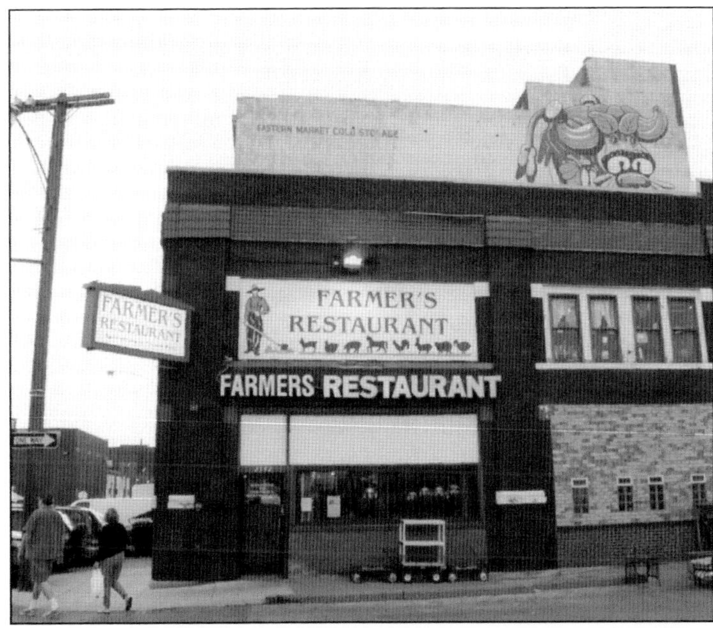

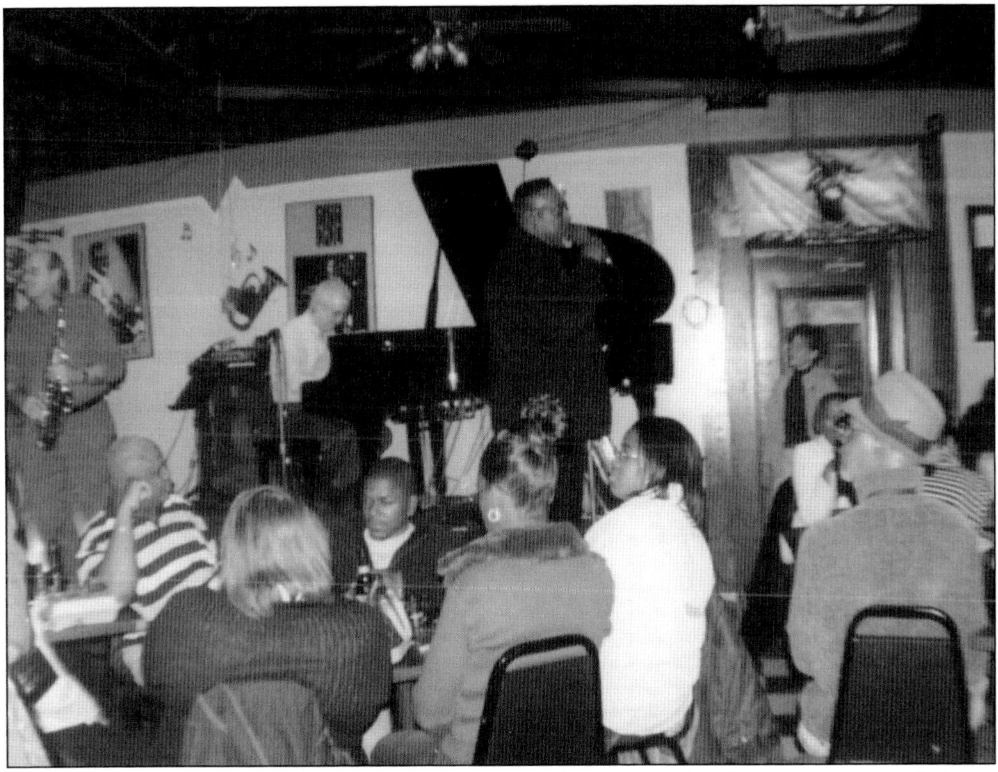

Bert's Marketplace. Jazz lover Bert Dearing opened Bert's Marketplace at 2727 Russell Street in 1987. Featuring a stage shaped like the hood of a baby grand piano, Bert's attracts both local and national jazz players and is a popular karaoke destination. The bar has grown over the years, and the complex, occupying most of the city block, now houses the original bar, a lounge, and another room large enough for concerts and large events. (Courtesy of Bert Dearing.)

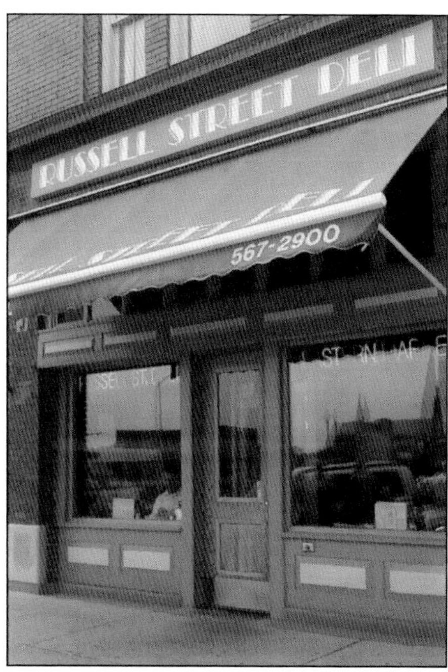

Russell Street Deli. The building that now houses Russell Street Deli was built in 1918 and was home to a grocery store for many years. It became the Mr. Pickles Restaurant in 1987 and was renamed Russell Street Café in 1989. In 1993, new owner Bob Cerrito renamed it Russell Street Deli. It gained a reputation for homemade soups and enormous sandwiches served at convivial communal tables. In August 2007, Cerrito sold the deli to Ben Hall and Jason Murphy, who have put their own stamp on the business, adding extended hours, off-site catering, and a soup cart that operates on busy Saturdays under the renovated Shed 2. (EMC.)

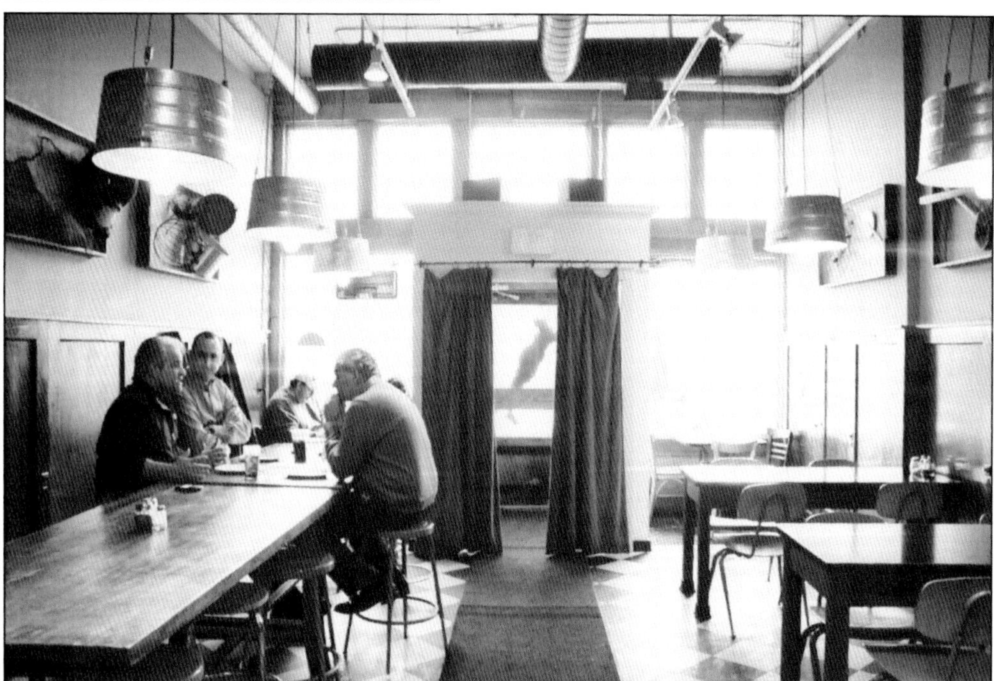

Supino Pizzeria. Dave Mancini opened this Supino Pizzeria on Russell Street, just north of the Fisher Freeway service drive, in 2008. The storefront had previously housed a different carryout pizza operation and a flower shop and was the longtime home of the Russell Provision Company. The name of the pizzeria is an homage to Mancini's father's hometown in Italy. Mancini furnished his restaurant with all reclaimed materials and specializes in hand-tossed, thin-crust gourmet pizzas. In 2009, the *Detroit Free Press* named Supino Pizzeria metropolitan Detroit's best pizza. (Courtesy of Ruth Synowiec.)

Eight

Public Art

The Eastern Market district has always attracted artists, perhaps drawn to the unique, round-the-clock mix of activities happening in the market district. The market offers colorful fruits and vegetables, the eccentric personalities of both customers and shop owners, a sense of history, and diverse architectural styles, which all come together to create a unique place.

The market also offers great building stock that often serves as inexpensive artist residences, similar to warehouse districts in New York and Chicago. Some of the first industrial buildings to experience loft-style housing conversions in Detroit were located in the market. In addition, these buildings often became artist's canvasses for large murals and installations.

In the early 1970s, super graphics—characterized by bright colors and cartoon-looking figures and objects—were added to many market district buildings. It could be said that Eastern Market was saved by art. These large paintings, applied directly on many market buildings, brought local and national attention to the district and helped attract new shoppers. In addition, in true artist fashion, all of this was done for a minimal cost. Although many of the murals painted in the 1970s have been removed as of this writing, some great examples can still be found around the market district. Eastern Market has also been home to many of the city's most interesting and creative gallery spaces, including underground venues, which attract creative people to the district.

The nearby Dequindre Cut Greenway, which occupies a former below-grade rail line stretching from the River Walk to Eastern Market, is a canvas for the work of modern graffiti artists. Moreover, since 2008, some building owners in the market district have chosen to offer up the walls of their buildings as canvases for this often-controversial art form.

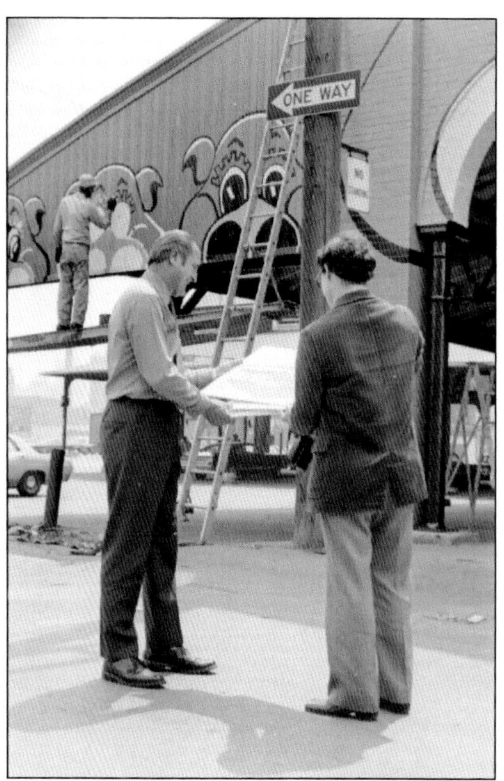

The Murals of Alex Pollock. Charles A. Blessing was Detroit's director of city planning from 1953 to 1977. In 1969, he hired Alex Pollock, a newly graduated young architect from Florida to help with the city's revitalization efforts. Pollock found himself drawn to Eastern Market, and the brightly colored murals he created for it became a visual symbol of the market for many years to come. (WRL.)

The First Murals. The proliferation of new, large, full-service grocery stores in the suburbs had been draining customers away from Eastern Market since the 1950s. Furthermore, years of deferred maintenance had given the market a rundown appearance, which did little to attract shoppers. Eastern Market desperately needed a face-lift and something buzz-worthy, but resources were scarce. The municipal department that ran Eastern Market, the Detroit Bureau of Markets, had a limited budget of $1,600—far short of the amount needed to do any major capital improvements. (AP.)

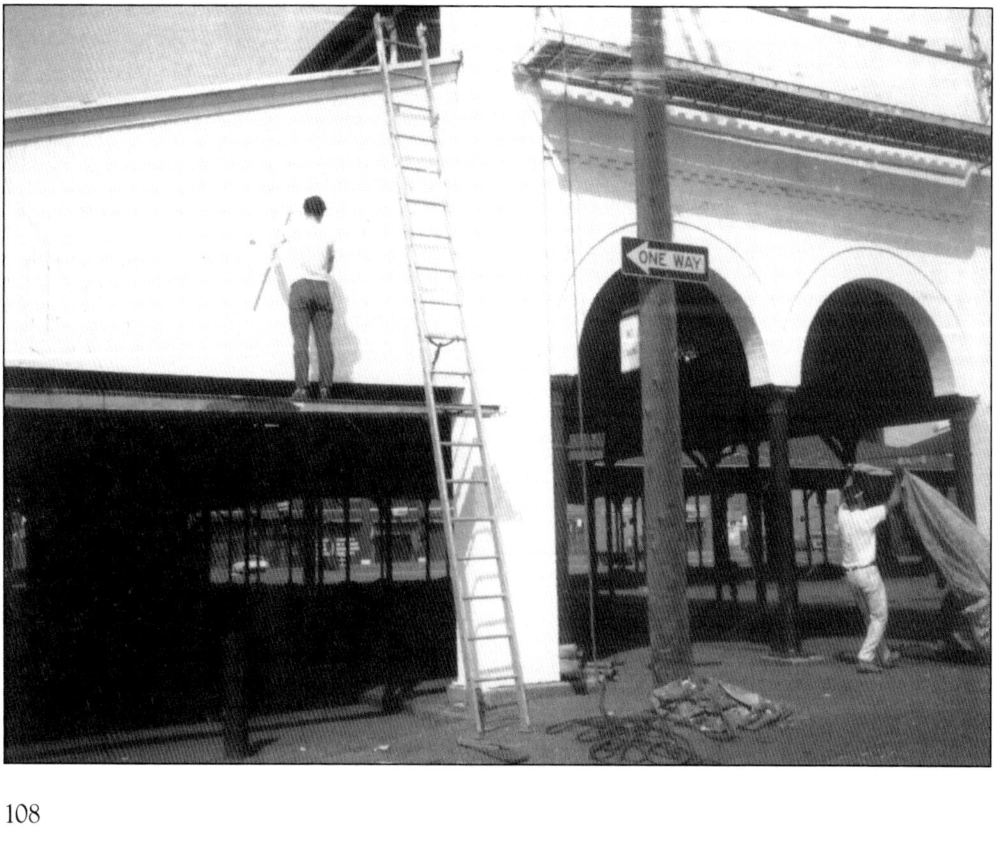

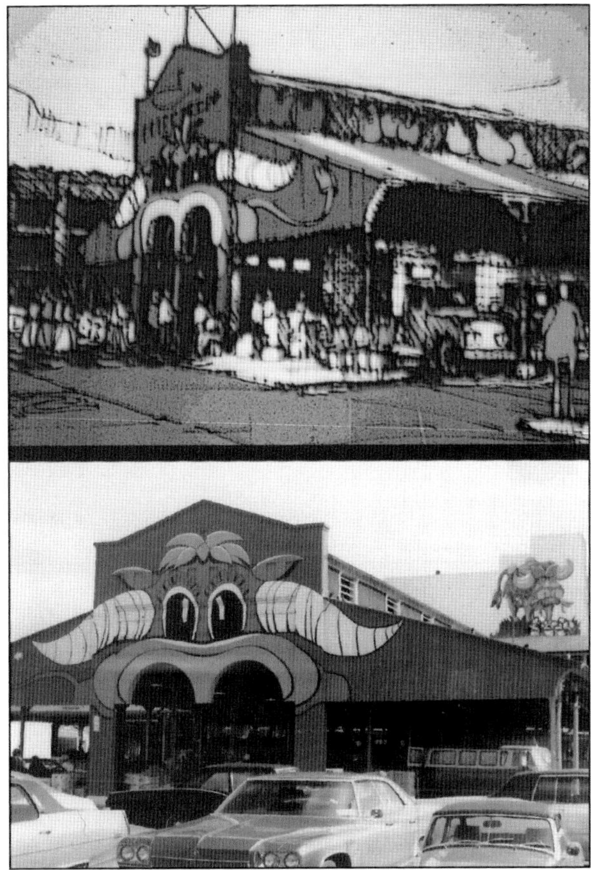

THE BULL. Alex Pollock envisioned a less-expensive, high-impact plan for Eastern Market. When he looked at the oldest building on the market campus, this Victorian-era shed built in the 1890s, he "saw noses where others saw arches," and, with this unique perspective, he designed the landmark chicken, bull, and pig murals for Shed 2. In early 1971, work began, and Pollock transformed the west side of Shed 2 into a bull. (AP.)

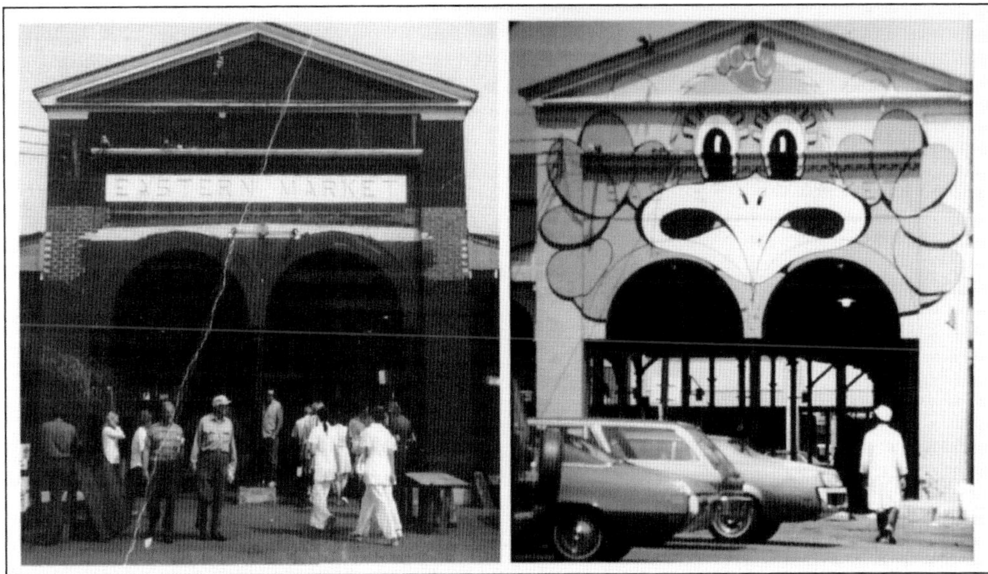

THE CHICKEN. The south facade of Shed 2 became a chicken, which had a look of shock and surprise. Although never completed, the original design included benches that looked like broken eggs, with the egg whites and yolks painted on the sidewalk below. (AP.)

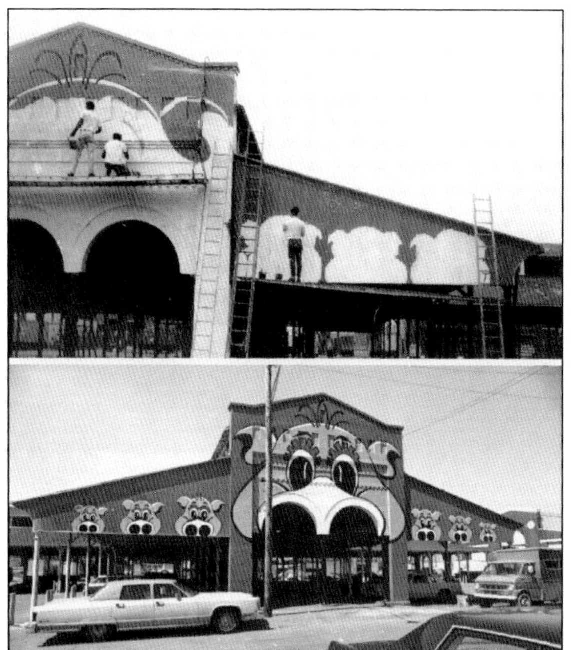

The Pig. The east facade of Shed 2 was transformed into a family of pigs. With paint costing just $4 a gallon, Pollock indeed made a big impact with his initial $1,600 investment. The chicken, pig, and bull murals were completed in six months. (WRL.)

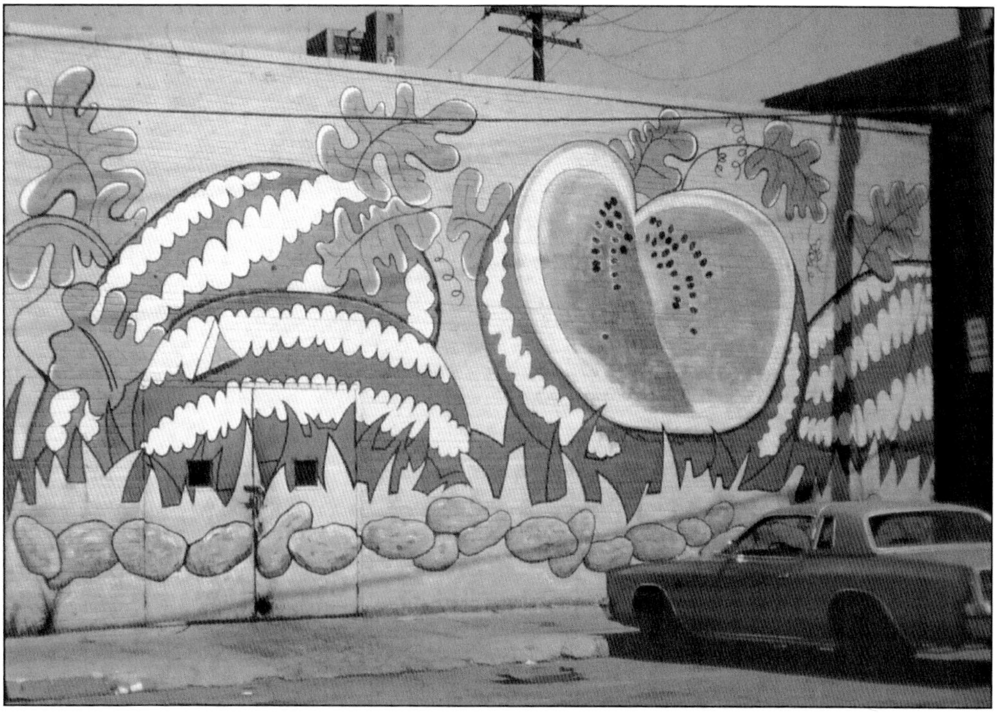

Vitale Watermelon. The Shed 2 murals were well received by both the public and the district merchants and were responsible for breathing new life into Eastern Market. In 1971, Jim Vitale, the owner of Vitale Watermelon, approached Pollock to design a mural highlighting the product for his building on Riopelle Street. Other merchants followed suit, and soon Rocky Peanut, on Russell Street, and Ciaramitaro Produce, on Market Street, had both been spruced up by Pollock's art. (EMC.)

POLLOCK IS FIRED. In 1972, the Detroit Planning Department was reorganized. After a federal grant expired, Pollock and several other low-seniority employees were fired. But, Pollock had a tremendous fan base, and his supporters launched protests. Within days, the artist was rehired by the city, and Detroit mayor Roman Gribbs named him co-coordinator for his Merchant Assistance Program. Pollock and his team of three architects designed additional graphics for Eastern Market and many other areas of the city. (AP.)

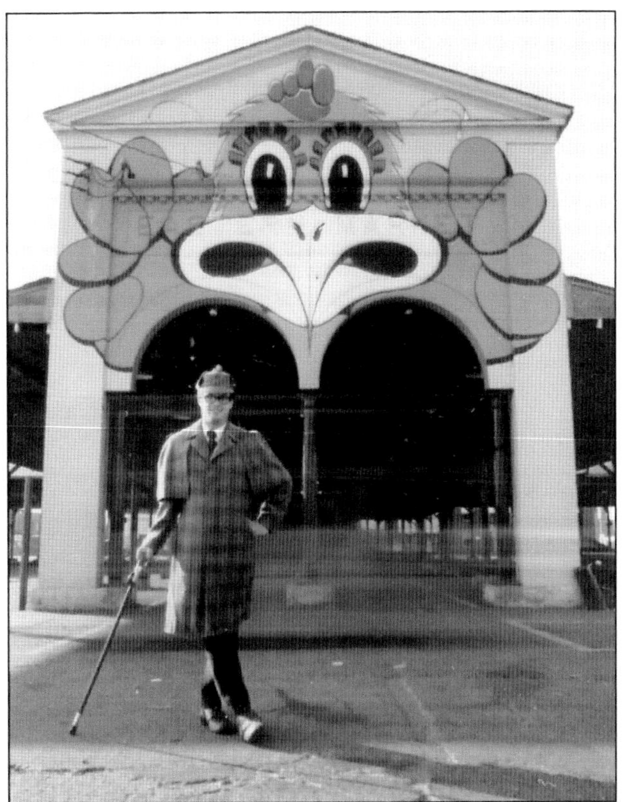

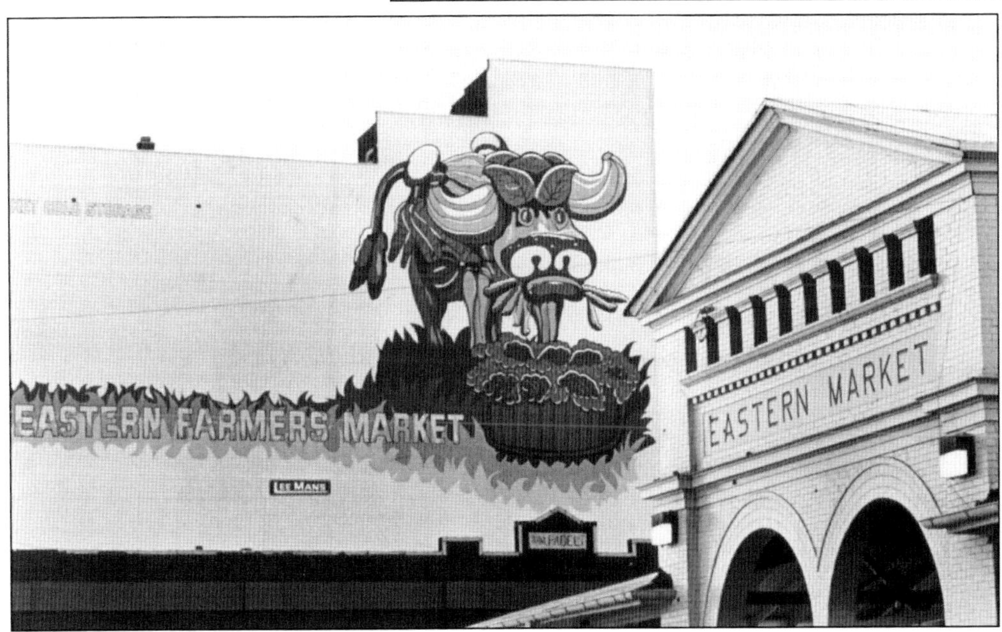

THE VEGETABULL. Commissioned by the Detroit-based Bank of the Commonwealth, which had a branch office in Eastern Market and later became part of Comerica Bank, this unique work by Pollock went up on the expansive wall of the Eastern Cold Storage Building. Pollock created the image of a bull made entirely of vegetables—hence the name. (WRL.)

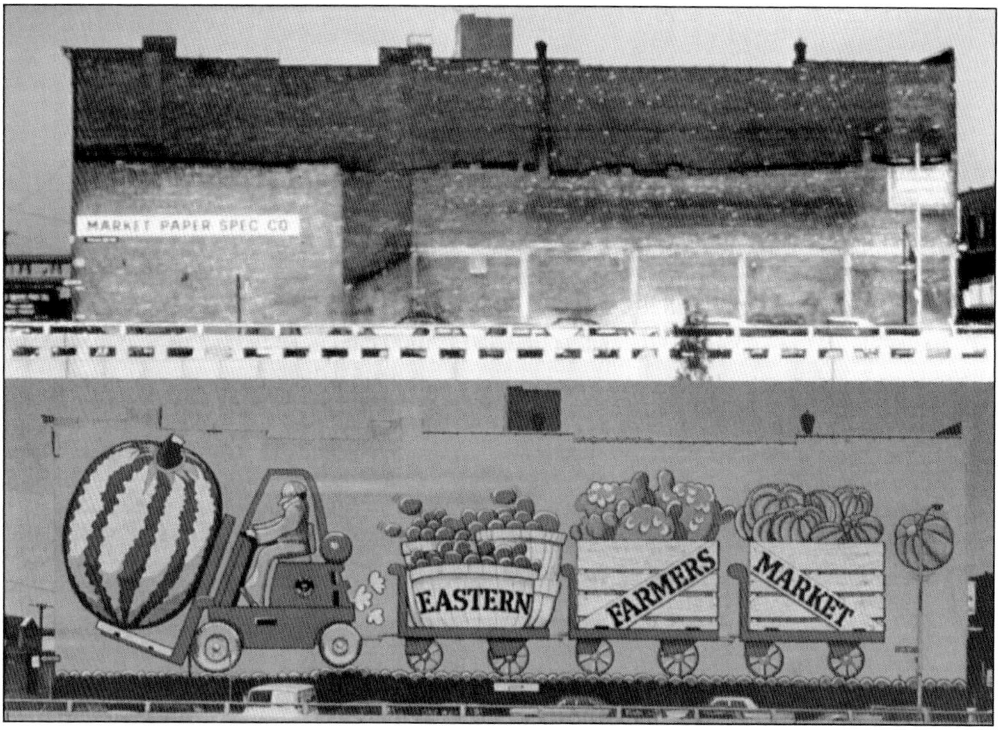

A Perfect Canvas. Several buildings were demolished for a new interstate highway connector in 1967 that ran through the Eastern Market district. This left a large unadorned wall on the north Fisher Freeway service drive. At the time, the building housed a company called Market Paper Specialty. It was a perfect canvas to create a landmark graphic to draw attention to the market. For this massive wall, Pollock created a unique mural featuring a forklift pulling carts of produce. The mural was painted by Lee Mans Outdoor Advertising. (AP.)

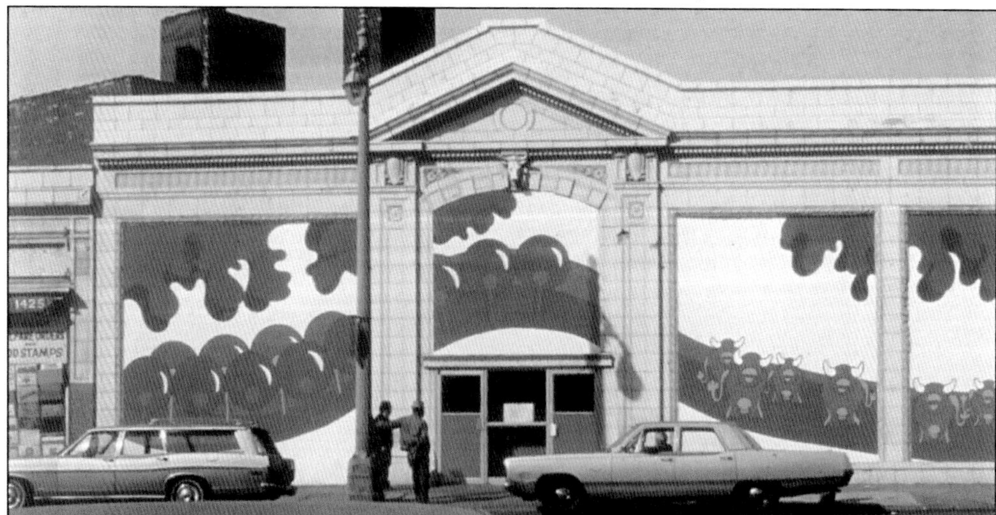

Gratiot Central Markets' Orchard. The long, blank, white wall along Gratiot Central Market became a mural of an orchard with grazing cows. Among the merchants in this space was Ronnie Bedway of Ronnie's Meats, who said, "We get people who come in who never knew this was a market—they thought it was a garage." (AP.)

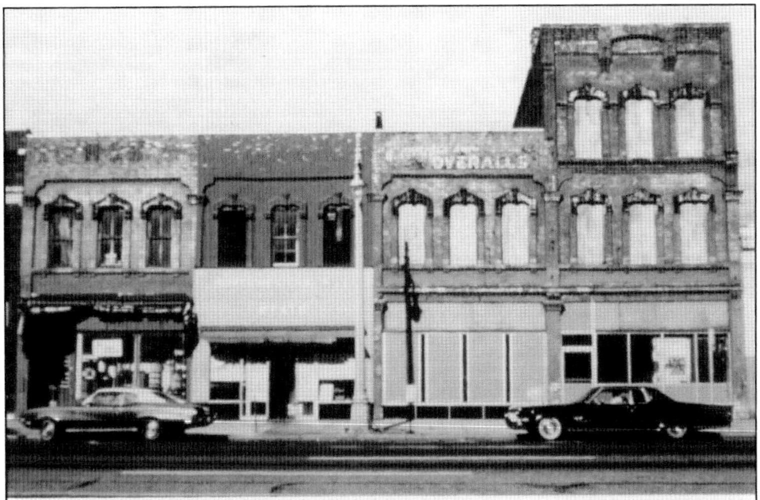

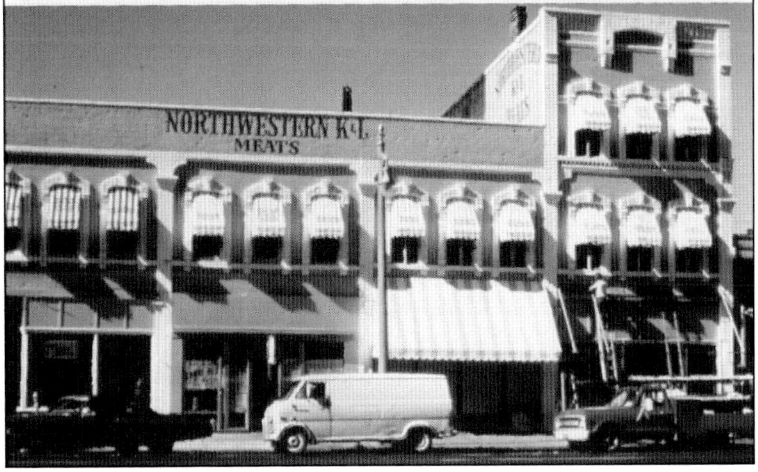

1409–1417 GRATIOT AVENUE. The four buildings on the north side of Gratiot Avenue that housed K&L Meats were refurbished into a single cohesive design that highlighted the Victorian-era details of the structures. (AP.)

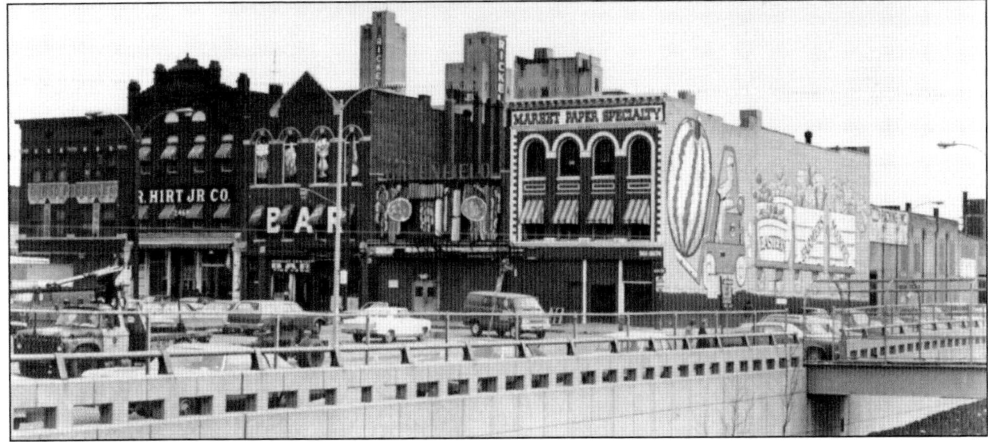

MARKET STREET. The buildings on Market Street between Winder Street and the Fisher Freeway service drive provided a rich canvas for Pollock's creative ideas. Each design incorporated the architectural features of the individual building and highlighted the products sold in that store. (BHC.)

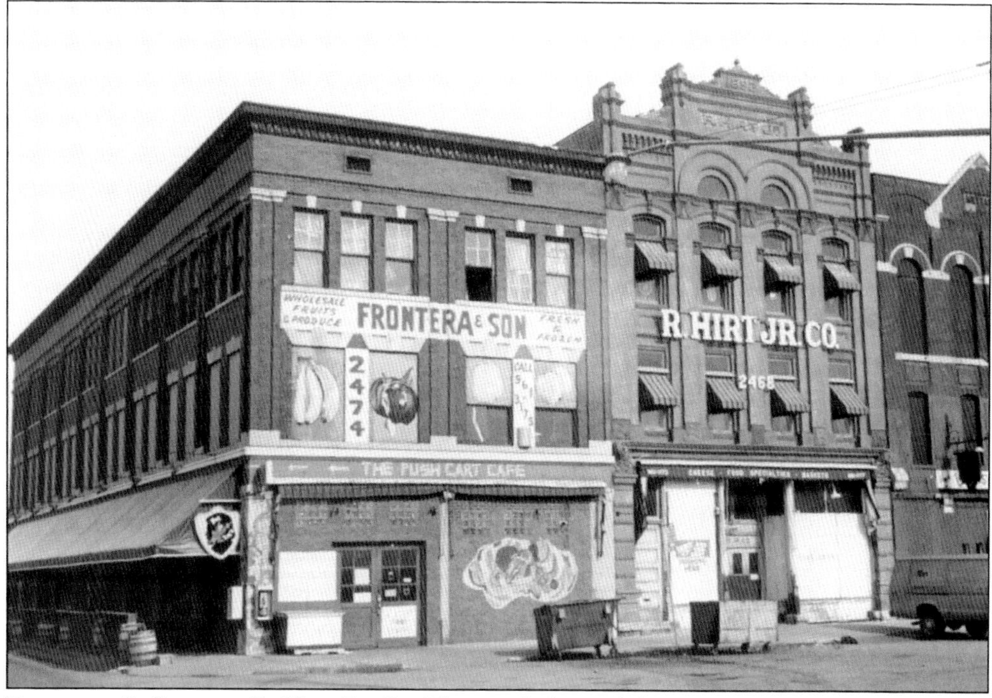

Frontera & Son and R. Hirt Jr. Co. The simple lines of the Frontera & Son building at the corner of Market and Winder Streets featured pictures of the wholesaler's fruits and vegetables. By contrast, only awnings were installed to complement the existing ornate redbrick facade of the R. Hirt Jr. Co. (DHS.)

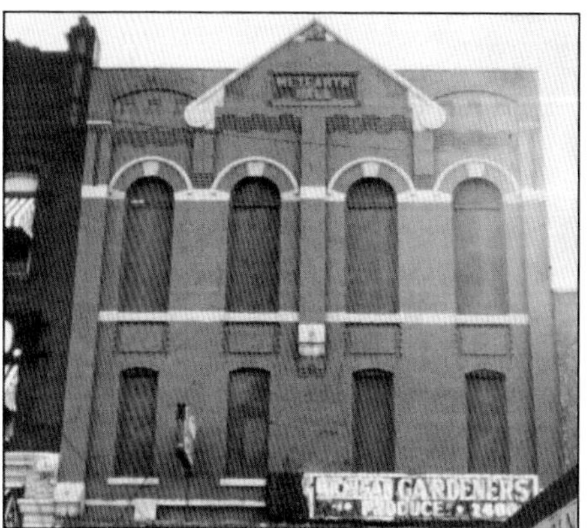

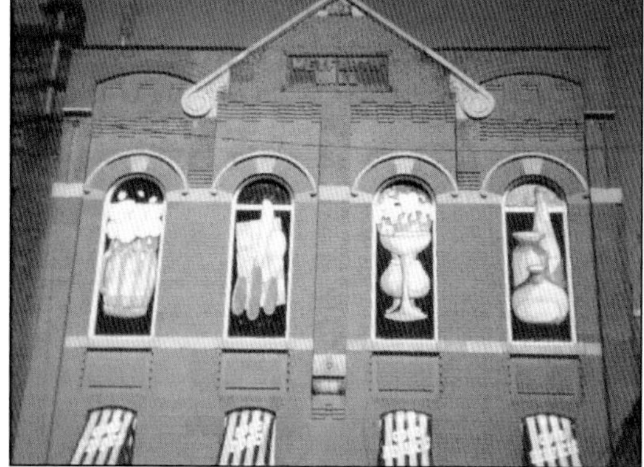

Market Center Bar/Vivio's. The design for this restaurant and bar featured items that could be found inside: a frosty mug of beer, a setting of silverware, an ice cream sundae, and bottles of wine and olive oil. (AP.)

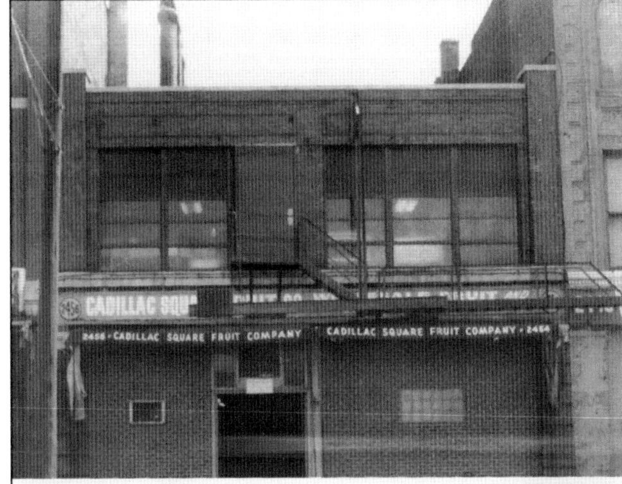

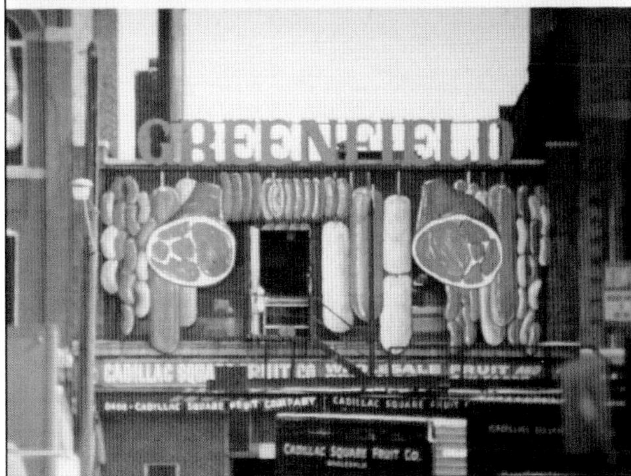

Greenfield Packing. The design for Greenfield Packing featured various sausages and meats sold in the store. (AP.)

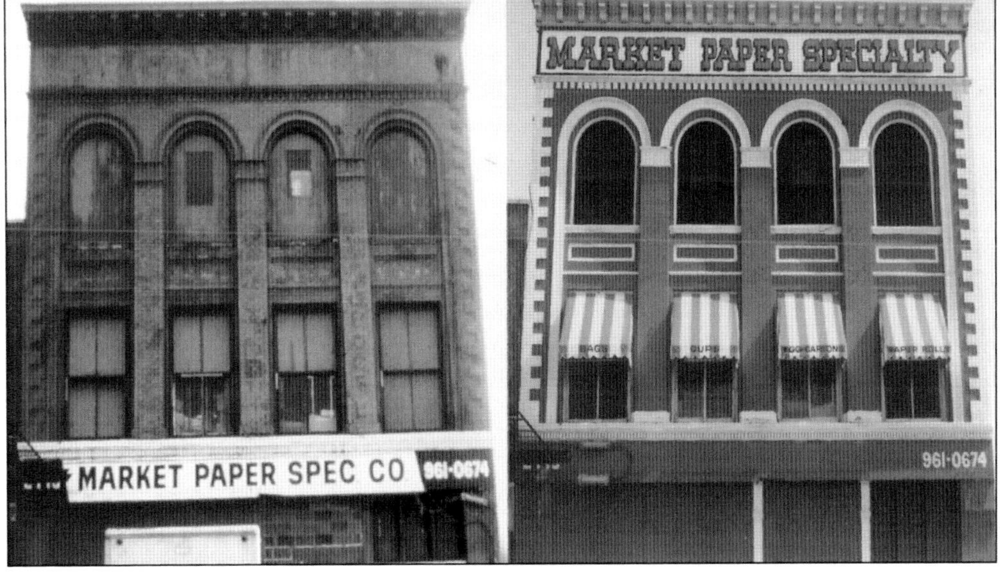

Market Paper Specialty. The design for Market Paper Specialty featured a bright red and white paint color scheme and a large sign and awnings listing items sold there: bags, cups, egg cartons, and paper rolls. (AP.)

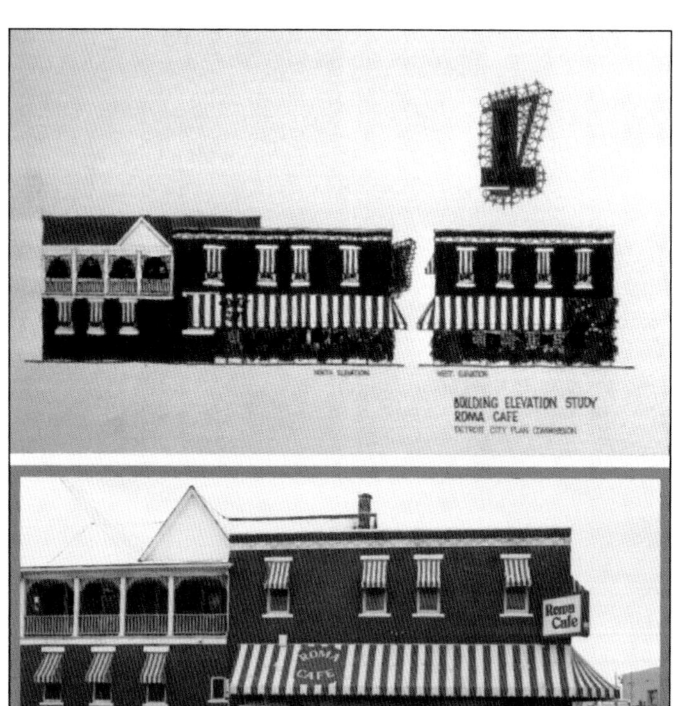

Roma Café. Alex Pollock designed a Venetian-style facade for Detroit's oldest Italian restaurant, Roma Café. The treatment for the building was a tribute to the owner's cultural heritage and also served to bring together the four different buildings under one unified design. (AP.)

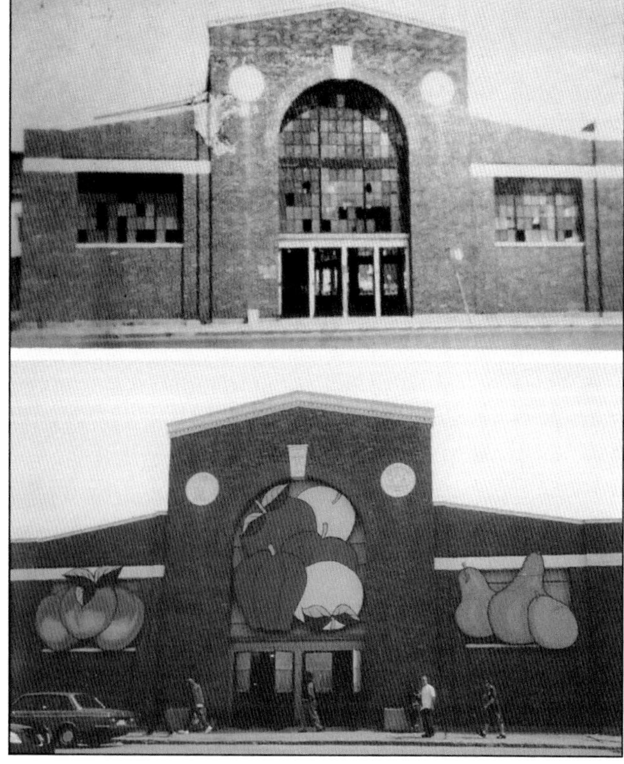

Shed 3's Windows. The city had a continuing problem with broken windows in Shed 3, and they were expensive to repair and replace. Pollock was asked to find a solution, and he decided to cover the windows with metal and more fanciful images of fruits and vegetables. With the renovation of Shed 3 in 2009, the cutouts were removed. Replicas of the originals were created that same year, with "face holes," and were hung on the south wall of the Eastern Market administration building. (AP.)

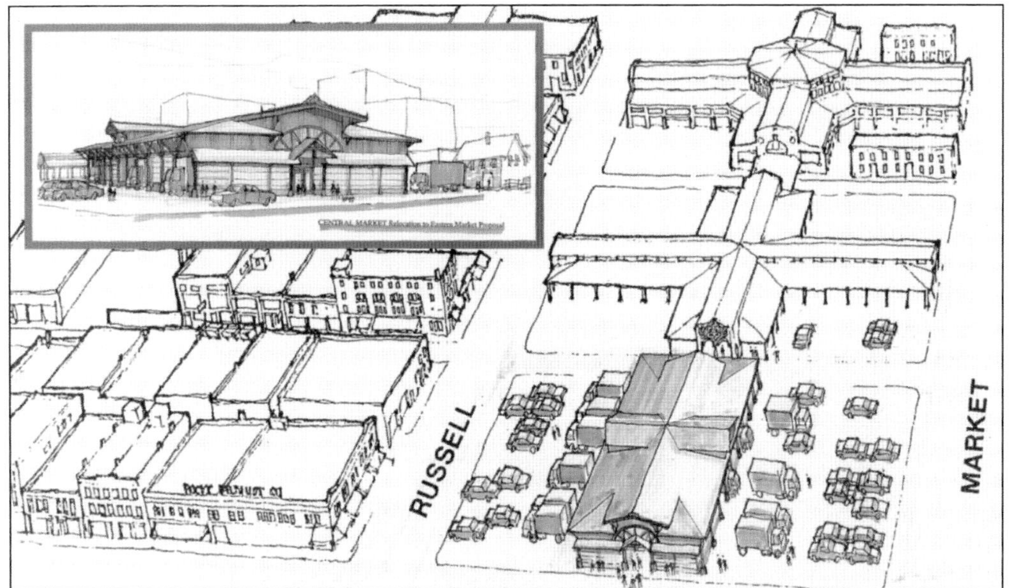

Pollock Envisioned a Restored Market. While many of Pollock's designs came to fruition, some were not. One of his most ambitious plans was to move the original Central Market shed to Eastern Market and situate it in the parking lot that had previously housed Shed 1 before it was removed for the freeway. The original Central Market shed had been moved to Belle Isle in 1891 to be used as horse stables and eventually closed in 1963. (AP.)

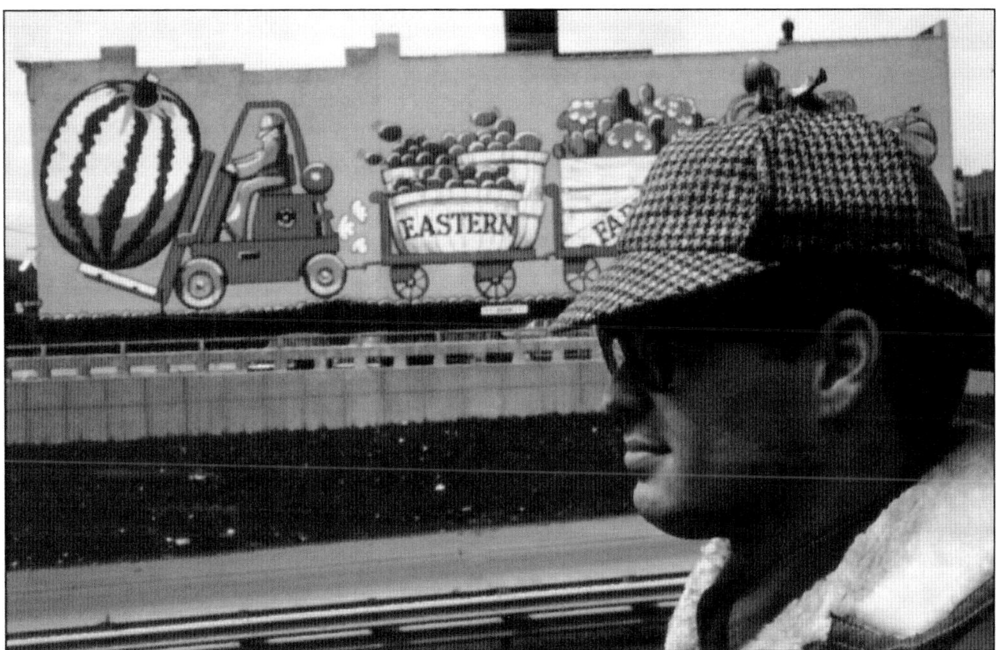

"Magic Alex." In all, Alex Pollock created 60 designs for Eastern Market, 38 of which were implemented, costing just over $60,000 in total. The mayor's Merchant Assistance Program ended after Mayor Roman Gribbs left office in 1974, but with the media and public interest, including a four-page color spread in *Life* magazine, Eastern Market enjoyed a resurgence through the mid-1970s. (AP.)

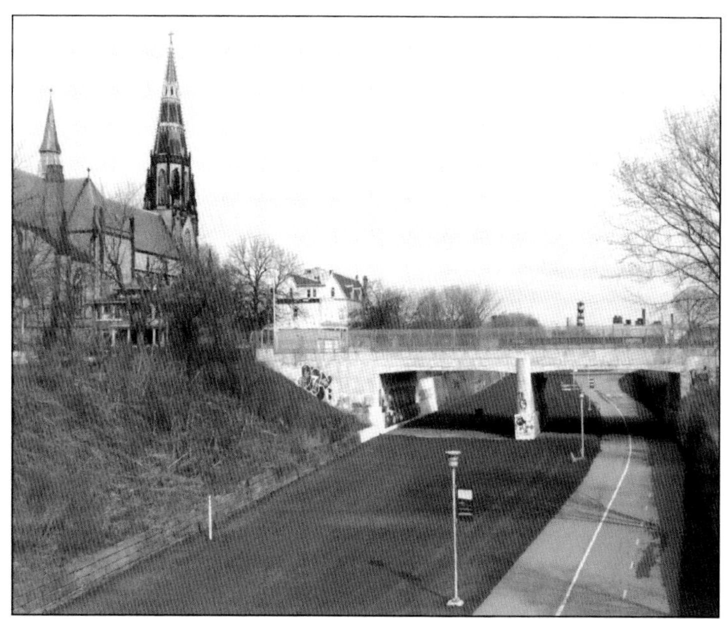

Dequindre Cut Greenway. By the 1980s, the rail line was no longer in use, and the bridge abutments became a canvas for local graffiti artists. In 2003, plans began to remake the Dequindre Cut into a greenway connecting the riverfront to Eastern Market. The greenway opened in 2009 as a bike and walking path and is still home to many of those same graffiti masterpieces. (EMC.)

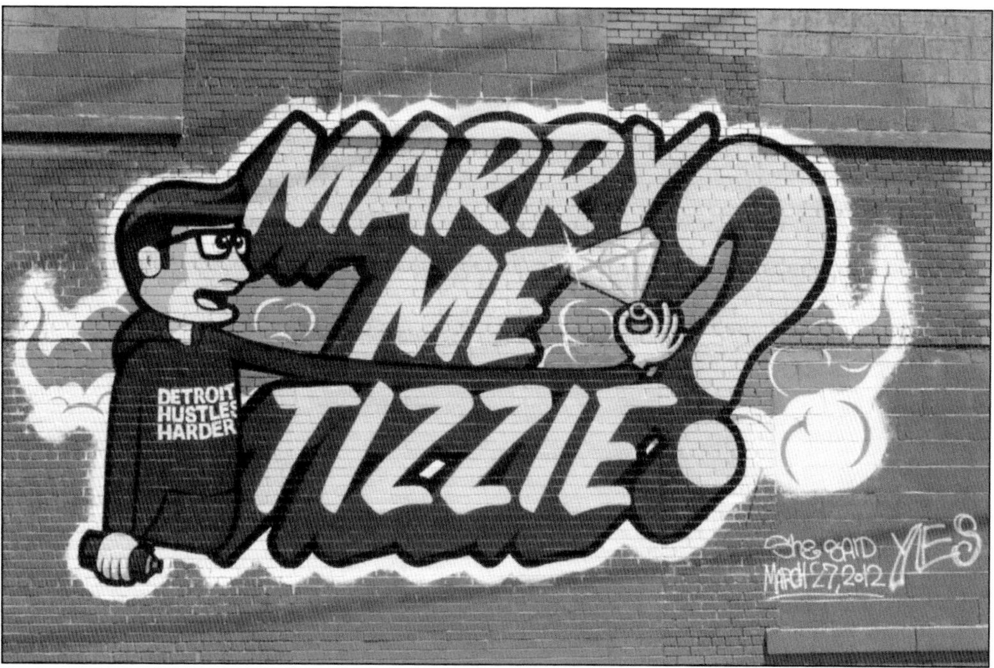

"Marry Me Tizzie?" When Tommy Daguanno, a professional cinematographer, decided to propose to his girlfriend, Tizzie Onderko, he chose to combine his artistic skills with the love that he and Onderko share for Eastern Market. He approached the owners of Greenbriar Foods, at 1801 Division Street, and asked about painting a mural on their wall. They agreed, and from March 22 to 25, 2011, Daguanno painted his marriage proposal. He documented the entire process with a time-lapse camera and turned it into a video. This was only fitting, as it was a video shoot in 2008 that had brought the two together. Daguanno brought Onderko to see the mural on Tuesday, March 27, and her response to his proposal can be seen in the mural's lower right: "She said yes." (EMC.)

Nine

Events

While the weekly Saturday market is an event itself, special events are also a great way to draw people and media attention to Eastern Market. Since the 1960s, local stakeholder groups have carried the torch of promotion and planned events to help show off the market to a broader audience. The first were relatively small community-based events that were mainly focused on special food promotions. Many of these events were specifically geared to setting records and garnering media attention. Throughout the years, events drew more people and included things like parades and festivals.

Today, many of the events celebrate the seasons. Springtime brings the annual Flower Day, on the Sunday after Mother's Day, and along with it acres of flowers and 140,000 visitors. Summer brings the seasonal Tuesday Market, as well as weekly Saturday cooking demonstrations featuring local chefs using seasonal Michigan produce and promoting healthy recipes. Fall brings many activities that celebrate another successful harvest, with activities such as pumpkin carving, apple pie baking and eating contests, and the annual Michigan Beer Festival. Fall is football season, and Eastern Market is the official home of Detroit Lions football tailgating during all Sunday home games. Metropolitan Detroiters still make special trips to Eastern Market merchants for Thanksgiving and the winter holidays. Children visit Santa Claus and help their families shop for Christmas trees, another annual Eastern Market tradition.

Year-round, buskers, an assortment of musicians, artists, and performers, provide music and entertainment in and around the sheds, serving as a soundtrack to a busy market day. In addition to the events sponsored by the market, the Eastern Market sheds, when not being used by farmers, are often rented for private special events like trade shows, fundraisers, photograph shoots, and family gatherings.

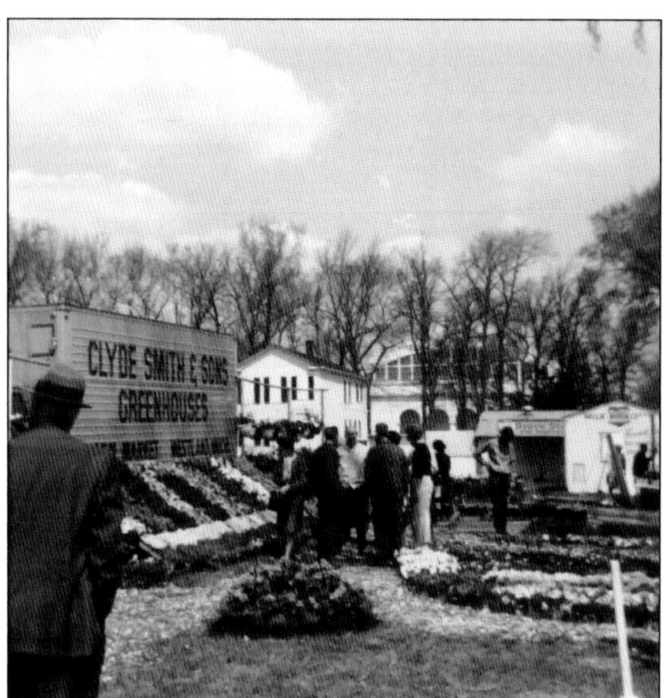

Flower Day: The Beginning. In the 1960s, southeastern Michigan had the largest production of bedding plants in the United States. Unfortunately, two-thirds of the crop was sold out of state. In 1966, a group of 20 flower growers in the metropolitan Detroit area formed the Metro Detroit Flower Growers Association (MDFGA) to promote awareness and local sales. Working with Don Juchartz of the Michigan State University Extension Service, the first Flower Day was held at the Michigan State Fairgrounds and featured displays, not sales, by local growers. (ES.)

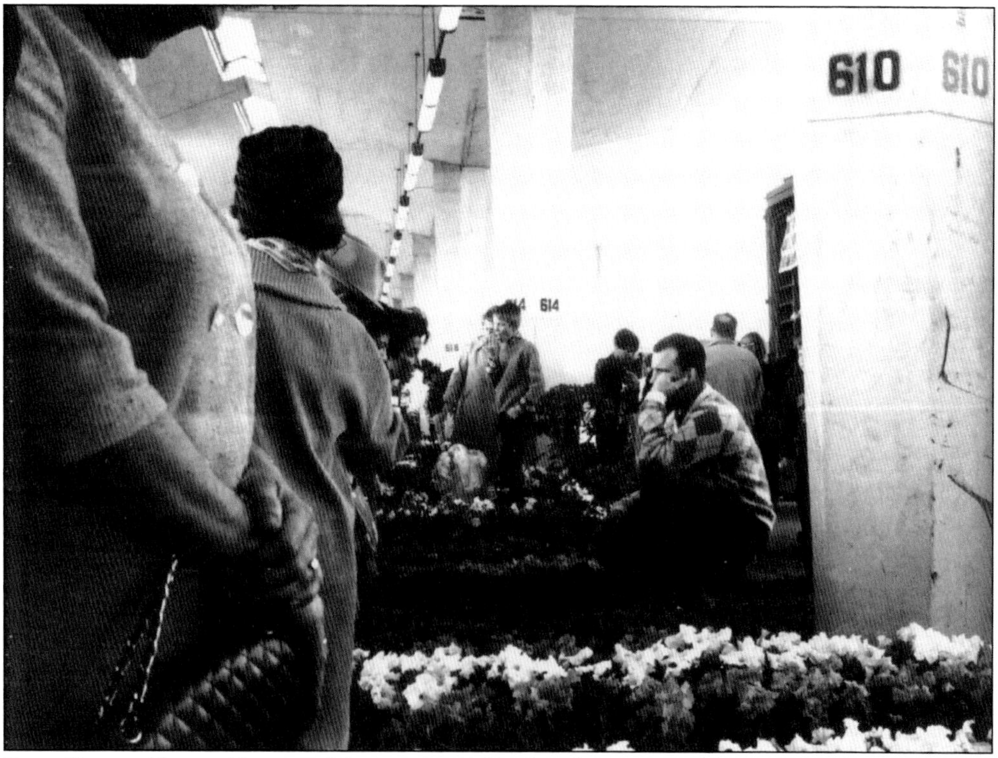

First Flower Day at Eastern Market. In 1967, after the success of the event at the fairgrounds, the MDFGA moved its event to Eastern Market, where growers could sell as well as display their products. (ES.)

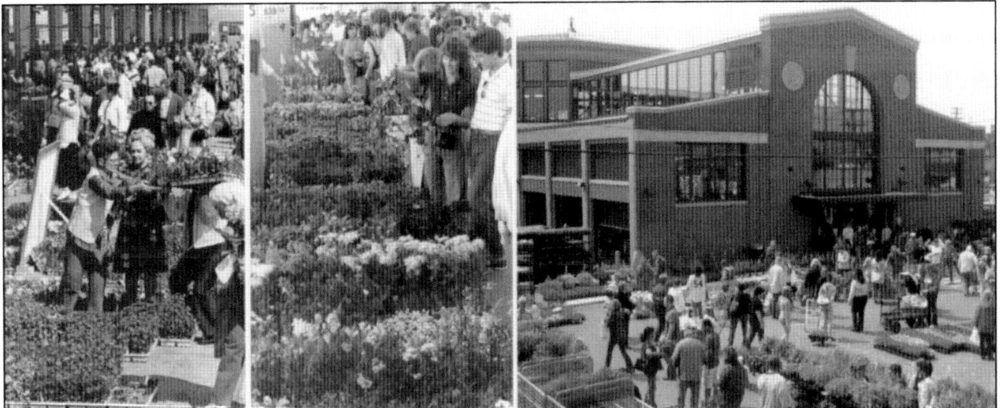

Rite of Spring. Since it was moved to the market, Flower Day has been held on the Sunday after Mother's Day and has become a spring holiday tradition for metropolitan Detroiters for more than 40 years. Annual attendance has grown to over 140,000 and includes more than 15 acres of flowers, bedding plants, trees, and shrubs, making Flower Day the largest outdoor, one-day flower event in the United States. (EMC.)

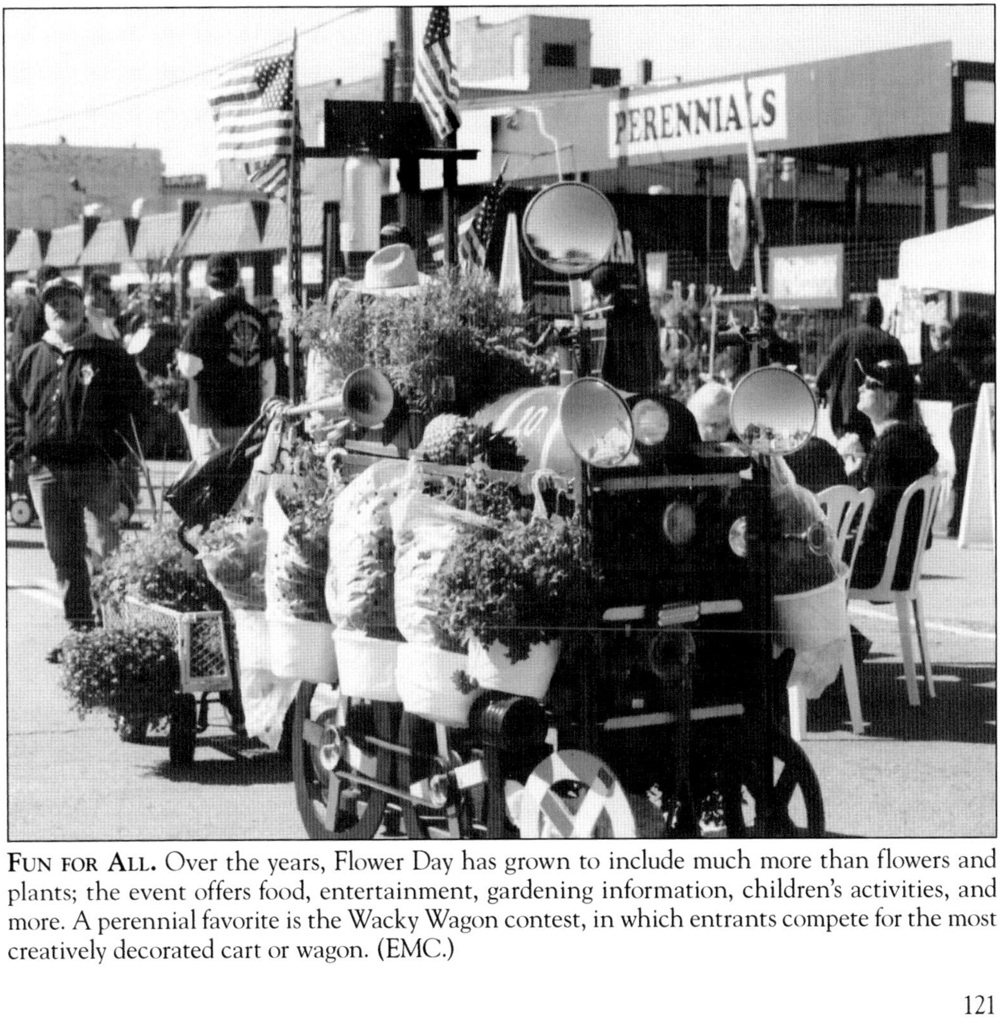

Fun for All. Over the years, Flower Day has grown to include much more than flowers and plants; the event offers food, entertainment, gardening information, children's activities, and more. A perennial favorite is the Wacky Wagon contest, in which entrants compete for the most creatively decorated cart or wagon. (EMC.)

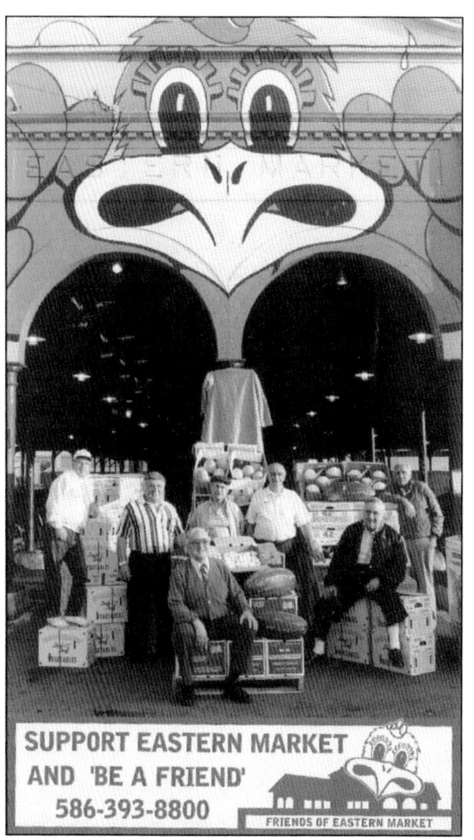

EASTERN MARKET MERCHANT'S ASSOCIATION. By the early 1980s, Eastern Market was again in need of attention. Several of the merchants were dismayed that they had no collective voice in municipal politics. With the help of Ed Deeb, the president of the Michigan Food and Beverage Association, the Eastern Market Merchant's Association (EMMA) was founded in 1984. Its first order of business was to petition the city to help make repairs to the sheds. EMMA also took an active role in producing and enlarging the annual Flower Day event. (Courtesy of Ed Deeb.)

EARLY EVENTS. The next task was to focus on attracting metropolitan Detroiters back to Eastern Market. Publicity and awareness were key to this effort. Events and activities of all kinds, including twice-yearly parades along Russell Street, unique attractions like the "World's Largest Fruit Cocktail," and special appearances by the Eastern Market Cowgirls, were all used to draw media attention and visitors to the market. (EMC.)

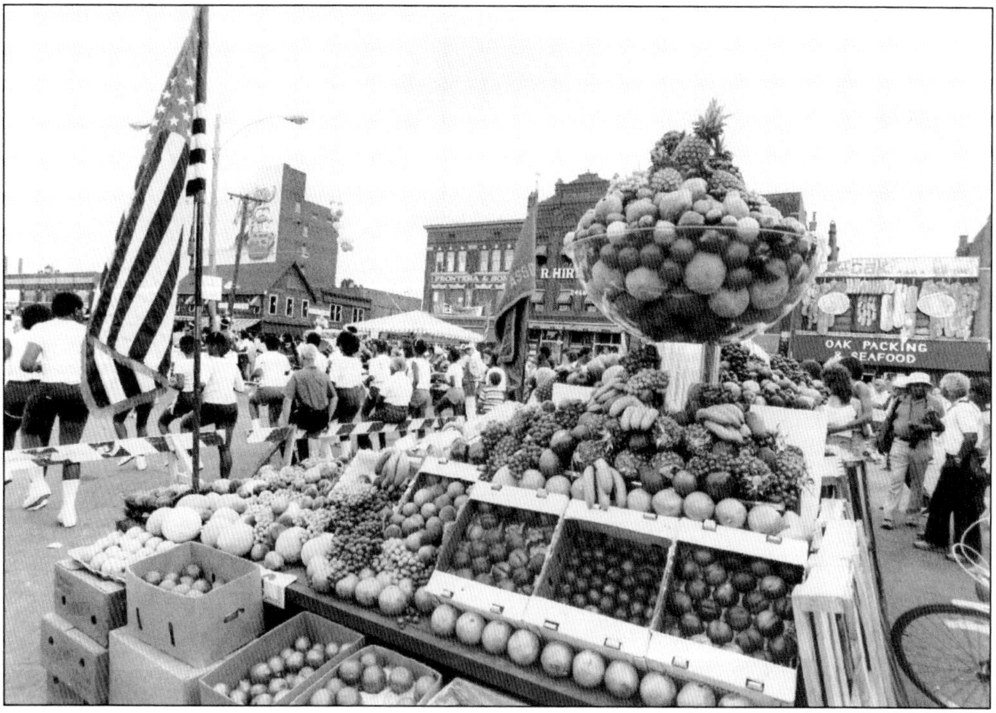

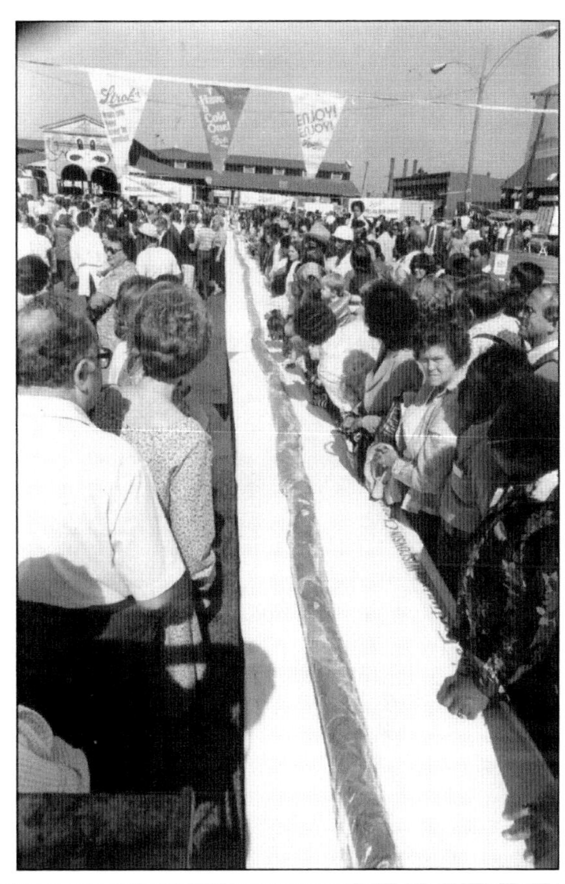

"World's Largest Sub." On September 26, 1979, as part of National Cheese Week, Eastern Market hosted the "World's Largest Sub" competition. A 200-foot-long submarine sandwich was assembled with 120 pounds of cheese, 40 pounds of tomatoes, 40 pounds of onions, four crates of lettuce, two gallons of mustard, two gallons of ketchup, and eight gallons of pickles. After being assembled by volunteers, the sub was moved to the street in sections, laid out end to end, and served to the hundreds of waiting spectators. (EMC.)

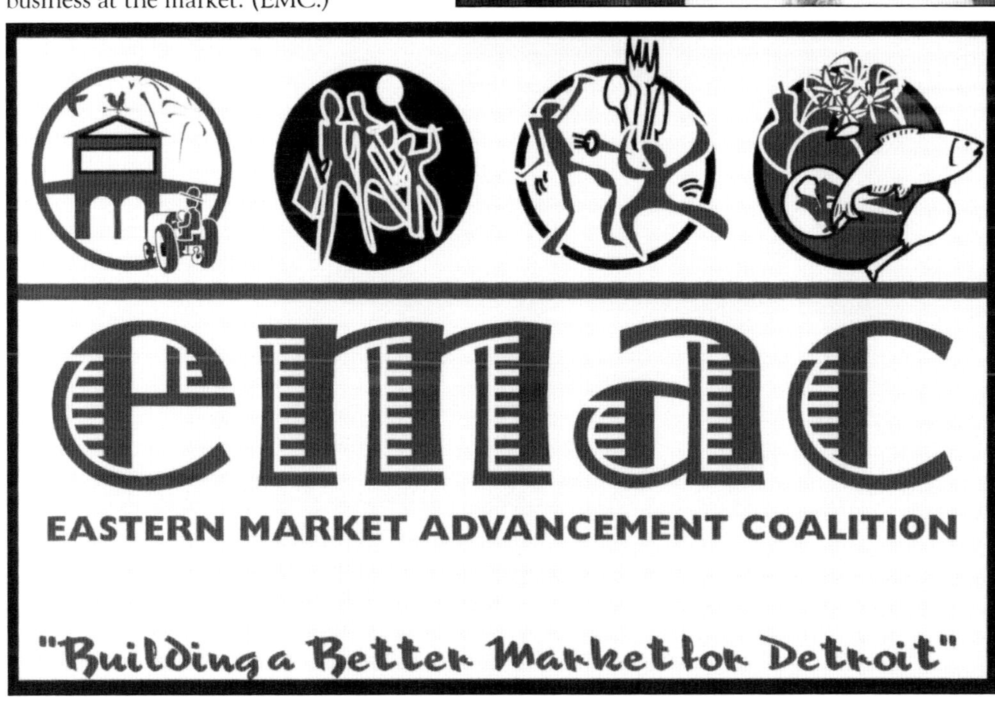

Eastern Market Advancement Coalition. The Eastern Market Advancement Coalition (EMAC) was formed in 2002 by local business owners and area stakeholders and was funded by a block grant from the Detroit Planning and Development Department. EMAC held events and ran promotions to help boost business at the market. (EMC.)

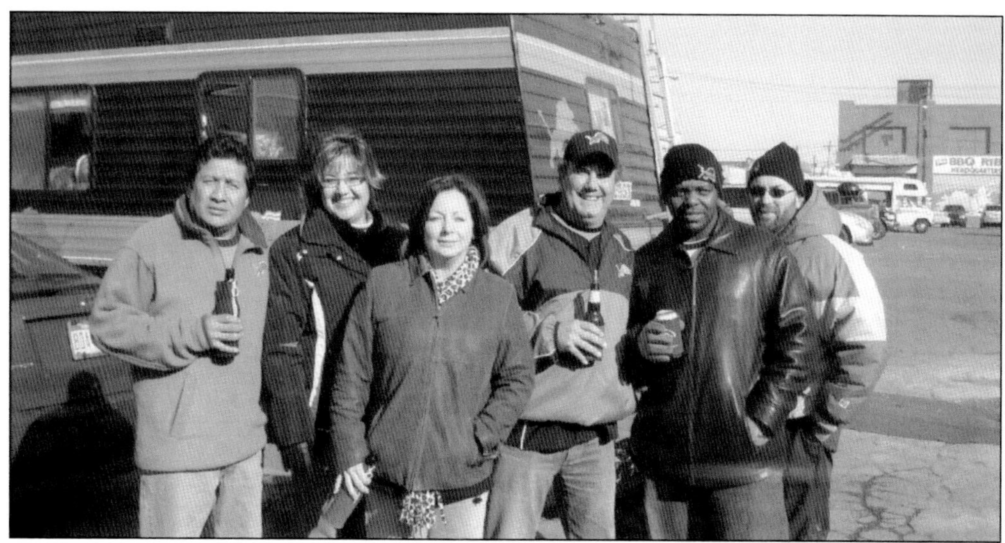

Tailgating. In 2002, the Detroit Lions moved from the Pontiac Silverdome to Ford Field in downtown Detroit, and Eastern Market became the official home of Detroit Lions tailgating. Featuring large open spaces and lots of parking, the market hosts 3,000 tailgaters for each Lions home game. It is just a short walk or shuttle ride to Ford Field. (EMC.)

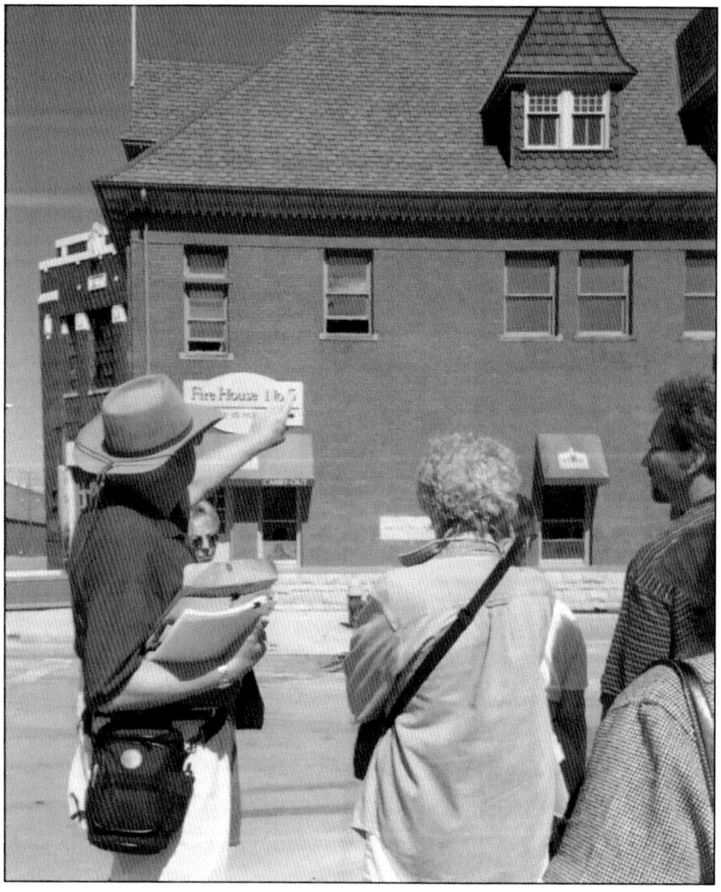

History Walking Tours. Each Saturday from May to September, the local historical preservation group Preservation Detroit conducts walking tours of the history of the market. The tour, which begins at the Eastern Market Welcome Center, allows visitors an in-depth look at Eastern Market's amazing 170-year history, from cemeteries to breweries, rumrunning to art galleries, and safe houses to prisons. (LR.)

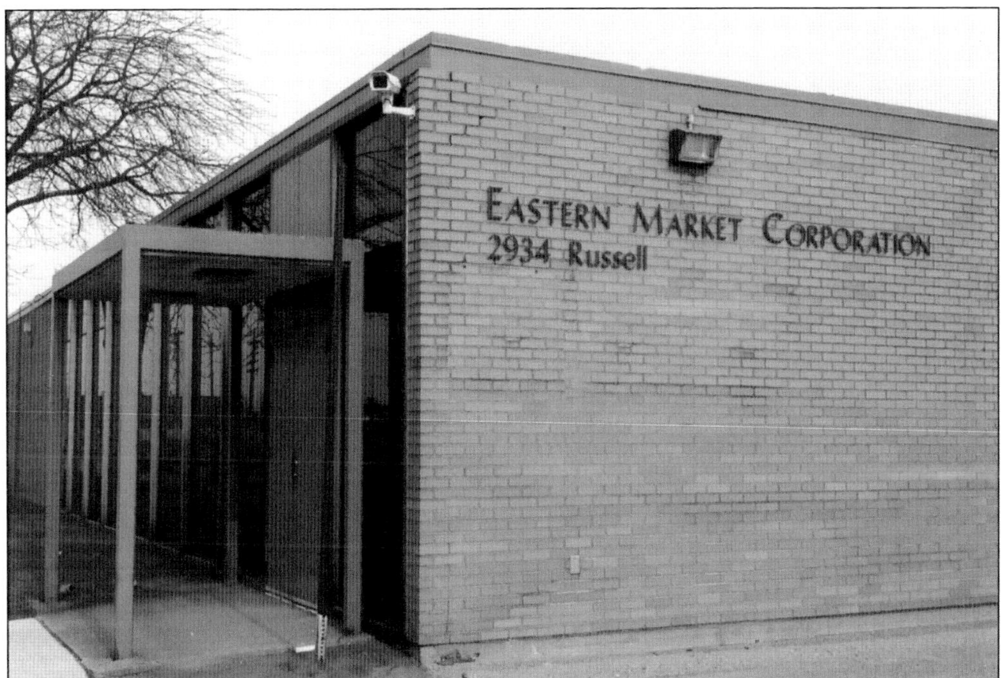

EASTERN MARKET CORPORATION. In August 2006, Eastern Market Corporation (EMC) was formed by combining EMMA and EMAC. Its purpose is to manage and promote the market and the market district under a management agreement with the City of Detroit. In addition to improving the physical market and market operations, EMC has brought a myriad of new and exciting events to the market campus. (EMC.)

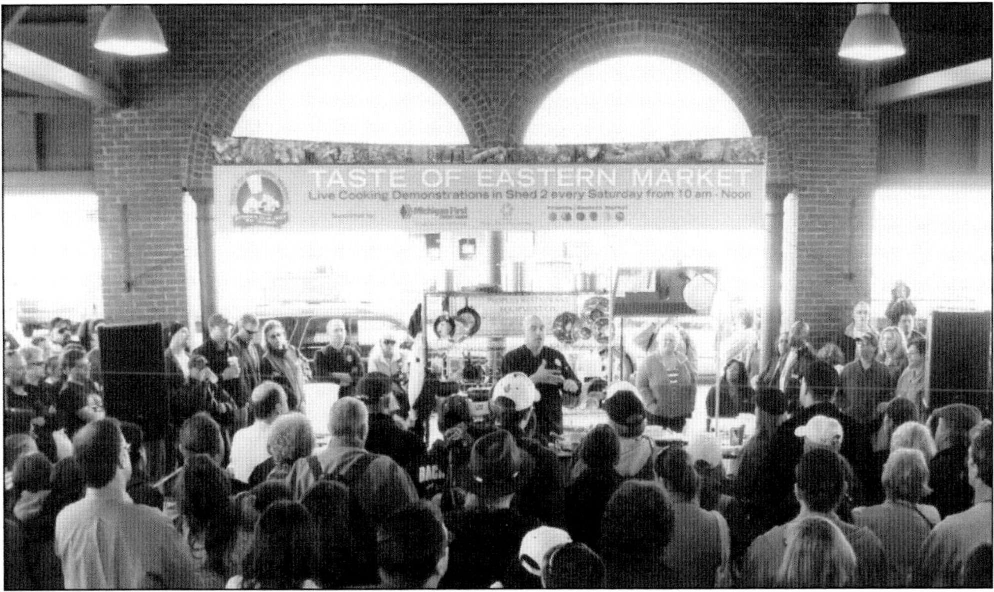

COOKING DEMONSTRATIONS. Eastern Market Corporation added weekly cooking demonstrations to the Saturday Market in 2008. Held in the middle of Shed 2, these hour-long demonstrations feature local chefs using local ingredients. In 2009, Food Network's *Iron Chef* and local restaurant owner Michael Symons kicked off the cooking-demo season. (EMC.)

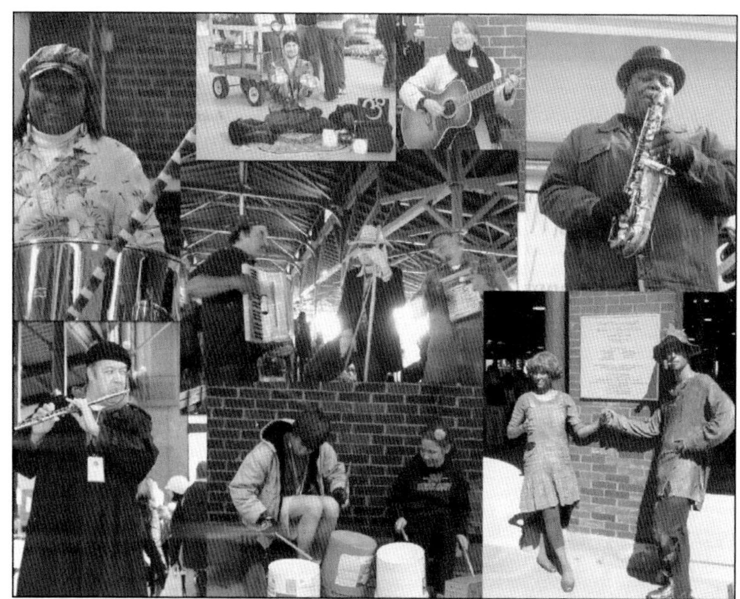

Buskers. Street musicians have always flocked to Eastern Market. EMC organized a program that allows buskers to perform throughout the market district. They are able to move throughout the market campus, performing at predesignated spots for one-hour intervals. (EMC.)

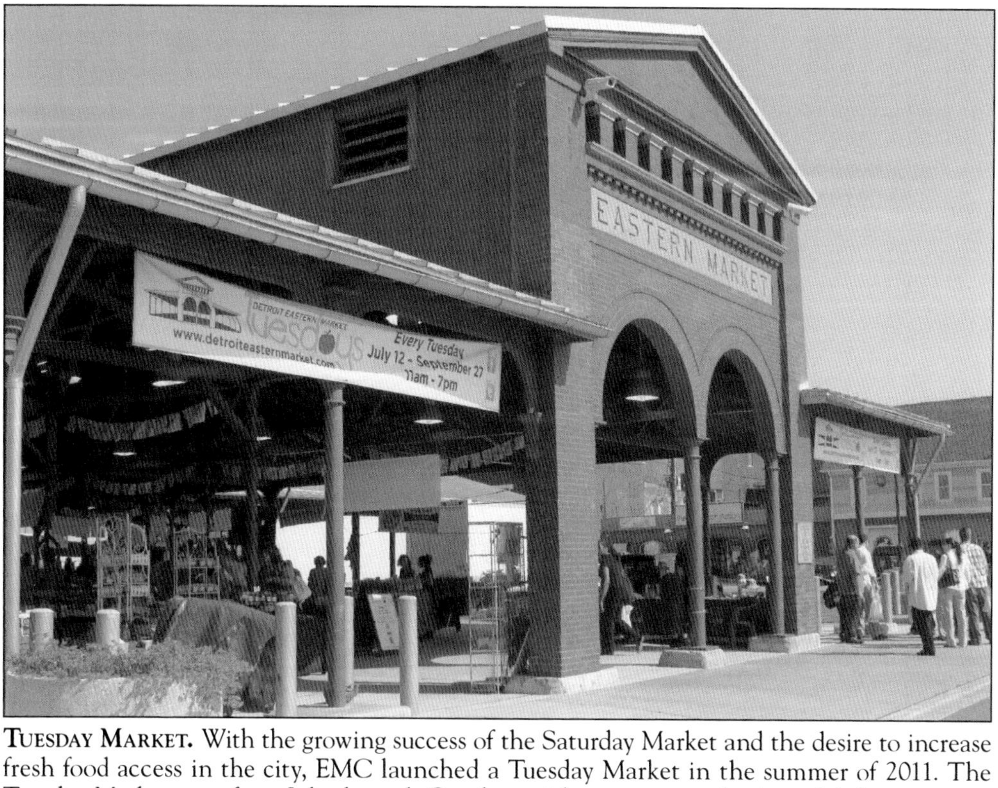

Tuesday Market. With the growing success of the Saturday Market and the desire to increase fresh food access in the city, EMC launched a Tuesday Market in the summer of 2011. The Tuesday Market runs from July through October, with a strong emphasis on Michigan-grown produce. (EMC.)

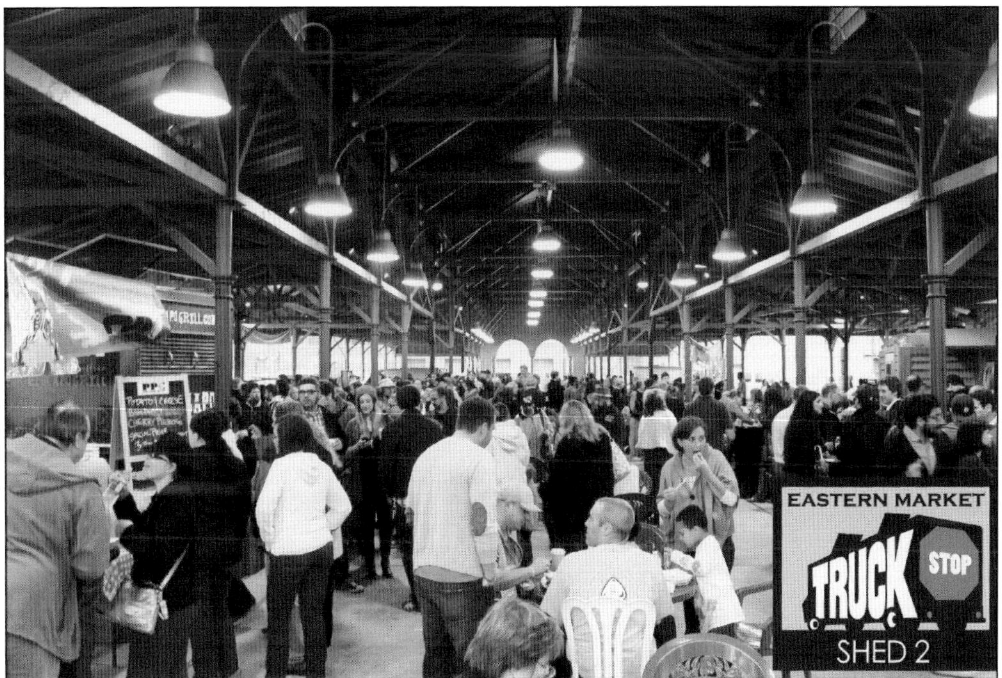

Eastern Market Truck Stop. Detroit's first food-truck gathering, the Eastern Market Truck Stop, was held on the last Tuesday Market of the 2011 season. The event gathered mobile food trucks from all over southeastern Michigan as a way to highlight the spirit of independent culinary entrepreneurship. The Truck Stop returned on the last Tuesday of every month as part of the 2012 Tuesday Market season. (EMC.)

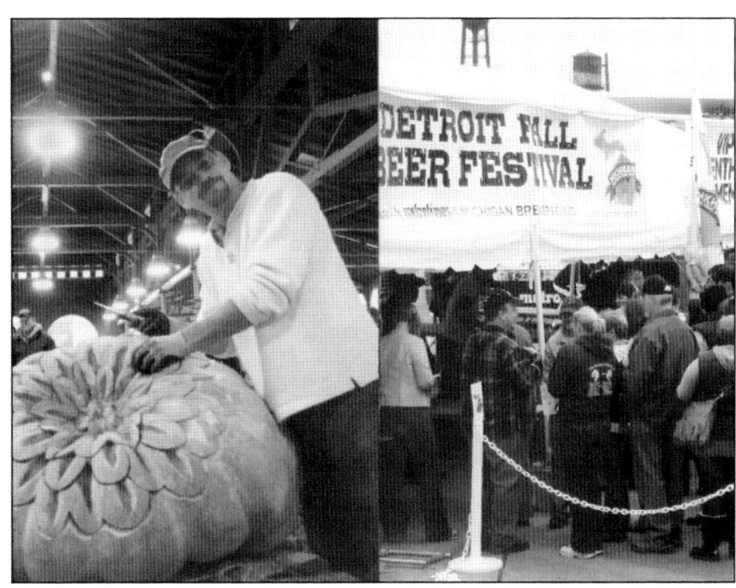

Harvest Season. The end of the growing season has traditionally been celebrated at the Eastern Market. Over the years, the market has hosted the traditional Blessing of the Harvest, Oktoberfests, an apple gala, beer tastings, and apple festivals featuring pie baking and eating contests, a petting zoo, hayrides, pumpkin-carving contests, and more. (EMC.)